BOLLINGEN SERIES LXV · 5

CARL KERÉNYI

Archetypal Images in Greek Religion

VOLUME 5

Bollingen Series LXV • 5

Carl Kerényi

ZEUS AND HERA

Archetypal Image of Father, Husband, and Wife

TRANSLATED FROM THE GERMAN
BY *Christopher Holme*

BOLLINGEN SERIES LXV · 5

PRINCETON UNIVERSITY PRESS
Princeton and Oxford

Copyright © 1975 by Princeton University Press

Princeton University Press is committed to the protection of copyright and the intellectual property our authors entrust to us. Copyright promotes the progress and integrity of knowledge created by humans. By engaging with an authorized copy of this work, you are supporting creators and the global exchange of ideas. As it is protected by copyright, any intentions to reproduce, distribute any part of the work in any form for any purpose require permission; permission requests should be sent to permissions@press.princeton.edu. Ingestion of any IP for any AI purposes is strictly prohibited without a license to do so; licensing requests should be sent to DigitalLicensing@press.princeton.edu.

Published by Princeton University Press
41 William Street, Princeton, New Jersey 08540
99 Banbury Road, Oxford OX2 6JX

press.princeton.edu

GPSR Authorized Representative: Easy Access System Europe - Mustamäe tee 50, 10621 Tallinn, Estonia, gpsr.requests@easproject.com

All Rights Reserved

Translated from the original manuscript of the author. Subsequently published in German: *Zeus and Hera: Urbild des Vaters, des Gatten und der Frau* (Studies in the History of Religions, XX; Leiden: E. J. Brill, 1972).

This translation first published in 1975
New cloth, paperback, and e-book Bollingen Recollections editions, 2026

Cloth ISBN 9780691281896
Paperback ISBN 9780691281889
ISBN (epub) 9780691290669
ISBN (PDF) 9780691281872

This is volume five in a group of studies of Archetypal Images of Greek Religion, which constitute the sixty-fifth publication in a series sponsored by Bollingen Foundation

The Library of Congress Control Number of a prior edition is 74-23858

To
GEO WIDENGREN

νεός ὁ Ζεὺς βασιλεύει·
τὸ πάλαι δ' ἦν Κρόνος ἄρχων.
ἀπίτω μοῦσα παλαιά.

New is Zeus who is king
In olden times Kronos was ruler.
Be off with you, old-time Muse.

—TIMOTHEOS OF MILETOS

in Athenaios III 122 D

Πλάσιον δή μ' [. . .
πότνι' Ἥρα, σὰ χ[αρίεσσα μόρφα . . .

Near then to me
[Come,] my lady Hera, your l[ovely form . . .

—SAPPHO 17

CONTENTS

Acknowledgments		ix
Introduction		xi
I	The Word *Zeus* and Its Synonyms, *Theos* and *Daimon*	3
II	The Beginnings of the Zeus Religion and Its Early History	21
III	The Emergence of the Olympian Divine Family	38
IV	Poseidon as 'Husband' and 'Father'	60
V	Zeus the Brother-Husband	91
VI	Hera Cults in the Peloponnese, Euboea, and Boeotia	114
VII	The Great Goddess of Samos and Paestum	148
Abbreviations		182
List of Works Cited		183
Index		197

ACKNOWLEDGMENTS

The publishers acknowledge permission to quote as follows: to the University of Chicago Press, for Richmond Lattimore's translation of the Iliad; to Harper & Row, Publishers, for Mr. Lattimore's translation of the Odyssey; and to Penguin Books, Ltd., for Aubrey de Sélincourt's translation of Livy's *History of Rome*. Grateful acknowledgment is also made to Ruth Spiegel, who carried through the editorial preparation of the manuscript, compiled and verified the bibliography, and revised the notes.

INTRODUCTION

IN THE VOLUME *Dionysos: Archetypal Image of Indestructible Life*, I offered a historical account of the religion of Dionysos from its beginnings in the Minoan culture down to its transition to a cosmic and cosmopolitan religion of late antiquity under the Roman Empire. This chapter of the religious history of Europe had been dealt with before—not, it is true, as a concrete, consistent, and coherent whole but at least in details or generalizations—in classical studies and archaeology, in philosophy and psychology. With this book on Zeus and Hera I aim to fill a gap in the account of Greek religion as *religion*, and thus once again, I hope, to fill a gap in our knowledge of the religious history of Europe.

The history of religion is the history of a correlation existing between man and beings worshiped by him, identifiable in history independently of whether such worshiped beings existed or not. The question has never been seriously asked, still less scientifically answered, what Zeus meant to the Greeks—or what Zeus and Hera meant to men and women—in terms of this correlation. The answer must be given, just as it was in *Dionysos*, from the point of view of the historian and of the humanist thinking about humanity. The historian reconstructs; the thinking humanist differentiates. The realities of history—here, the history of Greek religion—are in need both of reconstruction and of differentiation. It is a piece of luck that both procedures can operate in this field through very concrete media: through the medium of a rich and clearly transmitted language, the Greek, and through a medium that can be called, in a phrase combining landscape and monuments, the "sensuous transmission."[1]

Language in the history of religion is the scientifically intelligible boundary of the concrete. My earlier studies for a monograph on Zeus and Hera took as their starting point the human reference, as reflected in myth and cult. Such a reference is presupposed by the myths themselves, the linguistic structure that tells of these two deities and connects them with one another. The two earlier studies[2]—on the emergence of the Olympian divine family, and on Zeus and Hera as the nucleus of the Olympian divine family—indicated the group of human references in whose center the Zeus and Hera pair stood. The material discovered and presented in these studies forms part of the present book and has been reworked into what follows.

The human references that come to light in all cultures at all periods have an inherent tendency to show themselves above the relationship existing at any time between man and man, to appear as a self-realizing prototype and by this means to manifest themselves as an unchangeable primitive datum. Here it seems obvious to speak with C. G. Jung of "archetypes" or at any rate of "archetypal" data. The Greek word *archetypos*—from the language of the philosophers—is adjectival and I like to use it substantively only when greater intelligibility can be achieved. Language in its prephilosophic, natural condition is able to grasp human relationships simply and immediately, and it is also able to refer beyond what is at any time *merely* interpersonal. For this it

---

[1] See "Unsinnliche und sinnliche Tradition," in Kerényi, *Apollon*, pp. 72–89 (in H. Oppermann, ed., *Humanismus*, pp. 190–205). / For detailed information on footnote references, see the List of Works Cited.

[2] These were published in 1950 under the titles "Die Enstehung der olympischen Götterfamilie" and "Zeus und Hera: Der Kern der olympischen Götterfamilie."

has words whose full sense and currency are to be found in the correlation denoted in most European languages by the use and phonetic adaptation of the Latin term *religio*.[3]

Linguistic investigations showed me that for the better knowledge of Greek religion it would be insufficient to elucidate and give an account of the archetypal material, though even this would be more productive than the so-called "historical method" hitherto in use. There are words of archetypal content—such as "mother" or "father"—that are important for the understanding of Greek religion simply because of this content. The sense and currency of these words are given by an interpersonal relationship and they do not necessarily refer beyond it to that correlation called religion. An attempt has been made to derive religion from interpersonal relationships and to make this derivation psychologically plausible. This attempt of Sigmund Freud's is well known. But to derive all the religious statements of the Greek language from interpersonal relationships is not possible and the general validity of the Freudian explanation of religion founders on this point.

In a series of linguistic studies I came to the conclusion that the Greek language possesses its own inherent theology.[4] The fundamental word of this theology is *theos*. From a strictly methodological point of view it is consoling that in order to understand *theos*, no known or unknown god-concept, no "idea of god," need be introduced. All we have to do is to start from an experience in which this word is spoken predicatively. The experience can be recognized from the sentence in which *theos* is used predicatively, unless the word itself is already a sentence: *Theos! Ecce deus!* Between experience and word there is no third ele-

3 See Kerényi, *The Religion of the Greeks and Romans*, p. 160; also "Das Ungeschichtliche," in Kerényi, *Umgang mit Göttlichem*, pp. 68–78.
4 See Kerényi, "Die Sprache der Theologie und die Theologie der Sprache," pp. 81–91.

ment. No investigation about Zeus can afford to neglect this favorable situation, since it is given *by the word itself.*

The word *Zeus*, considered purely from the linguistic point of view, has no other sense and no other currency than that belonging to the same category as the sense and currency of *theos*. The fact that *Zeus* is a statement, the statement of an experience of the same category as *theos*, makes it unique among all names of Greek deities. It is immediately followed in the Greek religious order of rank by *theos*. In their linguistic foundations both *Zeus* and *theos* are concrete; they have the concreteness of an event. In the case of *Zeus* it was originally a definite event, while this limitation in the case of *theos*, just as originally, was not present. The number of events that could be *theos* was always infinite.

The conviction underlying my strict method, my "exclusion of a third thing between experience and word," belongs to linguistic philosophy and is in my opinion completely tenable. I repeat it here from the Introduction to *Dionysos*: "Human experience does not always give rise immediately to ideas. It can be reflected in images or words without the mediation of ideas. Man reacted inwardly to his experience before he became a thinker. Prephilosophical insights and reactions to experience are taken over and further developed by thought, and this process is reflected in language. . . . Language itself can be wise and draw distinctions through which experience is raised to consciousness and made into a prephilosophic wisdom common to all those who speak that language."[5]

Thus, the first chapter here is devoted to the word *Zeus*. The author of *The Cults of the Greek States*, Lewis Richard Farnell, began his chapter on Zeus by placing the investigator's impressions in the foreground:

5 See Kerényi, *Dionysos: Archetypal Image of Indestructible Life*, Introduction at note 1.

Introduction xv

"The study of the cults of Zeus is perhaps the most interesting chapter of the history of Greek religion, for it includes the two extremes of religious thought, the most primitive ideas side by side with the most advanced; and nearly all the departments of nature and human life were penetrated with this worship. Although the figures of Apollo, Athena, Dionysos, and Prometheus are of more importance in the history of external civilization and of the special arts of Greece, yet no character in Greek religion has such wealth of ethical content, or counts so much for the development of moral ideas, as the character of Zeus. At times he seems to overshadow the separate growths of polytheism; and at times in expressing the nature of Zeus the religious utterance became monotheistic."[6]

German scholars before Farnell spoke of a "monotheistic impulse in polytheism" that showed itself in the Zeus religion.[7] The uninterrupted density of the Zeus cult must have made at least as great an impression wherever in the ancient world Greek was spoken. It excludes at the outset any comparison with the primitive faith in a "High God" without a cult. Epithets and invocations, the enumeration of which in K. F. H. Bruchmann's *Epitheta Deorum* takes up twenty-two pages, in Roscher's *Lexikon*, forty,[8] are evidence of a currency enjoyed by no Greek deity other than Zeus. A. B. Cook's work on *Zeus* is devoted to the different aspects of the "sky god"—as one-sided a view of Zeus as the monotheistic would be—and became in five volumes a collection of the myths and monuments of the cult. And this work could be continued still further, however, less in respect to the myths than to the cult monuments. The

---

6 L. R. Farnell, *The Cults of the Greek States*, I, 35.

7 See the critical work of J. A. Overbeck, *Beiträge zur Erkenntnis und Kritik der Zeusreligion*, p. 4.

8 K. F. H. Bruchmann, *Epitheta Deorum*, pp. 122–43; W. H. Roscher, ed., *Ausführliches Lexikon der griechischen und römischen Mythologie*, VI, cols. 592–671.

disproportion between the immense mass of testimony to the existence of this religion and the content that could be ascribed to it as "worship of the sky god" would be astonishing. Would we then be confronted after all by a sort of "monotheism?"

It is a great historical religion that confronts us. Had it aroused our astonishment by the mere fact of its historical existence—and it did not do so only because it was approached from the standpoint of a monotheistic religion—it would have given rise to questions about the groundwork of such a religion. The evidences, the mere testimonies, were collected as if the existence of a religion so suggestive of monotheism were a matter of course, and as if no special thought need be given to the question *what sort of thing* it was that had prevailed and been preserved in it, in the same way as the monotheism of the Jews and Christians had prevailed and been preserved. Yet, in view of the overwhelming external evidence this problem can no longer be avoided. It had not even been noticed, let alone solved.

In what follows an attempt will be made to answer the questions: Who in reality was worshiped in the Zeus religion? Who was Zeus in correlation with the Greek world? And who was the goddess Hera, historically and archetypally united with Zeus as if they were a human pair? The archetypal forms what is permanent in history. It gave the history of Greek religion that plasticity which political history forms out of personalities. Plasticity, without the personalities of founders or proclaimers, is peculiar to Greek religion. In these volumes on the Archetypal Images in Greek Religion, the history of Greek religion is written from its earliest ascertainable beginnings up to that point where the condition of cult and myth ceased to exhibit any new historical development from an archetypal point of view.

The new is inevitable in the history of science, which cannot stand

Introduction xvii

still if it is to be science. It is equally inevitable that the new should encounter more resistance in its own field than ought to be expected from unprejudiced readers. The unprejudiced reader represents humanity, and history (as I at all events understand it) is always written with the view to a resonance in humanity, especially when the subject of this history is "a most human thing." As for the scholars who work in this field, I must refer them to the warning of a great physicist, Werner Heisenberg—in his *Der Teil und das Ganze* ("The Part and the Whole")—that it is often necessary, if science is to progress, to change our way of thought. In order to grasp even approximately the truth about such a rare phenomenon as the religion of the Greeks, the change is worth attempting.

By my chosen standpoint, however, keeping the archetypal in view, I chose also the limitation I have indicated. The book must come to an end at the moment when this point of view—so far as Zeus is concerned—would no longer pick out the essential feature in the portrait of the supreme Greek deity: where the "father" in the sense of the "father archetype" is no longer in the foreground of the thinking about Zeus. This is the case even in Hesiod, with whom the "father" has shrunk to a genealogical principle. Still more is it the case in the archaic philosophers, not to mention the men who thought about Zeus in fifth-century Athens and later.[9]

Rome
February 1971

C. K.

9 [The German manuscript continued here: "The Zeus of the philosophers and tragedians will be considered more closely in another book, in connection with Apollo and the religion conducted at Delphi in his name." Professor Kerényi did not write that book.—Ed.]

ZEUS AND HERA

Archetypal Image of Father, Husband, and Wife

I. THE WORD *ZEUS* AND ITS SYNONYMS, *THEOS* AND *DAIMON*

AFTER World War I, in a period when an intellectual expansion was expected in and from classical studies, the two most famous Greek scholars in Germany were invited to lecture on Zeus: Hermann Diels and Ulrich von Wilamowitz-Moellendorff. Their lectures summarized what was known at the time about the supreme god of the Greeks. The historical exploration of antiquity had reached its highest point. The two lectures are characterized as much by their mutual contradictions (and that of Diels also by an internal contradiction) as by a common limitation. They are limited by a narrowness of attitude toward religion, or in this case toward genuine religious possibilities among the early Greeks.

Diels, who gave his lecture in Copenhagen in 1922,[1] was himself to some extent aware of the contradictions in his conception, yet not enough to recognize all the illogicalities in his thoughts about Zeus. He began by observing that the comparative study of ancient religion and mythology on the analogy of comparative philology had not been successful. Yet he gave his opinion that there was a deity who can be assumed as a "common object of faith with the primitive Indo-European people." This deity, he says, is Zeus, the father of gods and men. Zeus is also the only one of the Olympic deities whose name is transparent and clearly reveals his original nature. "The language of our Indo-

---

[1] H. Diels, "Zeus," pp. 1–15.

European forebears denoted by *djeus*, accusative *djem*, the light of heaven."

Diels did not take account of a discovery made at about the same time by philology, not yet "language content analysis" but still a strict exploration of word forms that refused to be satisfied with the simplifying etymologies of earlier comparative studies. This discovery was that the Indo-European stem *djeu-* belonged to a verb *div-* of "perfective" aspect. "Thus, the meaning of *djeu-* which should serve as the basis of the study is that which comes closest to that of the verb." This is, according to the philologist Herbert Zimmermann, whom I quote, *djeu-* in a physical sense, that is, *aufflammen* (to flame up) " 'of the sun at daybreak' or—its result—'the bright sky of day.' "² With this addition, however, the linguist jumped out of language as it were and left the *content* of the stem *djeu-* —and thus also of the word Zeus—behind him. His choice of "flame up" for the content is in fact the crudest meaning, taken from fire, and this is not necessary. We can leave it at *aufleuchten* (to light up)³ and indeed we do not know that there is any closer expression than this. With the meaning "the bright sky of day . . . its result," Zimmermann departed even further from the grammatical content. He could not substantiate it from Greek. He wrote, "This meaning of a location is preserved above all in the Veda."

When Diels was preparing his lecture, linguistics had not yet advanced very far, or else its latest refinements were not known to Diels. It remained outside his field of study that the actual content of the

2 H. Zimmermann, "Das ursprüngliche Geschlecht von *dies*," p. 95.
3 See H. Frisk, *Griechisches etymologisches Wörterbuch*, I, 611: "*scheinen, hell glänzen, leuchten*" (shine, gleam brightly, lighten). See further J. Wackernagel, *Vorlesungen über Syntax*, p. 116; P. Kretschmer, "Dyaus, Ζεύς, Diespiter und die Abstrakta im Indogermanischen," p. 113. / For Zimmermann's appeal to the Veda, see his "Zeus," pp. 95–96.

word *Zeus* is the *moment* of lighting up. The great philologist, who was at home principally with the Greek philosophers, was not disturbed by the fact that none of the *static* meanings, like sky, day, brilliancy, brightness, which go beyond the actual decisive, *dynamic* moment of becoming light, could be found in Greek but had to be brought in from related languages. He made the observation—and did not see its contradiction with his method, which he believed to be exact—that "in the Greek the original meaning of sky, daylight, has almost completely disappeared."[4] The "almost" in this statement is an appeal to clues that must be regarded as highly hypothetical.

In Diels's view, however, it followed that Zeus must have been most closely identified with the sky in that place where the Greeks first constituted themselves Hellenes: in northern Greece, that is, in Dodona, where Zeus possessed an oracle that both was ancient and always remained archaic. At this spot, so Diels had to go on then to observe, Zeus had the epithet "Naios" or "Naos," "him of the spring." "Not in the canopy of the oak tree, the whispering of whose leaves passed for the voice of Zeus, did the god dwell but on its floor [*en pythmeni phegou*] as Hesiod expressly says."[5] So none other than the Dodonaean Zeus was originally not a sky god at all! If he had any characteristic trait it was this alone, that he was the god of the Hellenes, who there connected him with an older oracle. But why with an oracle? Diels does not ask this question. A lighting up, not in a physical sense, but as can happen through an oracle *humanly*, as an experience of the questioner, this must be the explanation here, often no doubt in the Greek meaning of *phos*, "light": "rescue."[6] For it must be remembered that in primitive

---

4   Diels, "Zeus," p. 2.
5   Ibid., p. 4. For the allusion to Hesiod, see *Fragmenta Hesiodea*, p. 117, fr. 240.
6   For this meaning, see Iliad VI 6, XVII 615.

languages no distinction need be expected between "physical sense" and human sense. Lighting up is lighting up whether this experience is caused by a material source of light or not.

From everything observed by Diels—the early presence in Dodona of the Hellenic Zeus as an oracle god who does not give his revelations from the sky—it could have been concluded that Zeus controlled not only the scene of meteorological phenomena but also the domain of consciousness in which he could be called "Panhellenios," the "god common to all the Greeks." This epithet is given prominence by Diels but in connection with the highest mountain of Aigina and its Zeus cult,[7] as if it meant a common weather god who had his abode *here* for the whole of Hellas, which the Greeks clearly could not have believed. "Panhellenios" means the god of all the Hellenes and nothing else: a god of at least as much spiritual and moral content as the consciousness of community is a spiritual and moral fact.

This simplest of all inferences, which does not even require a closer study of the language, Diels failed to make. The further historical inference would have been that the Hellenes generally made their first appearance in correlation with Zeus, and that this god, "who from Homer down to the end of antiquity stood at the head of the heavenly company,"[8] can be thought of *only* in correlation with the Hellenes. This inference was not made, in his 1923 lecture, by Wilamowitz either. He was more consequential than Diels in that he did not choose the quality of a sky god in Zeus for his starting point. "Roughly the first thing learnt by anyone who wants to understand Homer is that Zeus does not dwell in the sky but on the Macedonian Mount Olympos, whereas later poets, even the late Homeric poets, did equate Olympos

7 Diels, "Zeus," p. 5.
8 Ibid., p. 3.

1. *The Word* Zeus *and Its Synonyms,* Theos *and* Daimon

with the sky."[9] Let that be proof that Zeus only *became* a sky god. "He was the lord of the lightning"—that, according to Wilamowitz, was the original nature of Zeus. This seems a more dynamic view, yet it rested on very static foundations: on those ancient Olympian bronzes, which represent Zeus with the lightning in his hand. Only in recognizing the plasticity of attitude—a plasticity, however, which came rather late to the Greeks—did Wilamowitz advance further than Diels. Yet, the spiritual preconceptions that made it impossible to accept a spiritual and moral content in the Hellenic Zeus of the archaic period were common to the two men. They had in common, too, a certain fear of a scholarly kind, which was referred to by Wilamowitz at the beginning of his lecture.

He felt it necessary to dissociate himself from Friedrich Gottlieb Welcker, the author of the *Griechische Götterlehre* ("Study of Greek Religion") which appeared in 1857 and gave a systematic account of the religion of the Greeks. Influenced by notions of the Goethe period, this work had followed a long exchange of ideas between Welcker and Wilhelm von Humboldt and paid regard also to comparative philology. Wilamowitz devoted his opening words to the origination of this work: "In the year 1808 in Heidelberg the young Fr. G. Welcker waited on the then famous Professor Creuzer. He was on his way home from Rome, where he had become intimate with the Humboldts, husband and wife, as the tutor to their children, and had been much in the company of the great Danish scholar Zoega. Creuzer, who found in all religions the echo of a deep Oriental wisdom, was overcome with astonishment when the young man told him he intended to write a history of Greek religion. This plan of the young man's involved a much greater task than the old man had performed in his study of Greek religion. For

---

9 Wilamowitz, "Zeus," p. 2.

Welcker did give the world of scholarship a correct definition of its terms, though it is true the task is unlikely in a foreseeable time to find a solution that will satisfy religion and history alike, however vigorous the present traffic in what is called the history of religion.

"When Welcker published his *Götterlehre* it pained him deeply that his main theme was not believed. He had tried to show that the welter of innumerable deities had been preceded by a certain form of monotheism, and that the exalted primordial god was Zeus. This view is to be explained only by the fact that Welcker was still dominated by ideas that had become obsolete, drawn from the nature religion of the enlightenment and from Creuzer's symbolism. A further point was that the primordial relationship which had meanwhile been discovered among the Indo-European languages led to the assumption of a primordial Indo-European religion. . . ."[10]

Diels and Wilamowitz were guided in their view of Zeus by the fear that they would otherwise have to assume a monotheism of the same kind and the same origin among the ancient Greeks, or at the very least to assume an Indo-European primordial religion according to the ideas of the older philologists. Neither assumption was one they could have defended scientifically. It was strangely limited of them to believe that in Greek studies such a step into the unsure and unknown must be the only alternative to starting out from the crudest ideas about the supreme Greek god. Welcker's younger contemporary, Karl Otfried Müller, thought otherwise. In 1825, in his *Prolegomena zu einer wissenschaftlichen Mythologie* ("Prolegomena to a Scientific Mythology"), he made it a principle "in the investigation of myths not to close our minds to anything—not even to thoughts of original beauty and purity—and especially not to begin explaining them with a one-sided slant

10 Ibid., p. 1.

1. The Word Zeus and Its Synonyms, Theos and Daimon

towards a limited class of concepts."[11] If "beauty and purity" can be qualities of a language, then they are probably to be attributed to every primitive language, including that in which the Zeus religion makes its appearance.

The sentence with which Welcker in his *Götterlehre* began to discuss Zeus may well stand at the beginning of a scientific account. "At the furthest bounds of Greek antiquity we encounter the words *theos* and *daimon* and the names *Zeus* and *Kronion*; nothing more ancient exists for us in Greek religion."[12] What is scientific about this is the way in which Welcker restricted himself by marking out the particular science appropriate for the next step. As I have already indicated, this is the science of language, not only with reference to word forms but also as the investigation of content. It became possible to define the content of the stem *djeu-* exactly—in terms of a "perfective" action—as the event of lighting up. An investigator who wants to keep his mind open to any result, even if it should turn out closer to Welcker's views than to those of Diels and Wilamowitz, must start here.

A treatise of Paul Kretschmer, a sequel to that of Herbert Zimmermann, confirmed the exact content of the word *Zeus* but was less precise on the perfective aspect. It also offered an amplification that went beyond the linguistic data. "So we reach the conclusion that the fundamental meaning of the stem *djeu-*, in its weaker form *div-*, was that of 'lightening,' 'illuminating.' According to what has been said, therefore, *djeus* originally meant the 'illuminator' or 'illuminatrix,' the *daimon* of 'lightening,' of heavenly light."[13]

The introduction of a *daimon* as the agent of "lightening" and of a

11 K. O. Müller, *Prolegomena*, p. 80. (In the 1970 edn., see p. 24.)
12 F. G. Welcker, *Griechische Götterlehre*, I, 129.
13 Kretschmer, "Dyaus, Ζεύς, Diespiter," p. 113.

"demonic stage," which Kretschmer claims to recognize in the Rig-Veda in its ideas about Dyaus, are assumptions not justified by language. They cannot be based on Sanskrit any more than on Greek. What the Greek *daimon* is remains to be discussed in connection with Zeus. With the ancient Indians a demon was associated with evil, which lighting up and the bright light of day are not. "Lighting up" or "lightening" is *for the man to whom it happens itself* also the "illuminator"—whether simultaneous with the happening in nature or only in it. It is something altogether concrete, not it is true like a body bounded and substantial, nor yet like anything abstract either. Among the linguists as among the philologists, it was a restriction of thought not to bring under consideration the *concrete happening*.

It was also false and superfluous, in the case of the so-called "Indo-European weather impersonals," to deny that the subjectival expression "*Zeus hyei*," "Zeus rains," was preceded by the impersonal expression *hyei*, "it rains."[14] In all probability the opposite is true.[15] Apart from Wilamowitz in his Zeus lecture,[16] two great philologists have expressed themselves affirmatively. Karl Brugmann wrote, in 1925: "For such natural phenomena, phrases would already have existed before the mythological viewpoint found expression in them."[17] And Jacob Wackernagel, in 1926, stated: "We have no right to assume that the religious viewpoint is automatically older than one according to which people were content to state the event without asking about the agent."[18]

   14   W. Havers, "Primitive Weltanschauung und Witterungsimpersonalia," p. 105.
   15   T. Siebs, "Die sogenannten subjektlosen Sätze," p. 266.
   16   Wilamowitz, "Zeus," p. 3.
   17   K. Brugmann, "Die Syntax des einfachen Satzes im Indogermanischen," p. 17.
   18   Wackernagel, *Vorlesungen über Syntax*, p. 116.

What the philologists did not consider was the possibility that the religious view of a natural event or even of an event occurring uniquely in man does not necessarily require an agent apart from and outside the action. Such a division of experience into action and agent is excluded by the immediacy of the experience, at any rate in its first actual moment. In the second moment language comes on the scene. But it is an unproved and improbable assumption that there was also a third moment, that of abstraction. For the correlation called religion, event and man are enough.

The exact linguistic view of the word *theos* proves this. By the linguistic observations of two such Greek experts as Wilamowitz[19] and Wackernagel,[20] it is established that the substantive *theos*, with masculine ending, always retained part of its original predicative character, the character of a statement that can refer to something suggesting predication. There are examples even in the relatively late language, in Euripides and Menander, where *theos* is said of an event, or in Sophokles' *Ichneutae* where "Theos!" is called out four times in the sense of the Virgilian "Deus, ecce deus!"[21] On the other hand, in the whole Greek language, so far as it is not spoken by Jews or Christians, *theos* has no vocative[22]—for one does not address an event. The word *theos* is a precultic word and it proves that the correlation which religion is, even without cult, could appear at any moment of Greek existence.

Compared with its nearest relative in another Indo-European language, *theos* is the word specially characteristic of Greek religious ex-

19   Wilamowitz, *Der Glaube der Hellenen*, I, 17.
20   Wackernagel, *Vorlesungen*, p. 297.
21   See further Kerényi, *Griechische Grundbegriffe*, p. 17.
22   Wackernagel, *Vorlesungen*, p. 297.

perience. The most nearly related word is the Hittite *teshas*, "sleep" and "dream."[23] The correspondence of sound between *teshas* and *theos* is regular and complete. From the strictly phonetic point of view, a mathematical equation can be set up. The Hittite word is, moreover, a noun of the same declension as *theos*. Yet in sense, on the other hand, the correspondence is between *teshas* and *thes-*, a shorter form of the same word. This form survived only in compounds—*thes-* in the Homeric words *thesphatos, thespesios, theskelos*. In *thesphatos*, which means unmistakably "that which is uttered by an oracle," *thes-* is equivalent to *teshas* with the meaning "truth-dream." The second half of these three compound words has the sense of "saying" (the roots *pha-* and *sep-*) or of "impelling" (the root *kel-*).

The characteristic which here distinguishes Hittites from Greeks consists in this, that in Hittite the truth-dream is itself a masculine, like *oneiros*, "dream," which in the Greek can also appear as a person.[24] Phonetically *teshas* can be equated with *theos* but semantically only with *oneiros*, and *thes-*. The *theos* of the Greeks is not limited to appearing in sleep. If a dream, then it can be a daydream that enriches the dimensions of sense experience with a further non-sensuous dimension. It is more than the indefinite *thes-*, which in Greek could only have been a neuter word. *Theos* with masculine ending had already taken for the Greeks a step in the direction of personal appearance. *Theos*, moreover, was experienced not only in dreams but also in the waking condition. The demarcation of the dream experience from what was always and everywhere a possible event fell away the moment the step was taken to personal appearance.

With the Greeks the event at which "Theos!" could be called out

23 See further J. Friedrich, *Hethitisches Wörterbuch*, p. 222.
24 See Iliad II 6, 8, and 22.

1. The Word Zeus and Its Synonyms, Theos and Daimon

could happen not only in dreams but also in nature and in history and *simultaneously* in the additional dimension of spirit. Thence is understood the slogan attributed in the literature to Thales, the first philosopher: *Panta theon plere*, "Everything is full of gods!"[25] There was for the Greeks no moment and no place where men could not be confronted by a god. In clarity, sharpness of outline, and plasticity he could vary, according to the capacity of whoever was having the experience for seeing and fixing shapes. It can be presumed that this capacity with the Greeks was highly developed. But if we ask about the *Greeks*, ask at what (chronologically not absolutely definable) moment—a moment of prehistory with the greatest historical effects—there were Greeks in existence, the most probable hypothesis is this. There were Greeks, we may say, from the moment of that great event when lighting up, outside and in, was comprehended as a special experience in the word *Zeus*. No god is *historically* thinkable without that correlation in which he affected men and to which men also belonged, to experience him and take him over and receive him from earlier experience. Yet, equally, no men are any longer thinkable without their god or gods once the correlation has come about. Correlation with several gods was possible. In this respect the Zeus religion is not comparable to the relation of the people of Israel to their god. And yet it *is* after all comparable. (Indeed, the historical analogy—independent of the content of Zeus and that of the god of the Israelites—is so evident that it must now become a subject of general scrutiny among scholars.)

All the more important is it to assess what is specifically Greek in the correlation "Greekhood and Zeus," insofar as its nucleus, the Zeus-experience of the Greeks, actually admits of any assessment. The word

25 H. Diels, *Die Fragmente der Vorsokratiker*, 11 [1] A 22 (vol. I, p. 79, line 27).

Zeus contains two elements: experience of light and the modality of this experience, of which the Greek light is an essential precondition. There is no excluding it. Another precondition was the perceptual and spiritual sensibility that never left the Greeks as long as they remained spiritually creative. The transition to the "Greek light," from a region where the light is less intense, is the experience of everyone who comes to Greece from the north and possesses a certain degree of the same sensibility.[26] "A light the like of which the eye has never beheld and in which it feels blissful, as if it were awaking for the first time to the sense of seeing" is how Hofmannsthal describes it.[27] This light is ineffably sharp and at the same time mild. It brings out the finest details, so Hofmannsthal continues, finding beautiful words for the clarity of the light. For the Greeks, light was the element of truth, as night was the element of thieves.[28]

Yet, if *Zeus* is considered with linguistic precision—which here means to reach the extreme limits of scientific contemplation but not step over them—then the word makes it impossible to take as its content this actual light and the experience of it. All the same, the experience is not far off from that which was Zeus. The modality contained in the word is that of an *actio perfectiva*. Thus, the word *Zeus* stood in opposition to an *actio inchoativa*, in which nothing is produced, but in no kind of opposition to an *actio iterativa*, a self-repeating event. An event that repeats itself automatically causes the same "agent" to appear again and again. A highly dramatic appearance this actor made, in the person of Zeus, on the stage of nature and the whole universe. There is, on the other hand, a distinction to be noted

26 See further "Auf Spuren des Mythos," in Kerényi, *Werke*, II, 182 ff.
27 See Hugo von Hofmannsthal's Preface to Hanns Holdt, *Griechenland*, pp. v ff.
28 See, for example, Euripides, *Iphigenia in Tauris* 1026.

1. *The Word* Zeus *and Its Synonyms,* Theos *and* Daimon

between Zeus's appearance and the function of Helios. The sun shines down on us from the sky, looks on from a distance, and thus consumes days and years.[29] An event made visible to men by Zeus and at the same time absorbed into their spirit is not separated from him by any distance. To him who in his essence is *consummating event*, that which happens, again and again another event, spontaneously returns, whether from the movement of the clouds or on to tranquil brightness, the *eudia*. The element *eu-* in this compound word asserts that it is now "good," but at the same time that it has once been less good and can be less good again. *Eudia* happens no less as rain or a snowstorm. Not the sky or the light, in themselves, are Zeus. Events are evidence of him, like the drama of light to which shadow also belongs, and like lightning and thunder, not only by day but also at night. The sky black with clouds was quite especially *his* place (as alluded to by Homer with the epithet *nephelegereta*), the place of lighting up.

Welcker stated at the beginning of his account of Zeus an idea which he called the "greatest fact when we go back into the remotest Greek antiquity." We must hold fast to this "greatest fact" and also to the contradictory picture that emerged from it. This initial fact according to Welcker was the "idea of god as the supreme being, combined with a worship of nature which had never entirely been submerged but out of which early on a family of deities, sprung from Zeus and outside nature, had begun to take shape."[30] In place of Welcker's idea of god, Zeus must be put, as a concrete experience. Still, the difficulty remains as indicated by Welcker. There were three realities—the initially "greatest fact," the "worship of nature," and the "family of deities"—and yet one of the three always seems to exclude the others.

29 Kerényi, *Töchter der Sonne*, pp. 23, 60–61.
30 Welcker, *Griechische Götterlehre*, I, 129.

Here, then, in preliminary sketch is the task of a historical treatment, of which the linguistic principles were indicated by Welcker. We already see that *theos* and *Zeus* in fact do belong together in sense.

In the historical Greek religion, *Zeus, theos, daimon* denote the pole to which man corresponds as antipole. Linguistic scrutiny of these words leads us to the extreme bounds of what can be counted as "Greek religious studies"; indeed, they themselves form these bounds. Of the three words, paradoxically, it is *Zeus* which is at once the most impersonal and the most singular—almost as impersonal as *thes-*. It is a masculine, like other Greek words ending in *-eus*. Yet, the words *dyaus* and *dies* in Sanskrit and Latin respectively, which exactly correspond to *Zeus* phonetically, testify to a wavering of the gender between feminine and masculine, that is to say, to the absence of a necessary gender,[31] which in the case of an agent would be rather masculine than feminine. In the case of Zeus this impersonality is combined with a striking singularity. Though plurals of Zeus have come down, the examples show that they are mere grammatical possibilities which have a much more complicated relation to Zeus than *theoi* to *theos*. The plurals are no longer situated at the level at which Zeus as *actio perfectiva* (perfective aspect) was originally situated and which he finally reached as highest god.[32]

In contrast to Zeus, *daimon* is the most personal and at the same time the least singular of the three. Whenever the word occurs in the singular, it is a special *daimon*. Its ending alone makes the *daimon* personal; the formative *-mon* most decidedly expresses an agent. A "dispenser" is the meaning of *daimon*, but not a human one. In the

31 See further Zimmermann, "Das ursprüngliche Geschlecht von *dies*," pp. 79 ff.

32 Diels, "Zeus," p. 2; E. Fehrle, "Zeus," col. 575; Wilamowitz, *Der Glaube der Hellenen*, I, 215–16.

1. *The Word* Zeus *and Its Synonyms,* Theos *and* Daimon   17

plural, in the language of Homer, *daimones* is completely equivalent to *theoi,* "gods."[33] *Daimon* in the singular also is personal in sense. It appears in a personal occurrence, in a personal fate, we might say, although we must not understand "fate" here as a being existent on its own.[34] The "dispenser" occurred only in a personal case; it was a personal dispensation each time it happened. It had to be seen from the point of view of the person to whom it occurred and in this respect the *daimon* was the most personal of the three. Yet the word *daimon* was at the same time the most general expression, the word in the mouth of all unknowing persons.

Who was it who knew the name appropriate to whatever *theos* occurred there? Only a person familiar with the gods, *such as a poet,* could know. (It can almost be laid down as a rule that where Homer is himself narrating he can give the name of the god who appears, but that where we find an unnamed god in Homer it is one of his characters who is speaking.[35]) For people to say "The Dispenser!" was the most obvious thing in cases that seemed like an individual fate characteristic of a person. A further step was to assign the *daimon* as an individual deity of a lower order to people as individuals.[36] This, too, is a phenomenon of Greek religious history, but not until a relatively late date.

Zeus can be *daimon,* in the old original sense of the word, for a mortal.[37] The *daimon* reaches as far as the human being has his fate,

33 Iliad I 222, VI 115, XXIII 595.

34 Fate is understood as "that aspect of the divine in which it appears to man as destiny"; see Kerényi, *Die antike Religion,* p. 103 (in *Werke,* VII, 75). See also Wilamowitz, *Der Glaube der Hellenen,* I, 362 ff.

35 This disposition has been verified by O. Jörgensen, "Das Auftreten der Götter in den Büchern ι–μ der Odyssee," p. 366.

36 See Hesiod, *Works and Days* 122.

37 E. Heden, *Homerische Götterstudien,* p. 86.

in the words of the German poet Hölderlin, "to the abyss."[38] The *daimon* can be apostrophized; *daimon* has its vocative. The vocative form is also possessed by Zeus. The vocative makes sense where man experiences god in himself. To "father Zeus" he addressed himself from a greater distance. The *daimon* he experienced as the "dispenser." In tragedy, where it was later found possible to recognize "fate," the *daimon* reigned like an almighty god. There are instructive parallels in related languages. In Old Persian *baga-* and in Old Church Slavic *bogŭ* is the word for god, while in Avestan and Sanskrit the same word means "share," "lot," "destiny," "dispenser," "lord."[39] In the same way *daimon* can stand for Zeus.

Beside *Zeus*, *theos*, and *daimon* Welcker put the name Kronion, a patronymic, "son of Kronos." This was correct inasmuch as the succession, the connection with a new epoch after that of Kronos, was characteristic of Zeus. By the original content of his name, "lighting up," Zeus was connected for the Greeks not with the beginning of the world but with the time of which they themselves had historical consciousness, a "new" time contrasted with an "old" time not yet ruled by Zeus. The dithyrambic poet Timotheos of Miletos testifies to the quality of "newness" attached to Zeus. In the words quoted as a motto at the front of this book, Timotheos justifies his own modernity, a renovation of Greek music. His appeal to Zeus may have been a dithyrambic audacity. Yet, he must have been able to count on its finding a resonance in fourth-century Athens.

The time of the Persian Wars, and of the greatest spiritual brightness experienced by the Greek world since Homer, had gone before, in

   38 The expression appears in both the first and second versions of the poem "Mnemosyne." See F. Hölderlin, *Werke*, p. 393.
   39 See Frisk, *Griechisches etymologisches Wörterbuch*, I, 341.

1. *The Word* Zeus *and Its Synonyms,* Theos *and* Daimon

the sixth and fifth centuries. The emergence of a consciousness of common history went further than the consciousness of a comprehensive community. The scene of menace and rescue was no longer primarily the sky and nature but the earth and its seas, on which Greeks lived and died. It was not a "physical" but rather a "moral" event when in the sixth century B.C. the Greeks first saw in Zeus the god of their history. There are evidences from the time in which this history occurred—evidences not of contemplation but of the Zeus religion.

Herodotos reports the utterance of a Greek at the Hellespont, a witness of the great operation by which Xerxes brought his army across the Straits. He cried out: "O Zeus, why have you taken the shape and the name of Xerxes in place of Zeus if you wanted to overthrow Greece with all these people? You could have done it without that!"[40] And Herodotos also quotes an utterance of the Delphic oracle about a certain Spartan—Leonidas understood it to refer to him—who would resist the Persians, saying that he had the "courage of Zeus," *Zenos gar echei menos.*[41]

From the tragedians a single verse—the last line of Sophokles' *Trachiniae*—may be quoted here, for with it this view of history is transposed to heroic myth. After all the horror that has happened in the tragedy, down to the self-burning of Herakles, the son of Zeus, indeed *of this very event*, the poet says,

κοὐδὲν τούτων ὅτι μὴ Ζεύς

and nothing of all this is not Zeus—

a saying of the Zeus religion that makes you catch your breath. And yet it is a quite plain, outspoken utterance of Sophokles, who does not

---

40 Herodotos VII 56.   41 Ibid. VII 220.

philosophize like the other tragedians. Behind what his chorus declares here with such immediacy is the assumption that for the normal Athenian of the Classical period, of whom Sophokles himself counted as one, and without doubt also for the normal Greek, Zeus was the "meaning" that lighted up more or less in every great happening.

II. THE BEGINNINGS OF THE ZEUS RELIGION AND ITS EARLY HISTORY

THERE IS no question that Greek religion was primarily Zeus religion and no question that the Zeus religion was the religion characteristic of the Greeks. In what follows this is shown in detail. The most probable hypothesis is that the rise of the correlation Zeus at one pole with the Greeks at the other constituted a beginning *before* which it is not possible to speak of the existence either of Greek religion or of the Greeks whom we know in history as the bearers of that religion. The question is when this correlation arose. Were the Greeks who first invaded the world of Minoan civilization already Greeks in this sense? Did the correlation already exist among the invaders and did the other Greeks take it over from them, or did it arise among a tribe that arrived later, or in Crete first of all?

The most probable theory is that the correlation arose once and once only. The more closely and accurately the historical phenomenon of the Zeus religion is studied, the less probable it becomes that the correlation arose repeatedly—two or three times, say—among the Greeks. That it arose early is suggested by the memorials of the so-called Mycenaean Greek language, where the name Zeus in its uniqueness of meaning and singularity of number is present in various small contexts. The important texts are those from Knossos, but not for statistical reasons, as being more numerous than the references in Pylos. The random nature of this kind of transmission does not allow us to draw inferences of this character. What there is must be evaluated and interpreted singly.

Most important of all is the evidence of a *month of Zeus*, from that period of higher civilization in Crete (after the middle of the second millennium) when the lords of the palace of Knossos were already Greeks. The expression *di-wi-jo-jo me-no*, *Diwioio menos*, stands there clear and unambiguous.[1] In the Zeus month, oil is offered "to all the gods," *pa-si-te-o-i*, a collective grouping of the gods already well established. A month Dios is otherwise attested in northern Greece, in the Macedonian calendar as the first month explicitly,[2] and among the Greeks, from whom the Macedonians may have taken it over, without indication of its position in the year. It is found especially in the Aiolic linguistic territory, such as Thessaly and Lesbos and among the Aitolians.[3] As in a great arc the Zeus religion extends from the northern frontier of Greece, a territory of closely related language, as far as Crete. Since no Zeus month occurs among the tribes or cities of the center, whose calendar is well known to us, we must appeal here to the *argumentum ex silentio*. Zeus as the god of one month in the calendar is probably older than Zeus in his exalted position over all the gods. And not until the Zeus religion had penetrated Greece did the whole festival calendar in a manner belong to Zeus.

According to a text from Knossos, Zeus got grain as an offering.[4]

1   Knossos Fp 5. See further G. Pugliese Carratelli, "Riflessi di culti micenei nelle tabelle di Cnosso e Pilo," p. 602.
2   See E. Bischoff, "Kalender," col. 1595.
3   Perrhaibia, in Thessaly, is listed by Bischoff, col. 1598; see there also Lesbos and Aitolia.
4   On the offering to Zeus, see, for example, Knossos F 51.2 (*di-we*). For the genitive *di-wo*, see E 842.1. Further, see P. H. Ilievski, "Two Notes on the FR-Tablets," p. 149. The proposed forms are put together by H. Mühlestein, "Panzeus in Pylos," p. 88. (The assumption of a "Panzeus," however, was based on an uncertain reading and had to be given up.)

II. The Beginnings of the Zeus Religion and Its Early History 23

A wider prospect is opened up by a list of oil offerings. In the month Deukios, which is probably to be understood as Leukios, "month of lightening," the offering is carried to the "Dikte"[5] for Zeus Diktaios.[6] Mount Dikte stands at the eastern tip of Crete.[7] Its associations were rather with the childhood of Zeus than with his birth.[8] If it was the case that Zeus's birth was transferred there, the event took place not in a cave (it was found impossible to identify a cult cave there despite a careful search) but on the mountain itself,[9] a place of morning light, corresponding to the name Zeus. The expression "of Dikte" probably directed the sacrificers to a holy precinct with a little mountain temple, of which we know some examples from pictures.[10] The myth of the Cretan birth of Zeus, which for more than one reason would fit a cave, did not appear until the Zeus religion was already in existence. As it was older than the arrival of the Greeks in Crete and was no doubt already firmly associated with them, the birth myth was able to supply the framework of an early and genuine syncretism.[11]

It is less easy to decide whether it was in Crete that the Zeus religion first became enriched with mythologems of birth and childhood, marriage and fatherhood. Or had this "agent" implicit in lighting up

---

5 Knossos Fp 7.2. See also Pugliese Carratelli, "Riflessi di culti micenei," p. 602.

6 Knossos Fp 1.2. See further L. R. Palmer, *The Interpretation of Mycenaean Greek Texts*, pp. 235-36. The proposal of a missing letter before the name of the month is certainly mistaken.

7 See P. Faure, "Nouvelles recherches de spéléologie et de topographie Crétoises," p. 189.

8 See Apollonius Rhodius, *Argonautica* I 508-509.

9 ἐπὶ τῆς Δίκτης, according to Agathokles of Kyzikos, fr. 1, in Jacoby, *FGrHist*, III, B, p. 430 (472 F 1 16).

10 See Kerényi, *Dionysos*, ch. I, the concluding remarks on "Visionary Crete." / For the form "of Dikte," see above, note 5.

11 See "Flaming New Year," in Kerényi, *Dionysos: Archetypal Image of Indestructible Life*, ch. II.

Zeus and Hera 24

and illumination—whom the Greeks experienced with worship—been translated at a still earlier stage into such archetypal situations? This question must be posed quite concretely in regard to the situation in Pylos, as reflected by texts in the same script and language as those of Knossos, and in regard also to the highly ancient Zeus cult of Mount Lykaion in Arcadia. The answer would perhaps be easier if the radiative influence of the mainland upon Crete[12] were not just as much a factor to be reckoned with as the reaction on the mainland to the much-enriched Zeus religion from Crete.

A priest of Hera, *Heras hiereus*,[13] is not certainly attested for Knossos; the reading *era* is doubtful[14] and a priest instead of a priestess of the goddess would be surprising. Derivatives of the name Hera do seem to occur in Knossos, but they are more likely to be derivatives of a place name *era*.[15] The first appearance of Zeus and Hera visibly united side by side is in Pylos.[16] Among the gifts for a *di-u-jo* (*Divion*, shrine of Zeus), these are mentioned: to Zeus (*di-we*) goes a golden bowl and a male attendant, and to Hera (*e-ra*) goes a golden bowl and a female. In third place in the same context a son of Zeus is mentioned, *di-wo i-je-we* (*Dios hyiei*), similarly in the dative case and with a golden gift. His particular appellation *di-ri-mi-jo* is mysterious.[17] That he was also a son of Hera does not follow from the text. If a family is referred to here,

12   S. Marinatos, "Die Wanderung des Zeus," cols. 903–916.
13   L. A. Stella, *La civiltà micenea nei documenti contemporanei*, p. 15.
14   Knossos As 821.2 and L 1649 are equally uncertain.
15   See M. Gérard-Rousseau, *Les mentions religieuses dans les tablettes mycéniennes*, pp. 95 ff.
16   Pylos Tn 316.9 (tablet 172). See M. Ventris and J. Chadwick, *Documents in Mycenaean Greek*, p. 289; L. Palmer, *Mycenaean Greek Texts*, pp. 262 ff.
17   The appellation is referred to Apollo by L. A. Stella, "La religione greca nei testi micenei," pp. 26–27. A dark god must be considered if the word is related to δριμύς (see δριμὺς ἀλάστωρ in Aischylos, *Agamemnon* 1501). Διόνυσος

II. The Beginnings of the Zeus Religion and Its Early History 25

then it must be one such as the family of Zeus was in Homer, where Hera and a son not hers belonged to Zeus.

In a text from Pylos there occurs also an "Eleuther the Zeus-son"— *e-re-u-te-re di-wi-je-we*.[18] This name can be connected with the Dionysian village Eleutherai[19] that lies on the way from Pylos to Athens,[20] the shortest geographical connection between these two sites of the Dionysos cult. The village's founder hero, who erected a statue of Dionysos there, bore the name Eleuther.[21] The Pylian bearer of the same name was probably so called after "Eleuthereus," a name of Dionysos.[22] His appellation *di-wi-je-we* comes closest to the Greek *diogenes*, "sprung from Zeus." The name by which he became generally known appears in Pylos for the first time on two tablets[23] as *di-wo-nu-so-jo*; by the syllables *di-wo-* he is clearly connected with Zeus and subordinated to him. This presupposes at least a divine order, and one that was certainly of Cretan origin. It must have come into existence on the great island[24] during Minoan times and by 1300–1200 B.C., the period of the Pylian tablets, the compound name was already in such general use that in both texts

---

ὠμηστής is one possibility; see C. Gallavotti, "La triade lesbia in un testo miceneo," pp. 227 ff.

18 Pylos Cn 3.2. See J. Puhvel, "Eleuther and Oinoatis: Dionysiac Data from Mycenaean Greece," esp. pp. 161 ff. For the linguistic form, see C. Gallavotti, *Documenti e struttura del greco nell'età micenea*, p. 40.

19 On the countryside of Eleutherai, in Boeotia, where the goddess Mnemosyne is at home, see Hesiod, *Theogony* 54.

20 On the road from Pylos, through Aigosthena and up the mountain pass to Eleutherai, see Kerényi, *Dionysos*, ch. IV, at note 102.

21 The bearer of the name (see Puhvel, above, note 18) and of the epithet was certainly a man, as is made clear from the evidence assembled by H. Mühlestein in his review of *Inscriptiones Pyliae*, p. 278.

22 See *Suidas Lexicon* s.v. Μέλαν, and also Kerényi, *Dionysos*, in ch. IV, the section, "The Arrival in Athens."

23 Pylos Xa 102 and Xb 1419.1.

24 See further the section, "Ariadne," in Kerényi, *Dionysos*, ch. III.

Zeus and Hera

it could mean wine.²⁵ "Eleuther the Zeus-son" denoted in pure Greek form the rank of the wine god among the gods of the Greeks, and was rather evidence of the radiation of the Dionysos religion from south to north than of the actual spread of the Zeus religion which constituted the framework of that event.

Yet, this at least can be established with precision in Pylos. Tendencies are present toward the formation of the Olympian family of gods and goddesses around Zeus on an archetypal footing. The fatherhood of two sons is attested. The marriage of Zeus and Hera is made plausible by the fact that the masculine quality of the one and the feminine quality of the other are clearly expressed in the cult. A male attendant goes to Zeus and a female to Hera, as specified by one of the Pylos tablets.²⁶ But this does not yet associate the fatherhood of Zeus with marriage. The same Pylos text, one of the longer ones, earlier mentions a goddess closely related by name to Zeus, *di-u-ja* (Divia, or Dia), and her shrine *di-u-ja-jo* (*Diviaion*), second in the list after a goddess *i-pe-me-de-ja* (Iphimedeia)²⁷—certainly a lunar goddess—and also her shrine. This seems to be a reflection of the circumstance that a goddess had already been assigned to Zeus in his northern home—in Dodona she was called Dione²⁸—and that Hera did not take her place till later. The original "Zeus-wife," as plainly declared by the name Divia, was in Pylos an independent goddess, provided with a cult (golden bowl and female attendant) similar to Hera. Here in the southern Peloponnese, if any-

---

25 See Kerényi, "Möglicher Sinn von *di-wo-nu-so-jo* und *da-da-re-jo-de*," pp. 102–103.

26 Pylos Tn 316 (see above, ch. II, note 16). For the goddess (*di-u-ja*), see Tn 316.6.

27 The name is related to "Iphigeneia." There are no linguistic difficulties; see V. Georgiev, "Mycénien et homérique: le problème du digamma," p. 123.

28 The linguistic connection is similar to that of Dia with Diana; see F. Altheim, *Griechische Götter im alten Rom*, p. 98.

II. The Beginnings of the Zeus Religion and Its Early History   27

where, was the place for this Great Goddess to move from her sanctuary in Argos into union with Zeus.

No compelling reason has turned up in the texts for transferring the foundation of the marriage between Zeus and Hera, and their family, to Crete. The goddess Divia accompanied Zeus to the island and had her special festival[29] there, just as Hera probably had her Heraia. A marriage feast of Zeus and Hera near Knossos on the Theren River is reported by Diodorus Siculus quoting a late Cretan author, but again, a compelling reason would be needed to put this back into the pre-Greek or the earliest Greek period on the island.[30] As for the fatherhood of Zeus, it cannot with certainty be presumed from the name *Dio-nysos*. Even though this name was one that came into use for the god who in Crete preceded Zeus in his all-surpassing power,[31] the *-nysos* still does not necessarily mean that he was thought of as a son. "Dio" perhaps simply gave prominence to this "Nysos" (with his Nysai, the mountain goddesses or nymphs who reared him) as to a Zeus-like being, after the Zeus religion had already invaded the island.

The question of the beginnings of the Zeus family may therefore be answered with some probability in favor of the mainland. An open question is that of the original scene of Zeus's birth. The place of his birth was questionable even for the Greeks themselves. Kallimachos states this. He supports the claims of Arcadia against those of Crete. He depicts in his Hymn to Zeus the scene of a universal lighting up that

29   On this festival, see Knossos X 97 and 284: *di-wi-je-ja di-wi-ja*.
30   For the marriage feast on the Theren, see Diodorus Siculus V 72 4. Cook, I, 523, assumes "ritual pairing of the solar bull with the lunar cow." The assumption is unfounded. Even if it were valid, it would not be evidence of a wedding of Zeus and Hera in the Minoan period. In the vicinity of the river the cult of Demeter and Persephone is attested in a cave with a Christian chapel; see P. Faure, *Fonctions des cavernes crétoises*, pp. 147–48.
31   See "Mythology of the Leather Sack," in Kerényi, *Dionysos*, ch. II.

filled the whole sky.[32] It lay at a great height, practically on one of the peaks of the *Lykaion oros*, the Arcadian mountain of Zeus's birth, which was reputed to be a special place of light. There Rhea, the mother of Zeus, sought out the spot most protected by the scrub. No birth might ever take place there in the future, neither human nor animal. In a special way the spot remained forever holy.[33] That a tradition of a birth in the open air existed is proved by the fact that it was transposed even to Crete. In Crete, caves were the places proper for lighting up; the light broke out of the depth and darkness simultaneously with the early rising of Sirius. This can be established with exactness in the case of one Cretan cave that is not otherwise identifiable.[34]

As mentioned earlier, on Mount Dikte, from which Zeus got the epithet "Diktaios" in the Knossos tablets, no cult cave has been detected. Among the caves on Crete that were connected with a divine child— originally not Zeus but the god who as *Dio-nysos* was to become his son —was the Idaean Cave. According to Kallimachos, who here accepted the Cretan claim, Zeus was born not in the cave but "in the Idaean Mountains."[35] The Hellenistic poet, however, was certainly not the first to have transposed to Mount Ida the description of the birth in the open air. This description has been preserved in mythological literature as an explanation of the name of the Idaean Daktyloi. "When the time appointed for the birth arrived and the pains began, Rhea in her suffering supported herself with both hands on the mountain. The mountain thereupon bore the Daktyls in numbers equal to the fingers of the goddess, to assist her as obstetricians."[36]

32 Kallimachos, *Hymnus in Jovem* 10 ff.
33 See further, in ch. II, the section on Mount Lykaion.
34 See "Flaming New Year," in Kerényi, *Dionysos*, ch. II.
35 Kallimachos, *Hymnus in Jovem* 6.
36 R. Schoell and G. Studemund, eds., *Anecdota varia Graeca et Latina*, I, 224. Also see Kerényi, *The Gods of the Greeks*, pp. 83–84 (Pelican edn., p. 73).

II. The Beginnings of the Zeus Religion and Its Early History   29

This could have happened also in a cave. Yet, it was not the breaking of light out of a cave with which this extraordinarily archaic mythologem[37] was combined but with the universal lighting up. The mythologem became its framework and gave the lighting up human form. This could scarcely have happened further north than the range of influence of the Great Mother Goddess Rhea, which united Crete with Asia Minor. The most probable assumption in this case is that the archaic mythologem of the primordial woman and goddess giving birth in solitude[38] became in Crete an extension of the other myth which gave a permanent name to the divine event of lighting up and called it Zeus. A divine event like this had no definite location. It did, however, occur above all on mountain peaks lit up by the break of day.

The cultic situation on Olympos, mountain of the Homeric gods, corresponded—so far as it has been possible to discover traces of a cult—to this simplest myth. On the highest peak no traces of any ancient cult site have been found, but one such site was uncovered on a spur that stands about an hour's walk south of the 9,500-foot main peak and is itself some 300 feet lower. Archaeologists in the summer of 1923 thought they had detected an altar there and were able to pick up a few hundred shards to prove that there had been a lively sacrificial traffic at the place in ancient times.[39] Thus, sacrifice was offered not on the main peak, which was reserved for the happening of the god, but opposite it. The rock thrones found on other mountains, in Greece and especially in Asia Minor, are evidence of a more cumbersome style of expectation of the god's coming. The style of Greek religion did not always or everywhere entail a ritual form for a divine event. But where

37   See Kerényi, *Umgang mit Göttlichem*, p. 75.
38   Kerényi, *Werke*, I, 70 ff.
39   See H. Scheffel, "Eine antike Opferstätte auf dem Olymp," p. 129.

a throne awaits the deity, a well-developed ritual for the epiphany is present. Such a ritual can hardly be dated to the beginnings of the Zeus religion. Yet, an early encounter between this religion and that of another supreme god could well have taken place—in addition to that encounter with the life cult of the Minoans, which became the Dionysos religion in Greece, and in Crete itself produced the myths about a childhood of Zeus.[40]

We do not know what picture was conjured up, in the ninth and eighth centuries, Homer's own time, by a mysterious line of the Odyssey. The line occurs in a passage dealing with the peoples of Crete and King Minos.[41] For Homer, Minos was a son of Zeus by the daughter of Phoinix.[42] She, in the mythological tradition, is called Europa. That Homer names as her father the eponymous representative of the Phoenicians, an Asian people, must mean at least that the mythical high king of the Cretans, with the un-Greek name of Minos, was known in Greek tradition as a non-Greek, if not actually as an Oriental, king. The mysterious line of the Odyssey says of Knossos, where Minos ruled, that

ἐννέωρος βασίλευε Διὸς μεγάλου ὀαριστής.[43]

Enneoros is the ambiguous word. Was the nine-year-old Minos the ruler? Did he rule for nine years, or for nine other periods? Or does the word belong to the most mysterious part of the whole line, to *oaristes*? *Oaristes* presupposes partnership, in this case not, as elsewhere, an erotic one, since Minos was the son of the god, but a spiritual one; this, therefore, also presupposes a spiritual content of Zeus. Plato understood Homer to mean that Minos was accustomed to foregather with

40 On these myths, see Kerényi, *Dionysos*, ch. II; also *The Gods of the Greeks*, pp. 92–95.
41 Odyssey XIX 172–79.   42 Iliad XIV 321–22.
43 Odyssey XIX 179.

II. The Beginnings of the Zeus Religion and Its Early History 31

Zeus every nine years and that he derived his wise government and lawgiving from these meetings.[44] The missing clue is the place of the meetings. Did they happen on a mountain, in a cave, or in a building? According to the small dialogue *Minos*, the place was a Zeus cave.[45]

The question cannot be resolved. There seems to have been a custom that the Minoan king could visit some place where he was together with Zeus. Whether only Minos, as a mythical exception, took part, or not only he, but all the kings of Knossos of whom he was only the mythical type—this also must remain unresolved. The idea of a place where one could be outside time, above human life and death, was part of the religion of early times in the Mediterranean. Life contains the experience not only of lighting up, internally and externally, but also of low points and high points of existence. Culminations of life allow us to imagine the form of existence that is exhibited at regular intervals by the sky, at the apparent turning points of the sun, when time itself seems to stand still. Such is the form of existence of the gods in mythology. Men read it from the sky[46] and connect it with the experience of light and sweetness, unreflectively, in complete spontaneity. The experience of this form of being, above life and death, was derived from the experience of immediate timelessness when it occurred. It was the spontaneous, positive indication of the cessation of the time experience.

The experience of timelessness has been recorded in ancient writings. Aristotle exemplifies the fact of timelessness by the case, for him already mythical, of those who slept among the heroes in Sardinia.[47] Those who did so participated for a brief moment in the condition of

---

44 Plato, *Laws* I 624 AB.
45 *Minos* 319 E (of uncertain Platonic authorship).
46 See "Das Mythologem vom zeitlosen Sein," in Kerényi, *Niobe*, p. 195.
47 Aristotle, *Physics* IV 11 218b 21–26.

eternally incorruptible sleep of the Sardinian heroes and themselves dropped out of time even as the heroes had.[48] The classical example, however, was the myth of the Cretan Epimenides, who as a historical personage, priest and sage, was assigned to the seventh century B.C. The young Epimenides, so it was related in the oldest discernible form of his story,[49] was looking for his father's sheep and in the hour of noon had turned off the path to lay himself, tired by the heat, to rest in a cave. There he fell asleep. The hour of noon is no less important in this story than the place, a Cretan cave.

It is the time of noon when the shadows of things cease by their length and direction to serve as a measure of time. The shadows withdraw. The culmination of the sun makes it seem as if time had stopped. The actual time-measurer, the sun, stands at its peak and really does seem to "stand still." Epimenides woke up fifty-seven years later and went on looking for his father's sheep. He did not realize how long he had slept. It was three times the nineteen years of the Metonic cycle, the greatest unit of time among the Greeks. Fifty-seven years are time *itself*, increased threefold. Epimenides lived to be a hundred and fifty-seven. Thus, he lost out of his lifespan (rated, in the view of antiquity, at a hundred years), by the insertion of timelessness symbolized by the fifty-seven years, nothing.

A birth cave of Zeus in Crete, characterized by the lighting up of the fire, but geographically not identified, was marked out in the same sense as a place above life and death. Nobody was allowed to die in it.[50] Nor might it be entered. It was a place of immortality pure and simple,

---

48 See further Kerényi, *Niobe*, p. 206.

49 The Epimenides story is related by Theopompos of Chios, fr. 67, in Jacoby, *FGrHist*, II, B, p. 548 (115 F 67 12 ff.).

50 Antoninus Liberalis, Μεταμορφώσεων συναγωγή XIX.

II. The Beginnings of the Zeus Religion and Its Early History 33

on its own. The honey of the holy bees, which had fed Zeus there and still occupied it, filled the cave. If their honey overflowed, then the light of a great fire burst forth from the cave. The immortality that had its place in the cave implies timelessness. The bursting forth of the fiery glow once a year had its explanation in calendar and ritual.[51] In another case, timelessness and "standing light" (*statheron phos*),[52] like the sun's light at the point of noon, appear on a Zeus mountain—very much a mountain, of Zeus's birth, not in Crete but in the center of the Peloponnese. Here is a phenomenon in the history of Greek religion; the question is, What is the relation *between* the timelessness implied in "standing light" *and* Zeus the lighter up, with his mythology?

The Arcadian Mount Lykaion, 4,660 feet high at the summit, was connected with a light myth that made it a timeless place above life and death, a world beyond, set apart from earthly existence. "Lykaios" also was a name of Zeus, who had his altar there and his sacred precinct which it was forbidden to enter. The *Lykaion oros* has two peaks; Pausanias praises the wide-ranging view from the lower.[53] On this peak was Zeus's altar, of which all that remained was a mound of ash with bones of sacrificial animals. Somewhat lower down lay the sacred precinct, in the open air like the altar of burnt sacrifice. On this terrace Kallimachos pictured to himself the thicket in which Rhea gave birth to Zeus.[54] The association of this spot with timeless, standing light certainly reached

---

51 See Kerényi, "Licht, Wein, Honig," pp. 200–214; also "Flaming New Year," in *Dionysos*, ch. II.

52 See the expression in Plutarch, *De facie quae in orbe lunae apparet* 934 E; see also Plato, *Phaedrus* 242 A.

53 See Pausanias VIII 38 7. On the reference to the lower of two peaks, see J. G. Frazer, *Pausanias's Description of Greece*, IV, 382. On the altar and sacred precinct of Zeus, see K. Kourouniotes, Ἀνασκαφαὶ Λυκαίου, pp. 152 ff.

54 Kallimachos, *Hymnus in Jovem* 10 ff.

back into the ancient Mediterranean and Minoan regime of the goddess and found expression in the mountain's name. *Lykaion* can be regularly derived from *lyke*, an early Greek word for light.[55] At the same time, through a characteristic association of the peak of light with extreme darkness—an association that can be called early Greek[56]—*Lykaion* also alludes to *lykos*, the wolf, the nocturnal animal, whose Indo-European name and etymology have nothing to do with light.[57]

The myth of the place speaks of a condition characteristic of this kind of light. Man or animal, it was said, anything that set foot in the forbidden area, lost its shadow. No hunter would follow his prey into it. If a beast set foot on the sacred ground, the hunter would merely watch it from outside. So Pausanias described it.[58] It was the same phenomenon, he adds, as that in the Ethiopian Syene (modern Aswan) when the sun stands in Cancer. Only on Mount Lykaion it was always so. This story was roundly asserted, though it was not believed by the more critical minds.[59] Whoever crossed the bounds of the sacred precinct, so the story continued, was no longer allowed to live, surviving at most one single year.[60] For such a transgressor had fallen forfeit to what was beyond life and death. A further expression for this condition was a change of name for the transgressor. He was from now on looked upon as a deer[61]—a hunted animal—or, if he ate of the meat of that extraordinary victim sacrificed there, he was reputedly transformed into a

---

55   See Cook, *Zeus*, I, 64, notes 4 and 5, and the references there to Macrobius, *Saturnalia* I 17 37 ff., and to Iliad VII 433 (ἀμφιλύκη).

56   For a similar phenomenon in the religion of Apollo, see "Unsterblichkeit und Apollonreligion," in Kerényi, *Apollon*, p. 46.

57   Ibid., p. 44.

58   Pausanias VIII 38 6.

59   See Polybios XVI 12 7; Plutarch, *Quaestiones graecae* 300 c.

60   Pausanias VIII 38 6.

61   See Plutarch, *Quaestiones graecae* 300 CD.

II. The Beginnings of the Zeus Religion and Its Early History 35

wolf. Indeed, the belief in werewolves among the Greeks was likewise connected with the precinct of Zeus on Mount Lykaion.[62]

Pausanias refuses to name the victim that was sacrificed there "in secret."[63] It is however inexact to call it, as in the more recent literature, simply "human sacrifice."[64] Pausanias, at all events, relates the foundation myth of the sacrifice.[65] According to this it was Lykaon, the primordial king of the Arcadians—from his name, a "man of light"–who was the first to sacrifice an infant to Zeus Lykaios. Such a sacrifice was not and never became Greek, although on Mount Lykaion, if we rightly understand Pausanias, it was still performed in his time. Greeks and Romans explained this atrocity as similar to the crime of Tantalos and overlooked the senselessness of repeating an outrage that had been criminal from the outset. It would have been only a sin against the supreme god. The dialogue *Minos*, one of the possibly Platonic writings, quotes as the sole parallel the child sacrifice of the Carthaginians.[66] This was a well-known Phoenician custom, however, chiefly it seems in their colonies. The Semitic name for this sacrifice was *molek*.[67] (It was not a god called by this name—not "Moloch"–as was long believed.) The Semitic god who received sacrifices of this kind was equated by the Greeks with their Kronos. In the *Minos* dialogue we read that some of the Carthaginians sacrificed their own sons to Kronos.

62   See Plato, *Republic* VIII 565 DE, and the passages cited in W. Immerwahr, *Die Kulte und Mythen Arkadiens*, I, 10 ff. Also see Cook, *Zeus*, I, 70–72.
63   Pausanias VIII 38 7. What he learned about the secret sacrifice was not nice: οὔ . . . ἡδὺ ἦν.
64   See Kerényi, *Werke*, I, 109.
65   Pausanias VIII 2 3–4. F. Schwenn, *Die Menschenopfer bei den Griechen und Römern*, p. 20, assumes (not without reason; cf. Pliny, *Natural History* VIII 22, 81) that priests and victims belonged to the Antheadai, the family of Anthos.
66   See *Minos* 315 c.
67   See O. Eissfeldt, *Molk als Opferbegriff im Punischen und Hebräischen, und das Ende des Gottes Moloch*, pp. 1 ff.

The myth of the timeless light that could become dangerous to men and in its menace be transformed to darkness—and therefore demanded complete submission, the sacrifice of a human life—was the myth of an overwhelming divine presence. "Divine" in this case is not just an attribute of the overwhelming presence, not just one quality among many that clung to it. The overwhelming presence *was* the divinity and did not need to bear any personal marks. It is left to the working out of the myth, the mythologem, to add such details. The myth was grounded in religious experience and in the human nature that could have such experience. It cannot be maintained as a matter of course that this experience was peculiar only to one people or tribe. For the Greeks, bearers of their own original Zeus myth, this myth was something strange that they had to appropriate. The mythologem of father Kronos who swallowed his children represents an addition to the Zeus myth. It remained a mythological tale without religious substance, and without ritual consequences, unless it was indeed this that justified the child sacrifice to the supreme god. All the Kronos myths show evidence of remoteness from the Zeus era. And here lies the answer to the inevitable question, Who was this Kronos? Where did Zeus get a father from whom the pregnant mother Rhea had to flee in order to save her child?

The pre-Greek god with the name of doubtful meaning, "Kronos,"[68] was the El of the West Semites[69] and received from them the sacrifice of human children as part of the first-fruits offering made to him of everything that was born or grew. That was the sense of the sacrifice of human posterity, particularly in colonial territories. In this way the god was paid for the new land—probably with the first-born from the best of the conqueror families. Evidence of this is to be found in the *tofet*, the

68 See W. Fauth, "Kronos," col. 359.
69 See W. Fauth, "El," cols. 226–28.

II. *The Beginnings of the Zeus Religion and Its Early History* 37

burial places of the sacrificed infants.[70] They give the incidental meaning of the sacrifice. The primordial meaning, however, lies in the *correlation between* the bearers of a religion *and* a god such as the West Semites and their El were—a highly intensive correlation even in that form in which it was not yet spiritualized as it was among the Israelites.

We know nothing of any colonization on Mount Lykaion by the Phoenicians. All we have is the tradition among the Arcadians that the town of Lykosoura on Mount Lykaion was the oldest town in the world.[71] On the mountain there survived the secret sacrificial rite which among the Israelites had re-emerged from prehistory in the eighth and seventh centuries B.C.[72] They, however, had freed themselves from it by a more spiritual submission of the whole people; Israel itself became the "first fruits of God's harvest."[73] In the Zeus religion the requirement of total submission survived in its crudest form, that of the human firstborn sacrifice, on Mount Lykaion, hedged around and isolated as if on an island rising out of the seas of time past. The Arcadians called this mountain their Olympos.[74] The other, Macedonian, Olympos characterized the Greek religion from the beginning, all the more so when it had become the seat of an entire family of gods and goddesses. This was the family that had formed around Zeus the father.

70 See S. Moscati, "Il sacrificio dei fanciulli," pp. 61–68, and the literature cited there. The significance of the sacrifice, however, was not understood.

71 Pausanias VIII 38 1. V. Bérard, *De l'origine des cultes arcadiens*, is unrewarding.

72 See Eissfeldt, *Molk als Opferbegriff*, pp. 46 ff.

73 Jeremiah 2:3. See further M. Buber, *Israel and Palestine: The History of an Idea*, pp. 15 ff.

74 Pausanias VIII 38 2.

III. THE EMERGENCE OF THE OLYMPIAN DIVINE FAMILY

THE SIMPLE god-experience contained in the name Zeus requires no further analysis by the historian and in itself does not admit of any further development. It happened in the prehistory of the Greeks and it is not even important to assign the exact point of time and the exact tribe of Greeks in which it happened. According to the view put forward as the most probable in this book, it must have happened among the first immigrants, in the initial phase of that period of time filled with Greek prehistory, early history, and history, on the well-known scene of Greek history. Zeus possessed a history only insofar as the Greeks possessed one. He had no private history. Nothing could happen to him except what occurred in the correlation "Zeus and the Greeks." It is worth considering the lapse of time between the beginning and Homer, time enough for many occurrences.

This lapse of time cannot be exactly given. The latest dating for the pre-Doric immigration of Greek tribes, the first who were decisive for Greek religion and civilization, is the beginning of the so-called Late Helladic period (about 1580 B.C.).[1] Homer lived in the ninth to eighth century. Before Homer, in the second millennium and first century of the first millennium, the complex structure of Greek religion, which

---

1 See L. R. Palmer, *Mycenaeans and Minoans*, p. 25. It is problematical whether the beginning of the Middle Helladic period, 2000 B.C., the earliest possible date for the Greek immigration, is in fact to be assigned to Greek tribes or to others. The majority of scholars are in favor of the early date; see F. Schachermeyr, "Zum Problem der griechischen Einwanderung," pp. 105–120. On the other hand, it is incorrect (and therefore unprovable) to trace all the rites on Mount Lykaion back to rain making, as in G. Piccaluga, *Lykaon*, p. 87.

III. *The Emergence of the Olympian Divine Family*

was pre-eminently though not exclusively Zeus religion, was formed. There also appeared the Greek myth, the expressing of this religion in the telling of god tales, in mythology. The correlation between men and gods is never without ideas of the worshipers about the worshiped, and these are spontaneous ideas before they become tradition. Yet even where the myths, the expressions of these ideas, have already become tradition so that a traditional mythology is said to be in existence, this is not necessarily a systematic body of doctrine about the deities worshiped there side by side. It is not "theology" in the sense used today. Yet, insofar as *theo-logia* in the original sense of the compound is "god-saying," the Homeric mythology does contain a "Homeric theology" and also represents it.

With Homer the gods are not accommodated in a system. They do, however, appear as the members of a family, of which Zeus is the head. Olympos is the family seat. A kind of system can be seen even in this, not a conceptual system but only an order corresponding to the well-known human form of the gods. This human form is in itself evidence of the correlation between man and god without which no god could exist historically. A correlation was also assumed, moreover, between Zeus and the other gods and goddesses, in the form of an order which on earth comes about of its own accord quite naturally between rational beings.

The anthropomorphic grouping of the deities of a polytheistic religion seemed so natural to scholars in the past that they hardly gave it a second thought. Yet, it must be remarked that there is nothing in all the earth's religions with any real likeness to the Greek structure.[2] At first, indeed, the only aspect to be put in the foreground of research was that which showed a *state* of gods on Olympos, with Zeus as the ruler.

2 See M. P. Nilsson, *The Mycenaean Origin of Greek Mythology*, p. 221.

The other aspect, containing a human reference independent of the state or fundamental to it, the circumstance that here the *family* and its roots, both biological and social, the natural and human foundation, take the stage as outline and origin of a mythology—this was never adequately considered.[3]

All the same, the concern with the state aspect of the Olympian divine family did introduce one important consideration into the study of Greek religion. The fact that the family of gods and goddesses on Olympos under the supremacy of father Zeus also forms a divine state needs to be judged differently from the similar groupings of gods in ancient Egypt or in Babylonia. There were in various cities on the Nile and in Mesopotamia mythological stories, old and genuine mythologems, about the genesis of the world and the gods. They were the result of attempts to form cosmological and theological systems. Such attempts were required, perhaps even provoked, by political developments as soon as the city in question became the center of a greater state.

Yet, it can in no way be assumed that the divine system that came about in such historical circumstances was merely a copy of the political system of the actual state in question. Examples from east Asia and from living mythologies show that under archaic conditions, the actual earthly state can itself be trying to become a copy of a mythological order that was not a product of political thinking. At any rate, the closest relationship between the state order and the divine system would be the rule. Such a correspondence, however, or even the effort to achieve it, is lacking in historical Greece, indeed, is lacking even in Homer.

An assembly of gods on Olympos, like that depicted at the beginning

[3] For the first attempt at such a consideration, see the first version of this chapter, "Die Entstehung der olympischen Götterfamilie," pp. 127–38.

III. *The Emergence of the Olympian Divine Family*   41

of the twentieth book of the Iliad, in which all the gods except Okeanos took part, even the river gods and nymphs of woods, meadows, and springs, an endless multitude, can be compared with the great assembly of the armies catalogued in the second book. Zeus has the gods called together by Themis, who also performs the same function at human meetings[4] and natural concourses.[5] The same concept of law evoked by Themis for the assembly of gods also forms the foundation of earthly communities. Older than Zeus is this rule of law, which was expressed by the goddess' name and was in the archaic Greek world still a living thing. Zeus appropriated it, and the mythological expression of this was his marriage with the goddess Themis.[6] Zeus is only the second source of law, and this was established by his sovereignty—yet without displacement of the old law and its source, the older Great Goddess. So far as *themis* was concerned, a correspondence existed between the sovereignty on Olympos and that on earth.

The speakers who in Homer take the floor at the assemblies keep, "as from Zeus," those rules which are called by the ancient name *themistes*,[7] and they hold in their hand, when they speak "as from Zeus," a special long staff, the *skeptron*. Such a staff was also the symbol of the fact that Agamemnon held "as from Zeus" a higher position than the other kings and wielded the power of a high king. But this very thing goes beyond what we know about law and justice in historical Greece. It was a scepter hereditary in the house of Atreus, a work of art which Zeus had received from the master smith Hephaistos and had sent by Hermes to the father of Atreus. This conferment of power on the earthly king by the king of the gods himself belongs to an older pre-

4 Odyssey II 68–69.   5 See Kerényi, "Aidos und Themis," p. 278.
6 See Hesiod, *Theogony* 901; also C. M. Bowra, *Pindari Carmina*, fr. 10.
7 Iliad I 238–39.

historic state of Greece. Since the Atreids according to Greek legend ruled in Mycenae and the archaeological finds there do in fact testify to a great central power with a special older style of civilization, the inference can scarcely be avoided that the Mycenaean kingdom was the model of the Olympian divine state.

This inference has been drawn and supported.[8] I need not repeat all the arguments in its favor. A further inference can be drawn, however, from the historical situation of the Homeric mythology, which is after all a different situation from that of the Egyptian and Mesopotamian divine system. The Olympian divine family does not represent a system of Greek mythology. It is, however, a kind of systemization which, together with the "Homeric theology," Homer's view of the gods, did decisively influence for all subsequent generations the literary tradition and the artistic shaping of living mythology. The state aspect of this assembly of gods which kept its force throughout the history of Greek religion is the picture of an Olympian divine kingdom. This picture does not stand in the same close relation to the life of the historic Greek states as is usually the case in other cultures with an equally strong mythological religion.

On Olympos monarchy prevails, whereas life on earth is lived in republics.[9] The Olympian divine family—and to some extent the whole Greek mythology once it acquired general force—is, so to speak, left hanging in the air. Or more precisely, it is rooted not in real life but in the idealized life of warlike men of the past. The idealization is effected by the heroic legend. This is a typical phenomenon of the history of civilizations, not only among the Greeks. In Greece it forms above all the subject of the Homeric poems. However human this idealization

---

8 See Nilsson, *The Mycenaean Origin of Greek Mythology*, pp. 238–51.
9 Nilsson, *Geschichte der griechischen Religion*, I, 351.

III. *The Emergence of the Olympian Divine Family* 43

may have become in Homer, the one-sided masculinity of life in war as there portrayed led in a direction characteristic of saga and epic, but much less characteristic of mythology.

The distinction between legend, the mythology of heroes, a "mythology" only so called, and "real mythology," the mythology of gods, is necessary if we are to comprehend more precisely the Mycenaean origin of Greek mythology. The heroes of legend are warriors; above all, they are the kings of the warriors. The time depicted in heroic mythology is a historical time stylized in accordance with masculine ideals. The heroes of real mythology are gods and divine beings of primordial time. The time of real mythology is, in genuine primary mythological tales, the primordial time in which everything had its origin. Greek heroic legend, and its highest poetic representation in the epics of Homer, largely reflects the time of Mycenaean civilization in the well-known Homeric stylization. Genuine mythological tales of primordial time are embedded in the fourteenth book of the Iliad, for example, in the passage where Hera describes the separation of Okeanos and Tethys and, several lines earlier, where the poet recalls the first love trysts of Zeus and Hera "at their parents' home."[10] Where gods appear alone as in the tale of the deception of Zeus here in the Iliad, it is primordial time that shows up.

The origination of the Olympian divine family, a truly historical occurrence, was not a theme for a mythological tale, which would have had to take place in primordial time. We encounter the complete divine family in Homer, and if it was not created by Homer himself—this cannot be clearly determined—it did originate in heroic legend. Hence the Mycenaean origin of the state aspect of the Olympian divine family and its dissociation both from a mythological primordial time and from life

10   Iliad XIV 295–96, 305–306.

in historical Greece are accounted for. As to the other aspect, the fact that the Olympian family of gods and goddesses is a *family*, the case is rather different. We must concern ourselves with this aspect in order to understand at all the origination and historical possibility of a divine dynasty in Greek religion. We have already seen how concerned Homer was to make an assembly of all the gods acceptable through the appearance of the goddess Themis. This structure, state and family in one, of which it can be said that it was the embodiment and ground plan of the whole of Greek mythology—how was it rooted in Greek life?

The Greek word for "king," *basileus*, had a long prehistory before it reached Homer. He distributes the title very generously. In Ithaka alone there were many, old and young, thus addressed.[11] It was just the same in Knossos and Pylos, in Mycenaean times, according to the evidence of the tablets on which the word *pa-si-re-u* and its derivatives appear.[12] According to Greek linguistic usage, *basileus / guasileus* was itself a derivative.[13] The original word from the same root in Greek was *basile*, an ancient queen's title and the name of a goddess.[14] Thus, the linguistic evidence is that the source of the rank borne by these "kings" was a "queen," and the system of law in which both titles were originally valid was a different one from the Greek. In it the "queen" stood higher than a "king." The title *basileus*, which in Homer is borne neither by Zeus nor by any other god, is like a key fossil opening the way back into a still more ancient time than that of the Mycenaean kingdom. If

11 Odyssey I 394–95.
12 See M. Ventris and J. Chadwick, *Documents in Mycenaean Greek*, p. 404.
13 See E. Bosshardt, *Die Nomina auf -ευς*, p. 8. Also see A. Heubeck, "Griechisch βασιλεύς und das Zeichen Nr. 16 in Linear B," pp. 113 ff., esp. p. 135, where Heubeck comes very close to the correct derivation.
14 For occurrences, see Sophokles, fr. 310 (in Pearson, ed.); Plato, *Charmides* 153 A.

III. *The Emergence of the Olympian Divine Family*   45

it is really the case that the supremacy of Zeus over all the other gods reflects the position of the Mycenaean high king, then in Mycenae a patriarchal order of society, no longer a matriarchal one, must have been in force.

In the fifteenth book of the Iliad, when a special reason is being given why Poseidon must give way to Zeus (the elder brother), the younger cries out that "Zeus should give orders only to his own daughters and sons," and yields obedience only after Iris has reminded him that the Erinyes are always on the side of the elders.[15] The Erinyes were originally the representatives and avengers of mothers. They guarded the matriarchal order. Now they are doing this also for the patriarchal order. The father's right, the *patria potestas*, is referred to by the remark that Zeus should give orders only to his own children. And where the father is the source of right and might, the eldest son has precedence. The sovereignty of Zeus is based on the fact that he is the eldest son of Kronos, his power over most of the other gods on the fact that he is their father. Homer calls Zeus "father of men and gods."[16] We may well ask, Why also of men? There is here, without doubt, a kind of generalization; this is the generalization of his procreative fatherhood, a peculiarity to which we must return later. The Roman epic, which would not acknowledge this peculiarity in Juppiter—although in the name itself, Iu-*piter*, he was always invoked with the epithet "father"—substituted for it more precisely *divum pater atque hominum rex*, "father of the gods and king of men."[17]

The most probable assumption is that in Mycenaean civilization a

---

15   Iliad XV 194–204.
16   This formula appears in Iliad I 544 (πατὴρ ἀνδρῶν τε θεῶν τε) and frequently.
17   This occurs, for example, in Ennius, *Annales* 175, and in Virgil, *Aeneid* I 65, II 648. See also Ennius, *Annales* 580: "divumque hominumque pater rex."

mutual interaction existed between kingship and a Zeus religion which had more original ties with a patriarchal order than with a matriarchal one. Zeus's kingship in Homer is a historical survival of Mycenaean origin. The judicial aspect of his kingship, however, is firmly based on Zeus's fatherhood, on a father image which may be called archetypal. It is the image of the father of the family among patriarchal peoples, as also among the Greeks of historical times. In Homer this father image dominates the Olympian divine family, over and beyond the actual fatherhood of Zeus.

"*All* the gods rose up from their chairs to greet the coming of *their father*," so it runs in the first book of the Iliad,[18] though not all the gods are his children. Thetis, the daughter of the sea god Nereus, had previously addressed him as "father Zeus,"[19] a description which occurs more than a hundred times in Homer.[20] Often, and with special emphasis, Zeus in the assemblies of the gods is called "father" by his children, as by Hephaistos,[21] or by Pallas Athena with her formulaic "our father, son of Kronos."[22] According to the archaic version of the birth of Hephaistos preserved for us by Hesiod, however, the Greek (and also pre-Greek) fire god had Hera as mother but no father.[23] This older mythologem was eliminated in deference to the patriarchal order on which the Olympian divine state in Homer is based. The sovereignty of a father gives this divine state continued credibility.

Yet, it was not the gods of the Olympian family who first addressed Zeus as "father." It was men, the worshipers of Zeus who, however, from the content of his name, "lighting up," did not automatically qualify as a father. The assumption that the father, as the strongest person

18 Iliad I 533–34.   19 Iliad I 503.
20 See G. M. Calhoun, "Zeus the Father in Homer," p. 15.
21 Iliad I 578, 579.
22 Iliad VIII 31; Odyssey I 45.   23 See Hesiod, *Theogony* 927.

III. *The Emergence of the Olympian Divine Family* 47

in a family or family group, became the "god" who Zeus was for the Greeks is ruled out by the meaning or content of the name. Not much more plausible is the attempt to explain the appellation "father Zeus" by assuming an intimate relationship with the weather god: "He was a god whom every immigrant Greek carried about with him and found again on the mountain, near his dwelling place, from which the thunderstorm burst forth and the rain came."[24] This would amount to a weather god whom you carried around with you and projected into nature from inside yourself! The appellation, like the god, according to this version, would have been brought along out of the Indo-European past.

With probability, indeed certainty, only this can be stated. The appellation "father" for that which Zeus was—the highest thing that a man could imagine in his correlation with him—could arise only in a patriarchal family. In a matriarchal family this highest thing would have to be called "mother" or, if masculine strength and wisdom had after all been recognized as highest, "uncle." This would correspond to the dominant position of the mother's brother in the matriarchal family. We cannot go on with certainty to infer that the patriarchal appellation of Zeus was already in existence among the Greeks before they settled in their historical places.

Life in patriarchal families was of itself sufficient to bring about the name Juppiter among the Romans—including the element "father" in the nominative (originally vocative)—and the name *Dyauḥ pitar* among the Indians. The Illyrian *Deipatyros*, which is attested for the Tymphaians, a tribe of the Illyrian Molossoi in Epiros,[25] could in that region have come about after the Greek *Zeu pater* or parallel with it, in the initial phase of the Zeus religion. In Homer Zeus makes just as little appeal

---

24 See Nilsson, "Vater Zeus," p. 712.
25 See Hesychios s.v. Δειπάτυρος: θεὸς παρὰ Τυμφαίοις.

to his *patria potestas* as to his kingship. That he is the father is as a matter of course the source of his power, but this aspect pales in comparison with what Zeus is for Homer and with the manner in which Zeus presents himself, in a scene striking in every respect, at the beginning of the eighth book of the Iliad.

An assembly of the gods on Olympos is pictured, summoned by Zeus. How he speaks is striking, and it is worth reflecting on the meaning of his speech. The poet thought it necessary to use the drastic language of an archaic mythology, indeed to appropriate for his purpose one that was probably taken from an older epic of Oriental style, the *Titanomachia*. Zeus's words in the Iliad passage are:

> *Hear me, all you gods and all you goddesses: hear me*
> *while I speak forth what the heart within my breast urges.*
> *Now let no female divinity, nor male god either,*
> *presume to cut across the way of my word, but consent to it*
> *all of you, so that I can make an end in speed of these matters.*
> *And any one I perceive against the gods' will attempting*
> *to go among the Trojans and help them, or among the Danaans,*
> *he shall go whipped against his dignity back to Olympos;*
> *or I shall take him and dash him down to the murk of Tartaros,*
> *far below, where the uttermost depth of the pit lies under*
> *earth, where there are gates of iron and a brazen doorstone,*
> *as far beneath the house of Hades as from earth the sky lies.*
> *Then he will see how far I am strongest of all the immortals.*
> *Come, you gods, make this endeavour, that you all may learn this.*
> *Let down out of the sky a cord of gold; lay hold of it*
> *all you who are gods and all who are goddesses, yet not*
> *even so can you drag down Zeus from the sky to the ground, not*

III. *The Emergence of the Olympian Divine Family* 49

> *Zeus the high lord of counsel, though you try until you grow weary.*
> *Yet whenever I might strongly be minded to pull you,*
> *I could drag you up, earth and all and sea and all with you,*
> *then fetch the golden rope about the horn of Olympos*
> *and make it fast, so that all once more should dangle in mid air.*
> *So much stronger am I than the gods, and stronger than mortals.*[26]

The last line says quite plainly, in Homer's own style, the thing he wanted to say, the sense of the speech, the immense superiority of Zeus over all divine and non-divine beings.[27] To indicate the immensity into which Zeus has grown under the influence of the colossal divinities of the Orient, Homer makes use of the world-girdling golden chain and the crude bodily strength of the supreme god. There is a different, milder superiority about the manner in which Zeus's daughter Pallas Athena confirms his wild untamed strength and at the same time, by the "our father" form of address, puts his *patria potestas* in the foreground.[28] Yet, if we ask about the purpose of emphasizing Zeus's superiority here in the Iliad, it is nothing else but the preservation and assurance of the undisturbed course of the fateful events on the battlefield before Troy. Zeus is involved in what happens in the world like an invincible higher knowledge and conscience.

In Homer he towers with absolute pre-eminence over every human order, whether patriarchal or matriarchal. The peculiarity of the Olympian divine family is grounded in this. The fact that this astonishing structure could be supported by a degree of credibility was only because, archetypally speaking, it was not unfounded. The archetypal facts that

26 Iliad VIII 5–27 (in the Lattimore translation). On the *Titanomachia*, see Kerényi, *Prometheus: Archetypal Image of Human Existence*, pp. 23 ff.
27 Iliad VIII 27: τόσσον ἐγὼ περί τ' εἰμὶ θεῶν περί τ' εἴμ' ἀνθρώπων.
28 Iliad VIII 31–32.

supported both the patriarchal and the matriarchal family were so powerful as to bring into correlation with one another and with their worshipers the historically originated plurality of Greek gods under the supremacy of Zeus, and to gain acceptance for this correlation—that is, the Greek religion in its comprehensive human form.

The Olympian divine family was no doubt a patriarchal family, but what sort of one? In the patriarchal order the father has a son. From the fact that he is eldest and therefore usually also next to the father in strength and manliness, this son gets his right to carry on the family and ensure the continued existence of the "house," the dynasty. One who has no son—"prince" or "heir to the throne"—beside him is not a proper father of a patriarchal family. There is the third person in this family picture; the father has a wife who bears him this son. She is distinguished from the ranks of other women in the house who perhaps have also borne sons to the master, children not first in the category of "sons." We have here a characteristic triangle formed by the "first husband," "first wife," and "first son" when mythologically transposed to primordial time or, in the corresponding state pattern, consisting of the king, queen, and heir to the throne. In the Olympian divine family this triangle characteristic of the patriarchal order could not, for historical reasons, be reproduced as in life. Yet it does determine the picture sketched by Homer, with whom, however, it is intersected by another, a matriarchal, triangle, and also for historical reasons.

We are justified in asking whether the picture of the Olympian family in the first book of the Iliad was a creation of Homer's that appeared for the first time in this passage. For the possibility does exist, though no certain answer can be given. The human model for Homer's portrait is the simplest patriarchal family, in which the father of the house can

III. *The Emergence of the Olympian Divine Family*

chastise his wife if he pleases.[29] Yet, just as Zeus is not an ordinary father of the household but the father of the gods, so Hera, who calls Zeus to account as a personage having equal or almost equal rights to his, must not be referred back merely to a general human model. Least of all may the historian do this, for the historian sees in the union of Zeus and Hera also the union of two divine cults. The union there shows itself in the archetypal form of marriage, of patriarchal marriage at that, on the way towards the realization of the patriarchal triangle.

Zeus and Hera are the archetypal couple, Zeus the man and husband, even the brother-husband, Hera the woman and wife, yet characterized *only* as woman and wife, not as mother. It is for this reason that the patriarchal triangle was not properly completed in the Olympian divine family. The union of cults is raised, however, to the archetypal level, and thus it becomes for the worshipers an acceptable reality. What is missing is the "son" who might unite this couple in a patriarchal sense as a worthy first-born. In vain Hephaistos, the limping smith-god, originally the child of a virgin birth of Hera's,[30] declares himself a lowly son of Zeus. Homer himself shows how little this son matches the parental couple. And then the poet *introduces* the "son" who besides Zeus, the head of the dynasty, must appear at least as "prince"–Apollo. Apollo plays no part in the scene, but he does embellish the divine banquet with his lute playing.[31] In him a matriarchal triangle intersects and overlays the patriarchal one, which remains incomplete.

A characteristic matriarchal triangle is formed by Leto, Apollo, and Artemis. In this triangle Apollo is the "son" with the luster appropriate

---

29 Iliad I 545–46, 565–67. 30 Hesiod, *Theogony* 927.
31 Iliad I 595–603.

to the crown prince in a royal family. In Homer Apollo is distinguished by the title *anax*,[32] which corresponds at one and the same time to the English "sir" and "sire." After he has been adopted into the Olympian family of gods, Apollo is called "son of Zeus," but only in the second place. In the first place he is "son of Leto,"[33] and indeed, "Anax Apollo, whom Leto bore" was his completely sufficient title.[34] We know matriarchal social orders from the conscientious reports of anthropologists.[35] In such orders the mother's husband must not even be named in the titles of the son. In a matriarchal family, where practically speaking the mother's brother rules, the knowledge of the true origin of the children and of the role of the husband in conception is repressed. Ignorance about the natural origin of children among "primitive" or so-called Stone Age peoples is generally assumed by anthropologists, but certainly not with complete justice. It is hardly thinkable that human nature, in this case womanly nature, could have no proper knowledge of such an important event, even though a full and self-assured consciousness of it may be lacking. "Ignorance" can arise also from repression. The reason for the repression was the myth that new life needed a higher or deeper origin than that provided by a chance lovemate. The woman in the matriarchal order reserved to herself the privilege of conceiving her children out of this broader origin of life.

The "father" was not lacking in the matriarchal family either. He could, however, not be the admitted husband and absolutely not be the

32 This occurs in Iliad I 390, without Apollo's even being named. See further Calhoun, "Zeus the Father in Homer," pp. 3 ff.
33 See Iliad I 9: Λητοῦς καὶ Διὸς υἱός.
34 Iliad I 36.
35 See, above all, the studies of Bronislaw Malinowski, an anthropologist noted for his psychological interest and a keen eye for everything human. Of particular significance is his work on *The Sexual Life of Savages in North-Western Melanesia*.

III. *The Emergence of the Olympian Divine Family*   53

brother. The matriarchal order is to be recognized above all by its incest prohibitions. The most prohibited, most feared incest in the matriarchal order is that between brother and sister. In the triangle Leto–Apollo–Artemis the virginity of Artemis is implicit. But in the Olympian divine family the virginity of Pallas Athena, who was born to the father without a mother, is patriarchally determined. In this case the father restricts himself by refusing to exercise his rights over the women of the family in the case of the daughters. Incest prohibitions presuppose incest desires. The desire to belong only to the father and the prohibition of incest produced the virginity of the father's daughter.[36]

In the Leto–Apollo–Artemis triangle, the two children of Leto, the brother and sister pair, Apollo and Artemis, could have formed a pair of lovers worthy of one another. If the triangle were not historically given, we should have to ask why the two deities, of whom Apollo was connected most closely with the sun and Artemis with the moon, did not become a loving or wedded couple but rather became a brother and sister pair. The reason is that they were historically the *model* brother and sister pair of a matriarchal order. Zeus and Hera, on the other hand, formed no such model matriarchal brother and sister pair. They not only were brother and sister but went lovingly to bed together behind their parents' backs.[37] They formed the archetypal "couple," *before* any matriarchal or patriarchal order—with Zeus himself being least bound by any such matriarchal or patriarchal ties. The Olympian divine family was able to form itself around Zeus because he was able to take on more than one single aspect of fatherhood. As the "broader origin of life" Zeus stayed outside the matriarchal triangle, which

36 See Kerényi, *Die Jungfrau und Mutter in der griechischen Religion.*
37 Iliad XIV 295–96.

through him, the originally anonymous procreative father, became a component of the Olympian family. If this had not been so, and if the perfect matriarchal family of Leto had not existed beside the imperfect patriarchal family consisting only of Zeus and Hera, we should not have been able to understand why Leto with her son Apollo did not assume the position of head woman of a patriarchal family. Indeed she would have *had* to assume this position, and with her son come out of a matriarchal world, if the patriarchal divine dynasty of Zeus had not been formed in the domain of sovereignty of another Great Goddess, Hera.

Closer study reveals the paradox that the fatherhood of Zeus had more concrete meaning in relation to the matriarchal part of the family than in relation to the family's patriarchal whole. The appellation "father" is by no means unambiguous in the history of religions. In the form *Zeu pater* it was a firm fact of the Zeus religion, originally in the patriarchal sense.[38] The reason for the combination of *Zeus* and *pater* is doubtless to be sought in the sphere of *spiritual* values, which were also possible in a primitive society, once man became human, and could be connected both with "lighting up" and with "father." The composition of the Olympian divine family shows that Zeus as "father" must earlier have stepped into the role of the "broader origin of life" in a matriarchal group, originally a "fatherless" family like that of Leto, Apollo, and Artemis. Zeus thus took on a greater concreteness than he might have had in the sphere of purely spiritual values—though concreteness, in the life of women in Greece, can equally be ascribed to Zeus by reason of the well-known myths about his fatherhood in connection with mortal women.

In the mythology of heroes, Zeus represented the non-maternal

38 See above, p. 47.

III. *The Emergence of the Olympian Divine Family* 55

origin of life. This was something no individual man could comprehend within himself, nor was it tied to any individual woman; rather, it distributed offspring as a divine gift. This is how the content of these myths can be formulated.[39] Historically, the formulation can be put more precisely. The belief in the fatherhood of Zeus in certain definite cases, perpetuated by hero mythology, was a legacy of a matriarchal past. And it is possible to say where this legacy was preserved more than anywhere—in Argolis, the countryside in which were located, besides the most famous Hera sanctuary of the mainland, also the characteristic fortified sites of Mycenaean civilization, and Mycenae itself. One of the famous myths about the patriarchally forbidden, matriarchally correct fatherhoods of Zeus was the myth of Danaë. Shut up in a bronze chamber in Argos, Danaë conceived Perseus, the founder of Mycenae, by Zeus who impregnated her in a golden rain.[40] In another myth of this kind, the story of the conception of Herakles on Alkmene's wedding night when Zeus took the place of her husband Amphitryon, the relationships are not so clear. This myth was transposed to Thebes, yet the original locality of the story was in all probability Tiryns, the neighboring citadel to Mycenae.[41]

The union of Zeus and Hera, a historical event before the invention of the Olympian divine family, must have formed the nucleus of the divine family. No other origin is conceivable. Otherwise Leto, the one among the goddesses who conceived Apollo, the worthiest son by Zeus, would have had to take on the position of patriarchal "head wife" of Zeus in place of her originally independent matriarchal motherhood.

39 See further Kerényi, *The Gods of the Greeks*, p. 158 (Pelican edn., p. 140).
40 Kerényi, *The Heroes of the Greeks*, pp. 45 ff.
41 Ibid., p. 128.

Hera herself did not fit at all well into the patriarchal family that the creator of the Olympian divine family must have had in view. She was connected with the older matriarchal world just as much as was the less sharply characterized Leto (who indeed lacked any special divine personality). Evidence of Hera's ties to this older matriarchal world can be seen in the fact that the archaic theme of parthenogenesis, the bearing of fatherless children, is found several times in connection with her, even though no son capable of entering the patriarchal triangle—as Apollo did—was ever born of Hera's conceptions.

It has already been mentioned that Hephaistos, who in the archaic version was known as the son only of Hera,[42] in Homer complies with the patriarchal order by appearing as the son of Zeus. By another fatherless birth, Hera, according to the Homeric Hymn to Apollo,[43] brought the monster Typhaon into the world. Her third son, who in Homer appears, just like Hephaistos, as a son of Hera and Zeus, is the war god Ares, of whom his father says that he is of all the gods the one he hates most, being much too like his mother.[44] Certainly the birth of this son was never the reason for the union. The reason must be looked for in the original nature of Hera, in her *Gestalt* or archetypal characteristics. These can be gathered from the descriptions of her cult and the myths connected with it.[45] Homer assigns patriarchal reasons for the special position of Hera among the gods. Hera had been, the poet says, the eldest daughter of Kronos and was the wife of the eldest son who rules over all the gods.[46] But Homer also hints that the relationship in Mycenae was different. Agamemnon in the seventh book of the

42 See Hesiod, *Theogony* 927.
43 The Homeric Hymn to Apollo 305 ff.
44 Iliad V 892–93.
45 On the Hera cults, see further chs. VI and VII.
46 Iliad IV 59–60.

III. *The Emergence of the Olympian Divine Family*   57

Iliad swears by Zeus as the "high-thundering lord of Hera."[47] So "Hera's husband" is one among the ceremonial titles of Zeus as a god of oaths. This whole apparatus of titles was clearly Mycenaean.

The historical situation in which the nucleus of the Olympian divine family came about is thus defined. The goddess Dia, whose traces we were able to discover in Pylos,[48] vanished from the union with Zeus. Her place was taken by the far more demanding Hera. The rulers of a great part of the Peloponnese were Hera's devotees. In the Iliad she names Argos, Sparta, and Mycenae as her favorite cities.[49] The features of a matriarchal order and the corresponding mythology even in the time of these Greek-speaking rulers still were strong enough in the environs of Hera's cult to contribute to a new structure inside the Zeus religion. This structure was certainly not yet the Olympian family we know, which contains as its matriarchal component a divine trinity as important as the Leto–Apollo–Artemis triangle. Yet, the tension between Zeus and Hera, which in this family gives expression to two legal titles ("king" and "queen") though to only one ruling patriarchal power, is not merely a poetic fiction created for the effective representation of the Trojan War.

The beginnings of the formation of the Olympian divine family can be discerned in the Pylos clay tablets,[50] although not in such a way as if the process of formation had begun in Pylos itself. Still, the conditions in Pylos in the thirteenth century B.C. in regard to cult and religion are important enough in themselves, and we shall study them more closely in the next chapter. The Zeus and Hera couple are cer-

---

47 See Iliad VII 411. The wording is picked up again at XIII 154 and XVI 88 and, in an unsuitable context, at X 329.
48 On the goddess Dia, see above, in ch. II.
49 Iliad IV 51–52.
50 See above, pp. 24 ff.

tainly mentioned in Pylos, but not in the first rank. We may rather look for the beginnings in the very place to which Homer led us—the kingdom of Mycenae and the sanctuary of Hera at Mycenae and Argos. In Homer we found the Olympian divine family as the order, valid for all later times, of Greek divine mythology in its developed form. Thus, the part which Homer may have played in creating this order does now remain to be considered as a conclusion to this chapter.

It is especially the fusion of the family of Leto with the incomplete patriarchal family of Zeus which makes it likely that the creator, at least in the last phase of formation of the Olympian family, was Homer. The Leto matriarchal triangle requires us to assume an author who possessed a comprehensive view of the religion of the Greeks on the mainland, on the islands of the Aegean, and in Asia Minor. Such a view can be assumed in the case of Homer. Negative evidence that Homer was the creator of the divine family is the circumstance that Dionysos and the Eleusinian deities do not appear in any of the family gatherings in Homer despite the fact that the religion of these deities goes back into Mycenaean times.[51] An attitude of reserve towards these gods characterizes all the Homeric poetry, but Homer would certainly not have gone so far as to eliminate them entirely if by his time they had already been taken up into Olympos, into the family structure.

How far Homer dared to go in creating his order is shown by the role he assigns to the goddess Dione in the divine family. In Dodona she was more or less the female half of Zeus. Her name, which is an expansion of Dia, the goddess who as we have seen was known in Pylos, is evidence of this. Neither Dia nor Dione had any other content

---

51 See "Dionysian Names," in Kerényi, *Dionysos: Archetypal Image of Indestructible Life*, ch. III; and *Eleusis: Archetypal Image of Mother and Daughter*, pp. 18 ff.

III. *The Emergence of the Olympian Divine Family*   59

but that of the "female lighting up." In Homer, however, she is the mother of Aphrodite. Thus Aphrodite, this Great Goddess of the Mediterranean and Near Eastern world, has become a daughter of Zeus. The poet therewith eliminated an archaic myth which would have broken right through the Homeric style not only in poetry but also in religion—the myth of Aphrodite's birth from the penis of the mutilated Ouranos as it fell into the sea. If Hesiod had not included this myth in his *Theogony* it would, so far as Homer's intentions went, have been forgotten. It was one of those inhuman (and in part also not anthropomorphic) components of Greek mythology that must be assumed to have been invented before Homer. Yet, these myths are nowhere alluded to by Homer, that Ouranos for instance wanted to prevent the birth of his children, or that Kronos swallowed his sons, or that Pallas Athena, who in the Olympian scenes is characterized as the father's daughter, sprang from the head of Zeus.[52]

Thus, the Olympian divine family—and with it the family generally—became the expression of a humane Zeus religion. This family does not contain a Great Mother, like Gaia in Hesiod, a mother earth by whose designs everything in the growing world was to come into being. The image of the Olympian family is determined by the image of the father, and if by any female image as well, then by the image of the woman and wife, Hera. While the image of Zeus is not the only father image of Greek mythology, it is the father image of the supreme god of Greek religion. What sort of father image is it?, we now ask.

52 For these myths, see Hesiod, *Theogony* 156–58, 459, 924–26.

IV. POSEIDON AS 'HUSBAND' AND 'FATHER'

IN ALL conceivable situations, for gods and men, Zeus was called "father." Among the numerous evidences of his worship, however, there is not one of a special cult of "Zeus Pater."[1] There was no cult that specially emphasized his fatherhood or defined it more precisely. It was Poseidon who bore the epithet "Pater" in a definite cult, and the myth upon which this cult was founded throws some light on the question as to what sort of "father" he was. Homer has Poseidon appear beside Zeus in the patriarchal family only in a rather subordinate position, which did not exclude his being a father too in his own domain. Yet, he is not a simple character as would be seemly, for instance, for an elemental being, even for the god of the sea himself or of the moist element in general. The Homeric characteristics attributed to Poseidon were very probably founded in the history of Greek religion. The pre-eminent position in relation to Zeus which Poseidon occupies in the tablets from the palace of Nestor at Pylos is a further reason for us to set up his image for comparison beside the father image of Zeus.

Homer gives no picture of rivalry or brother hate between the two, such as might allow us to infer a rivalry between two religions in that period—or even in the memories of men of that period. There can be no inference of rivalry, that is, between the Zeus religion and another in which Poseidon could have occupied a similarly high position. Nor is it a merely incidental question of how far a Poseidon religion is at all

[1] This was established by E. Fehrle, "Zeus," col. 652.

IV. Poseidon as 'Husband' and 'Father'

conceivable. Of the cult of Poseidon as it is known to us from history Farnell quite rightly observed: "It lacks the spiritual and ethical interest of some of the Olympian cults, and from the earliest to the latest period Poseidon remains comparatively a backward god, never intimately associated with the nation's intellectual advance."[2] Homer's description agrees with this general picture. In the Iliad Poseidon, like a faithful vassal whose job it is, unharnesses Zeus's horses and covers up his chariot while the king of the gods himself mounts his golden throne[3]—undoubtedly a scene from Mycenaean times. Poseidon gets angry, it is true, with his elder brother when Zeus does not favor the Greeks.[4] He does, however, even resisting Hera's incitement, acknowledge his own subordination,[5] so long as he is not carried away by his sympathy for the Greeks, who are dear to him. For the history of religion, nothing more can be got from this than the character of a national god tied to the material interests of his people, among whom he lives and has his being and exerts his often devastating power.

Yet in Homer, Poseidon does show himself anxious about his worship and, since he is of an irritable nature, irritated. The myth that made not only Zeus but also Poseidon and Hades sons of Rhea and Kronos was essential to the Olympian divine family. Whether the further tale—that the three brothers had shared out the world between them by lot and that this was how Poseidon got the sea as his domain—belonged to the same myth or existed separately can no longer be made out. This highly summary tale is quoted by Homer. It takes no account of the early history of Greek religion, in which the share-out was not yet so clearly indicated. Poseidon appeals to the tale of sharing by lot,[6] but

2 L. R. Farnell, *The Cults of the Greek States*, IV, 1.
3 See Iliad VIII 440–43.
4 Iliad XIII 351–53.
5 Iliad VIII 208–211.
6 Iliad XV 187–93.

it is not the extent of his great domain that worries him. His irritation is provoked instead by limitations in his cult, and this does reflect something of the relationship of his worship to the religion of Zeus.

In the seventh book of the Iliad, the Greeks fortify their camp by the sea with rampart and towers. It is a wondrous construction, completed in a single day. In order to emphasize its grandeur Homer has the gods look on and talk to one another about it.[7] Poseidon addresses Zeus. He recalls the walls of Troy which he and Apollo built for Laomedon. Thus, the fortified camp is compared with the besieged city itself. But will any mortal bother about the "intelligence and skill"—*noos kai metis*—of the gods now that the Greeks, otherwise so dear to Poseidon, have completed this work without even thinking of sacrificing hecatombs? This is his reproachful question to Zeus who, very annoyed, replies:

> *What a thing to have said, Earthshaker of the wide strength.*
> *Some other one of the gods might fear such a thought, one who*
> *is a god far weaker of his hands and in anger than you are;*
> *but the fame of you shall last as long as dawnlight is scattered.*
> *Come then! After once more the flowing-haired Achaians*
> *are gone back with their ships to the beloved land of their fathers,*
> *break their wall to pieces and scatter it into the salt sea*
> *and pile again the beach deep under the sands and cover it;*
> *so let the great wall of the Achaians go down to destruction.*[8]

In the Odyssey the gods, with Zeus at their head, did actually play a trick on Poseidon. Behind his back they saved Odysseus and had him conducted home by the Phaiakians, a mythical favorite people of Posei-

7 Iliad VII 436–63.
8 Iliad VII 455–63 (tr. Lattimore).

IV. Poseidon as 'Husband' and 'Father'

don's. The fear expressed in his words of reproach is not without substance:

> Father Zeus, no longer among the gods immortal
> shall I be honored, when there are mortals who do me no honor,
> the Phaiakians, and yet these are of my own blood.[9]

And again Zeus pacifies him, addressing him in the familiar formulaic style:

> What a thing to have said, Earthshaker of the wide strength.
> The gods do not hold you in dishonor. It would be a hard thing
> if we were to put any slight on the eldest and best among us.
> But if there is any man who, giving way to the violence
> and force in him, slights you, it will be yours to punish him.
> Now and always. Do as you will and as it pleases you.[10]

It is Zeus who has to remind Poseidon what power he commands. Let us look at a map of Greece on which the Poseidon cult sites are marked,[11] and let us remember how the whole Greek world was dominated by the sea, how Greek civilization was dependent on sea travel. Then the Homeric words quoted can have only one historical meaning, that in Homer's time the memory of an alternative was still alive: perhaps the worship of Poseidon will decline, *or* perhaps it will conquer this great territory. It is not Zeus in the Olympian conversations who is concerned about *his* worship. Zeus is no longer afraid of any rival, although according to an old myth, Poseidon too, with Hera and Athena, was one of the

---

9   Odyssey XIII 128-30 (tr. Lattimore).
10 Odyssey XIII 140-44 (tr. Lattimore).
11 See the frontispiece map in F. Schachermeyr, *Poseidon und die Entstehung des griechischen Götterglaubens*.

rebellious deities who wanted to bind him![12] For the Zeus religion, the sea also was and remained a place of fortunate lighting up. Zeus was seen alongside Poseidon as "him in the sea," Zeus Enalios.[13] But who was Poseidon, according to his name?

On a purely linguistic view, *Poseidon* is the absolute opposite of *Zeus*. Both, when looked at closely, are transparent and both belong phonetically and grammatically to the Greek language. Yet, *Zeus* is the simplest conceivable verbal noun, *actio perfectiva* become a person, on its own, in complete independence of any object or of a superordinate subject to which the acting person would belong. *Poseidon* is a compound word, formed from a vocative, *posei*, and a genitive, *das*.[14] The word *posis*, of which the vocative is here involved, probably corresponds to the Sanskrit *patis*, "master," and the Latin *potis*, "capable one," but in Greek it means exclusively the "capable husband of a wife." The wife in the compound is the goddess Da, with the meaning *ga* or *gaia*, the earth, and would still have been completely understood as such by the Greeks of the Homeric age. This is proved by the three variants *Ennosigaios*, *Ennosi-das*, and *Enosi-chthon* of the god's paraphrase. His name, equally paraphrastic, is attested in Mycenaean form as *po-se-da-o*,[15] Homeric *Posei-daon*, Doric *Potei-dan* and *Potei-das*.

Ennosigaios, Ennosidas, Enosichthon, with the meaning "Earth-

---

12 Iliad I 399–400.

13 See H. J. Mette, *Supplementum Aeschyleum*, fr. 178, for the epithet "Enalios" (with the predicate πέμπετε).

14 On the etymology of Poseidon, see P. Kretschmer, "Zur Geschichte der griechischen Dialekte," pp. 27–28; V. Georgiev, "Mycénien et homérique: le problème du digamma," pp. 112–13; C. J. Ruijgh, "Sur le nom de Poseidon," pp. 6 ff.; and finally, with an absurd mythological result, E. P. Hamp, "The Name of Demeter," pp. 198–204.

15 Ventris and Chadwick, *Documents in Mycenaean Greek*, p. 126; also see Liddell and Scott, *A Greek-English Lexicon* s.v. Ποσειδῶν.

shaker," is the more ceremonial paraphrase. In it the earth is the object. In the paraphrase that has become the god's proper name, the earth as goddess and wife is so to speak the possessor of the "shaker," who is described as her husband. Independently of the object of his activity as shaker and husband Poseidon *does not exist in the Greek language*. Zeus in a ceremonial formula is called *posis Heras*[16] and linguistically this is in exact correspondence with *posis das*. The correspondence, however, is limited only to the expression of a relationship (of Zeus to Hera) which came about historically and did not belong to his essence as stated by his name. The quality expressed by the name in Poseidon, *posis das*, does belong to *his* essence. The further paraphrase "shaker" (*enosis*) must be added to the *posis*, just as though the god's activity as a violent copulator were extended to include shaking generally. This means shaking of the earth and also—certainly from the earliest times— shaking of the mobile sea as well. An early experience of human beings living in the Mediterranean area was that earthquakes were not confined to the land. The sea often enough quaked too. From the "shaker" they expected security against earthquakes and gave Poseidon the epithet "Asphaleios," "securer."[17] His epithet "Gaiaochos"[18] retained in contrast a sort of ambiguity. The element *-ochos* "had the sound" of holding and also of having (by man of woman).[19]

Corresponding to this relationship, that Zeus exists alone as a divine being whereas Poseidon is never alone, never without earth or sea, is the fact that there is reason enough in the history of Greek religion to speak of a Zeus religion but only to a very limited extent of a "Posei-

16 On πόσις Ἥρης, see above, ch. III, note 47.
17 See Plutarch, Theseus XXXVI 1.
18 Ibid., γαιήοχον.
19 Cf. Liddell and Scott s.v. ὀχεία, a word that is equally ambiguous.

don religion." Analysis of the name itself shows that among Greek-speaking people Poseidon's connection with the earth had priority over his connection with the sea. This is not an absolute priority. For it is very possible that the name Poseidon—comparable in this respect with the similarly compound name Dionysos[20]—is the paraphrase of a god who had another name among non-Greeks and was already connected with the sea. Another result of word analysis is the clue that Poseidon among the Greeks was archetypally united with the earth as a *posis* with his *alochos*, a husband with his wife.[21] Such a union is characteristic of a religion with at least two deities as objects of worship: besides Poseidon an earth goddess who may even have been the principal deity of the religion. Such an order of rank is all the more probable the more the male partner is absorbed by the function he performs with his female. And in the case of Poseidon, the function of the *posis* actually gave the god his name.

We may speak here of an exact result, at first only on a linguistic basis. The religion to which Poseidon belongs inside Greek religion is characterized by a given cultic community and by the special archetypal function of Poseidon in this cult. The description "archetypal" seems more suitable here than "human" or "universally human" although by archetypal nothing is intended that does not form part of human nature. But a human function and connection could easily mislead us into thinking of something anthropomorphic, whereas the archetypal husband which Poseidon obviously was in his connection with the goddess Da could also appear as an animal husband. Indeed, this very thing was characteristic of Poseidon, in remarkable contrast to Zeus. Poseidon's association with animal form is so well attested historically that we must

20 See "Dionysian Names," in Kerényi, *Dionysos*, ch. II.
21 For the phrase πόσις καὶ ἄλοχος, see Aristotle, *Politics* I 3 1253b 6.

IV. Poseidon as 'Husband' and 'Father'

see more in it than a mere mythological theme, more than a god's game of disguises with his beloved.

A notion which went even further was that Poseidon's original shape *was* the horse.[22] This can be refuted with mathematical certainty. We instead derive the theriomorphic appearances of Poseidon from the "husband archetype." It is even possible here to borrow mathematical language, as exact as possible, and to suggest that the concept of the archetypal is like that of an imaginary square root, the mathematician's *i*. By this *i* a multiplicity and at the same time simplicity of meaning can be made intelligible. To be sure, if only for the sake of clarity of thought, the "husband archetype" must be strictly separated from the "father archetype." Such a separation clearly corresponds to the matriarchal way of thinking. In this the mother's husband is regarded not as the father of her children but *only* as husband, a view which again has its own universal archetypal validity. The female sex encounters the male in four relationships to which four archetypal images correspond: the father, the brother, the husband, and the son. Of these the form of the husband is reserved exclusively for the woman as wife. The activity of a divine husband does not imply fatherhood. Thus, unfruitful shakings, earthquakes and tidal waves, could with the greatest naturalness be referred to Poseidon the husband.

This activity, mating by the aggressive male, whether fruitful mating or not, was predominantly associated with a Poseidon in horse's shape from the time that animal appeared in the Mediterranean lands in the first half of the second millennium.[23] It was an obvious step for

---

22 For the original suggestion, see Wilamowitz, *Griechische Tragödien*, II, 227, note 1. The identification has been repeated by many after Wilamowitz without evidence.

23 See Schachermeyr, *Poseidon*, p. 53.

Poseidon, the "husband" and *only* the husband, whose being was entirely absorbed by this function, to assume the form of a stallion. He often bears the epithet "Hippios,"[24] sometimes also "Hippegetes," "horse-drover,"[25] and "Hippokurios," "horse-tender,"[26] but never is he called "horse" or "stallion" simply, as he would have to be if there were any substance in his identification with the horse.[27] In Homer Poseidon took care of Zeus's team of horses[28] and thus demonstrated not only his vassalage but also the range of his activity—the animal sphere. From a certain point of time onward, this sphere was represented in Greece principally by the horse and the breeding of horses. It was, however, hardly as a draught or riding animal that Poseidon loved the horse so much as in its perfect animal freedom. The myth expresses in its fashion the temporal priority of the god over his favorite animal. According to the Attic[29] and the Thessalian[30] versions of the myth, Poseidon made the first horse leap out of his split ankle, in the Attic version from his own semen which had fallen upon a rock.[31] No doubt the horse was for this reason regarded as a free offshoot of deity. In the area of the Poseidon sanctuary of Onchestos, in Boeotia, wagoners had to walk on foot alongside their team, and if the horses succeeded in breaking the wagon on the tree trunks in the sacred grove and thus freeing themselves, they were kept there ever after as free animals devoted to the

24   See Farnell, *The Cults of the Greek States*, IV, 74, note 4a.
25   Ibid., note 4b.
26   Ibid., note 4c.
27   See above, note 22.
28   Iliad VIII 440.
29   For the Attic version of the myth, see Servius' commentary on Virgil's *Georgics* I 12 (in G. Thilo, ed., p. 134).
30   See the scholium on Pindar, *Pythia* IV 246. The myth is also represented on Thessalian coins; see, for example, the *British Museum Catalogue* for Thessalia, table X 5, 6.
31   See the scholium on Pindar, *Pythia* IV 246.

IV. Poseidon as 'Husband' and 'Father'

god.[32] Horses represented with dragging bridles, on coin designs,[33] indicate their freed condition in the Poseidon cult.

All this was after the stallion had taken the bull's place in relation to Poseidon, "Taureios Ennosigaios," "bull-like Earthshaker," as he was called in Thebes.[34] The role of the bull in the Poseidon cult is no less well attested than that of the horse. Poseidon also had the same relation to the ram, whose shape he equally assumed as consort.[35] All this refutes the supposition of a primordial Poseidon in horse's shape, and sufficiently explains all the theriomorphic appearances of the consort. The priority of the bull, of tauromorphism over hippomorphism, is just as assured in the Poseidon cult as in the history of Mediterranean civilization, and proves the correctness of the archetypal view of the different, equivalent animal forms. What took place was only a "change of symbols," and so we may call it, without any wish to preach "symbolism" or refer everything back to archetypal images. The same thing happened in other cases[36] in Greek mythology and religious history when the Greeks encountered a new animal or plant world. The change from one to the other, from bull to horse, did not forever exclude the older symbolic animal. The process began, however, in the Mycenaean

---

32 The Homeric Hymn to Apollo 230–39. The Germans similarly kept horses as oracular animals: Tacitus, *Germania* X 10–11 (in Robinson, ed., p. 286).

33 See Paula Philippson, *Thessalische Mythologie*, coin table 1, 3.

34 See Hesiod, *Shield of Heracles* 104. Also see the metaphoric use of the bull sacrifice to Poseidon, lord of Helike, "Enosichthon," in Homer, Iliad XX 404–405. The cults in Thebes and on Mount Helikon are indistinguishable. The Hippokrene spring on Mount Helikon belongs, however, to the period of the later hippomorphism.

35 See Kerényi, *The Gods of the Greeks*, pp. 182–83 (Pelican edn., pp. 161–62).

36 For an example from Kos, see Kerényi, *Asklepios: Archetypal Image of the Physician's Existence*, pp. 55–56.

period. We must look more closely at this circumstance, all the more because the cultic community that has been revealed by the names is similarly Mycenaean.

The original meaning of the great sacrifice of the Greek religion, the *hekatombe* (in literal translation, the "hundred-ox" sacrifice) has not come down to us. The Greek idea that Homer and Hesiod derived from the rite can be formulated most briefly as follows: a being together and eating together with the gods, a feast of common nourishment in which the gods—in the *idea*, visibly—take part.[37] It was this idea to which the Prometheus myth also was attached, before Hesiod and probably also before Homer, with its interpretation of the difference between gods and men. The idea of *common* revelry is supposed to have been realized for the first time in Mekone;[38] it was the pre-existing condition of the sacrificial meal. This idea, however, in no way rules out the inference that the rite of the hecatomb was itself *not* of earlier, pre-Greek origin. The great sacrificial animal of the Minoan period in Crete was certainly the bull. Yet, there is still no evidence from Minoan and Mycenaean times of the sacrifice of a hundred animals at once.

This may be pure chance. All the same, the bull appears on Minoan and Mycenaean representations of bull-catching and the bull game and in the evidences of the tearing to pieces of a bull[39] as an individual animal and not as an animal of mass sacrifice. The dangerous bull game of the Minoan statues and paintings seems to be the ritual repetition of bull-catching. It was apparently the free animal that had to

[37] See further Kerényi, *The Religion of the Greeks and Romans*, pp. 187–88.

[38] On the original sacrifice, see Kerényi, *Prometheus: Archetypal Image of Human Existence*, pp. 42–44.

[39] On the Cretan bull game and capture, and the rending of a live bull, see the section "Zagreus," in Kerényi, *Dionysos*, ch. III.

IV. Poseidon as 'Husband' and 'Father'

play its own part, the part of the god torn to pieces, in a sacred game—and in a last scene not represented in the records so far recovered. It is hardly conceivable that a mass sacrifice developed out of this. It *is* conceivable that the individual animal was the representative at once of its species and of a divinity that chose this form in which to manifest itself even without the bloody outcome of its epiphany. The tauromorphic manifestation of a god as husband can be assumed in Minoan Crete by reason of its expression in Greek myth. In the myth of Europa, it is Zeus who assumes the shape of a bull.[40] It would be premature, however, to infer from this that the connection between Zeus and this manifestation in Crete was closer than mere chance. The bull with which Queen Pasiphaë fell in love and mated came from the sea, sent by Poseidon. This is the oldest version of the myth to be handed down to us, and is the one followed by Euripides in his tragedy *Cretan Men*.[41]

Later mythographers replaced Poseidon by Zeus in this relationship.[42] It is very improbable that Euripides would have given up Zeus for Poseidon if his version had not been the original one. For there are other respects as well in which this tragedy of Euripides gives genuine cult details from Crete, among them the meal of raw meat from a bull torn to pieces. Euripides' Pasiphaë calls the bull from the sea "apparition" (*phasma*),[43] the sacrificial animal destined for Poseidon. In all probability the Cretan myth of the appearance of Poseidon himself as a bull from the sea can here be identified. The role of the bull as husband was due to his representing the god who in this form approached the "lady who gives light to all"—this is the meaning of the

40 Kerényi, *The Gods of the Greeks*, pp. 108–110.
41 See Nauck, *TGF*, frs. 471–72.
42 See further C. Robert, *Die griechische Heldensage*, I, 362, note 1.
43 Ibid., p. 362, note 3.

name Pasiphaë, whether she was originally the moon goddess or an earthly representative—and "shook" her. It is his bellowing that connects the bull with the earthquake. The Cretan hears it frequently, as Kazantzakis testifies: "Megalo Kastro [Heraklion] often shook to its very foundations. A rumble [*mungrito*] sounded below in the world's cellars, the earth's crust creaked, and the poor people above went out of their minds."[44]

Besides *po-se-da-o-ne* on clay tablets at Knossos there also appears *e-ne-si-da-o-ne*, "Earthshaker," and thus the myth of the shaking, bull-shaped husband in Crete can be taken back at least as far as the time when Zeus was already there.[45] But of the origin and meaning of an entire hecatomb about which we are asking, this tells us nothing. It does seem, however, as would be expected in the nature of the case, that there had been ever since pre-Greek times a fundamental difference between the sacrifice of a single bull and the mass sacrifice of bulls. The single form is realized as an ambivalent occasion on which the sacrificial animal represented the god and the sacrificers were considered murderers and sinners, as with the bull sacrifice for Dionysos and the Bouphonia at Athens.[46] This form of sacrifice is contrasted—even in a theoretical consideration—with the other possibility in which the sacrificial animal is an equivalent value, the equivalent of the sacrificer and the goods which he renounces in order to secure their increase. The realization of this possibility is the offer of a hecatomb.

44 N. Kazantzakis, *Report to Greco*, p. 69. See also p. 70: "There's nothing to an earthquake, really . . . . It's just a bull beneath the ground. He bellows, butts the earth with his horns, and the ground shakes."

45 See above in the text, at the beginning of ch. II. On *e-ne-si-da-o-ne*, see Palmer, *Mycenaean Greek Texts*, p. 302.

46 See W. F. Otto, "Ein griechischer Kultmythos vom Ursprung der Pflugkultur," in *Das Wort der Antike*, pp. 140 ff.

IV. Poseidon as 'Husband' and 'Father'

Evidence of this is to be seen first of all in the naked fact of the value of a hundred or even several hundred oxen. For one hundred is only the basic number. In Homer the *teléessai hekatombai*, "complete hecatombs," is a recurring formula.[47] Neither a feudal lord nor the state would gladly squander so many picked beasts from its own stock without some special meaning. Secondly, entries in the Greek calendar show that the hecatomb also represented a special connection between man and god, evidently a god with extraordinary demands. These demands were fulfilled by the Greeks not only towards a single deity. In the calendar such fulfillment is attested as an important act on its own by festivals with the name Hekatombaia and a month Hekatombaion.

It was a living need among the Greeks—among Ionians and Dorians alike[48] and so probably among all the Greeks—to offer a hecatomb at least once a year. In Athens the month Hekatombaion was the first of the year, after the summer solstice, and had earlier been called Kronion, month of Kronos.[49] Kronos, insofar as he was identical with the Semitic El,[50] could have been a god of great demands. For the Greeks of historical times he was the god of a past represented by the slaves, the descendants of the oppressed aboriginal population. For that reason, the Greek Kronia—like the Roman Saturnalia—were festivals at which the servants played the masters, giving the celebrations a unique character.[51] The sacrifice of the hundred cattle was offered, in the historical

---

47 See, for example, Iliad II 306; Odyssey XVII 59.
48 M. P. Nilsson, *Griechische Feste*, p. 174.
49 *Etymologicum Magnum*, p. 321, line 4.
50 See above in the text, the end of ch. II; also W. Fauth, "El," cols. 226–28.
51 For the Kronia, see L. Deubner, *Attische Feste*, pp. 152–53. The festival was not a harvest festival. In this month in Greece, the only harvest to have

period at Athens, to Apollo.[52] But it was the god who was called "Hekatombaios" after the sacrifice, and not the sacrifice after the god! The priority of the sacrifice over the god to whom it was offered in the historical period is proved by the miserable nature of the substitute which often had to do duty for the hundred cattle—perhaps a bull and ten lambs on Mykonos.[53] It is more precise if we assume that the need to secure oneself—the people, the tribe, the race—by the greatest offering (expressed in the basic number one hundred) and to enjoy the condition of safety under divine protection had been received by the Greeks from an earlier age and *lived on*.

The sacrifice of a hecatomb to Poseidon is described in the third book of the Odyssey, the visit to Pylos. If Homer's account is not simply taken from an older, Mycenaean epic—to judge from the archaeological finds in the excavated palace of Nestor, this cannot be ruled out[54]— then it does have historical value. The sacrifice was of nine times nine bulls, by which the number one hundred is only nearly reached, although the ceremony is expressly called a hecatomb.[55] The fundamental number nine, however, corresponds to the number of provinces ruled by Pylos on one side of the Bay of Messene, as listed on the clay tablets which have been found at Pylos itself.[56] The seven provinces on the other side are evidently disregarded by Homer, and yet the simplified

---

just been completed is the fruit harvest, as is expressly stated by Philochoros (in Macrobius, *Saturnalia* I 10 22) in order to bear out his fallacious "harvest festival" interpretation.

52 *Etymologicum Magnum*, p. 321, line 5.
53 See J. de Prott and L. Ziehen, eds., *Leges graecorum sacrae*, I, No. 4, lines 29–30.
54 See "Im Nestor-Palast bei Pylos," in Kerényi, *Werke*, II, 260–65.
55 Odyssey III 59.
56 See Palmer, *Mycenaeans and Minoans*, pp. 82–83.

IV. Poseidon as 'Husband' and 'Father'

picture he presents is not without its reasons in the conditions now known to us.

It is the Pylians who at the beginning of the third book of the Odyssey perform the great sacrifice. That Poseidon, to whom they offer the sacrifice, is their forefather is nowhere said, but immediately afterwards Pylos is called the "well-founded"—and therefore also comfortable and civilized—city (*eüktimenon ptoliethron*) of Neleus.[57] Neleus was reputed, at least from the time of Homer on, to be a son of Poseidon. In Homer's time, on the other hand, the older tradition was still alive according to which the father of the founder hero of Pylos was the river Enipeus.[58] Poseidon's assumption of the role of forefather—*genethlios, genesios, patrigeneios*, as he is called exclusively in late sources[59]—is described in the eleventh book of the Odyssey, in the story of the ancestress Tyro, mother of Neleus and Pelias.[60] Homer has a special sympathy for Tyro, and devotes more verses to her than to the other mothers of heroes in the underworld. Homer probably worshiped her, indeed, as his own progenitress.[61] We learn that Poseidon approached Tyro in the shape of Enipeus because she was in love with the river god. Poseidon only revealed himself to her after the act of love. This revelation can be evaluated historically as Poseidon's entry into Thessalian

57 Odyssey III 4.
58 This is more probably the Thessalian Enipeus than the Elian. The love affair of Tyro, the wife of Kretheus, with the Thessalian river god was already established by the time she was given a father in the person of Salmoneus, who ruled beside the Elian Enipeus.
59 See Nilsson, *Geschichte der griechischen Religion*, I, 452.
60 Odyssey XI 235–52.
61 According to the tradition preserved in the *Vita Homeri* attributed to Herodotos, Homer's mother's name was Kretheis, a descendant of Kretheus. Her love affair with the river Meles mirrors the love affair of Tyro with the river Enipeus (see above, note 58).

genealogies.⁶² It cannot be safely inferred from it, however, that he was also worshiped in Pylos in such a capacity. All that is certain is that in Thessaly Poseidon had not always been the great forefather.

On the beach of Pylos, as the sacrifice and sacrificial meal are represented by Homer, nine places were marked out for groups of five hundred men each to sacrifice their nine bulls and to consume them without the portions that were burnt.⁶³ They were the people of Nestor, his sons and comrades, the nation offering itself to the god along with the hecatomb. The picture is completed by the sea and the black color of the bulls sacrificed to Poseidon. Homer names him, to emphasize the context, the "bluish-haired Earthshaker," "Enosichthon kyanochaites."⁶⁴ A hecatomb for Zeus, Hera, or Apollo consisted of white bulls. The great sacrifice was adapted for Poseidon, certainly not first by Homer, but it is here attested for the first time that Poseidon was entitled to a hecatomb just as these other deities were.⁶⁵ We recall that it was Homer who represented the god as being not so sure of his worship as Zeus.⁶⁶ Pylos is the right place to give us this concrete picture of the pre-Homeric condition of the Poseidon cult and of a further at-

62 C. Robert, *Die griechische Heldensage*, I, 39, interprets the Homeric story as an early "transformation of the oldest form of legend," and on p. 53 states the view, no doubt rightly, that Poseidon's father role in the family of Aiolos first took root among the Aiolians who had emigrated to Asia Minor, not in Thessaly. But tauromorphism still pushes through in the story of the daughter of Aiolos, Melanippe, the "black mare." According to Euripides, in the *Wise Melanippe*, a bull watched over the twins Aiolos and Boiotos, which Melanippe bore to Poseidon, and a cow suckled the infants. See further Kerényi, *The Heroes of the Greeks*, p. 70.

63 See Odyssey III 7–9.
64 Odyssey III 6; translation mine.
65 For hecatombs sacrificed to Apollo, see Iliad I 315–16; for hecatombs to the gods generally, see Iliad VII 450.
66 See above, the beginning of ch. IV, and note 6.

IV. Poseidon as 'Husband' and 'Father'

tribute included in the god's name—that is, his membership in a tighter cult association before he received panhellenic rank.

We may indeed say that Poseidon held a relatively pre-eminent position among the shorter entries (narrow clay slips) found at the palace of Nestor, but we must assess this correctly. For these clay tablets, dating to some four hundred years before Homer produced his great historical painting, we are indebted to the fire that by chance baked them hard. Their contents evidently cover only a short part of a year, probably only a month, of the year before the palace was burned down and destroyed. The name of the month may have been Plowistos, since *po-ro-wi-to-jo* has been read on the most important of the tablets.[67] This was the name of the first month of spring, when seafaring was resumed. This month could also have been specially dedicated to Poseidon, but such was not the case. It is characteristic that the entries on these tablets, which obviously belong together, name him almost without exception in a cult association with other deities. And what may well be decisive is the fact that in one context the name of *another* month precedes the name of Poseidon: *pa-ki-ja-ni-jo-jo me-no po-se-da-o-ne*.[68] So Poseidon was celebrated on his own, in an earlier or later month.

The deities named before Poseidon and in cult association with him in these documents from the last month of the palace of Nestor are goddesses. The most important is the document mentioned above in which the name of the month *po-ro-wi-to-jo* is followed by the offerings to *po-ti-ni-ja*, the goddess "Lady," Potnia. If the month belonged to a

---

67 Pylos Tn 316. See Ventris and Chadwick, *Documents in Mycenaean Greek*, pp. 286–87; Palmer, *Mycenaean Greek Texts*, pp. 261–63. The wrong interpretations have not been repeated.

68 Pylos Fr 1224.

Great Goddess, then it was the one who was not named but rather was designated by her exalted rank of "Lady," or "Mistress." There is so much agreement between some highly archaic cults of Arcadia and these Pylos observances that we can reasonably assume a connection and include it in our account from the outset.[69] It would be wrong, as some scholars have done, to regard the title *potnia* of the Mycenaean documents as having no other content than that she was mistress of a definite territory. Instead we must think of a content that was simply not easy to say aloud. It is certain that the religious scruples against uttering the real name and its content were no less powerful in early times than in late. The Arcadian parallel is the Great Goddess of Lykosoura, who is referred to only as the "Mistress"–*despoina*, a word synonymous with *potnia*. "The true name of the Mistress I fear to communicate to the uninitiated," says Pausanias.[70]

The greatness of the Mistress or Lady of this most important of the Pylos cult documents can be gathered from the names which follow; in close association first of all are two goddesses, *ma-na-sa* and *po-si-da-e-ja*. Goddesses in Greek lands often enough form trinities[71] and still more frequently pairs, which are attested both in Pylos and in Arcadia. The cult of the mysteries of Lykosoura, just as at Eleusis, is addressed to a pair of goddesses. One in Eleusis is Persephone, in Lykosoura the Despoina; the other is the mother, in both places Demeter. Only in Arcadia Demeter is closely connected with Poseidon, who mates with her. In the temple of the mysteries of Lykosoura, on the other hand, three goddesses were worshiped and represented: besides the Despoina and Demeter pair, Artemis as well. Pausanias understood

69 This is suggested in rough by Palmer, *Mycenaeans and Minoans*, p. 123.
70 Pausanias VIII 37 9.
71 See Kerényi, *Niobe*, pp. 29–31.

IV. Poseidon as 'Husband' and 'Father'

this trinity to mean that Artemis could equally be regarded as a daughter of Demeter.[72] In Lykosoura Poseidon, as "Hippios" and father of the Despoina, had an altar.[73] Together with Artemis Propylaia, Poseidon also received a temple as "father" in front of the Propylaia of the sanctuary of the mysteries at Eleusis,[74] and this reminder of his fatherly dignity was certainly in conscious agreement with the Arcadian mysteries.[75]

The trinity of goddesses *po-ti-ni-ja*, *ma-na-sa*, and *po-si-da-e-ja* in principle contains the trinity of Lykosoura plus Poseidon. In *ma-na-sa* we may probably discern a Mnasa, Mnemosyne in Mycenaean form. In relationship with the Mistress and with Posidaeia, the "Poseidon-wife," she would be the goddess who, like Artemis at Lykosoura, forms the third figure in a female trinity commanding the universe. The three-in-one universal goddess does not have to be invented. Hesiod portrays her as the great Hekate,[76] who participates in all three world domains. A large Boeotian vase of the seventh century B.C. shows her with animals of the air, the earth, and the water to represent the domains, and also with the severed limbs of sacrificial animals.[77] Such was the cruel fashion in which sacrifice was offered to the Despoina of Lykosoura in Greece.[78] Poseidon is not assigned to the whole trinity, but he "serves" it to the extent that for its own perfection it submits to a mate. That he is also the "father," as at Lykosoura and Eleusis, is not yet given by this quartet. Immediately after his entry the document lists the gifts for the

---

72 Pausanias VIII 37 3–6.
73 Ibid., par. 10.
74 Pausanias I 38 6.
75 See Kerényi, *Eleusis*, p. 70.
76 Hesiod, *Theogony* 413 ff.
77 This is reproduced in Nilsson, *Geschichte der griechischen Religion*, pl. XXX 3; see also pp. 257, 287; and Kerényi, *The Gods of the Greeks*, p. 35 (Pelican edn., p. 31).
78 Pausanias VIII 37 8.

"Ancestor," *ti-ri-se-ro-e*, the *Trisheros*, and for the "Lord of the House," *do-po-ta*, the *Dospotas*.

The votive gifts offered were as follows: to the Potnia a golden drinking bowl and a woman, to the Mnasa and the Posidaeia each a golden goblet and a woman, to the Trisheros and the Dospotas (Despotes in the more familiar vocalization) one golden goblet each. On the back of the tablet there follow the gifts offered in Pylos itself, not outside it, *pa-ki-ja-si*, as on the front of the tablet. Inside the city were the sanctuaries into which the following gifts were brought, first of all the *po-si-da-i-jo*, the Posidaion, which actually had a number of resident staff.[79] These entries are of the greatest importance when correctly understood.

Only the Posidaion, the sanctuary of Poseidon, is named, not the god himself, as in the previous entries where the three goddesses, the Ancestor, and the Despotes are all named. A golden drinking bowl went to the sanctuary—that is to say, a vessel of the same rank as that for the Potnia—and two women. Male deities otherwise receive, as they do also on this tablet, male servants. The two women are more closely identified as *qo-wi-ja* and *ko-ma-we-te-ja*.[80] The first word, probably in the plural, *qowijai*, must be translated female cow or bull herd, the second, *komawentjai*, as *komaessai*, "long-haired." In the sanctuary of the mysteries of Lykosoura it was prescribed that the women might not enter except with their hair let down.[81] Female cattle herds with hair let down were given to Poseidon in his sanctuary, where he himself perhaps was not present, though probably a sacred bull took his place.

79 Pylos Fn 187.18.
80 Palmer, *Mycenaean Greek Texts*, p. 362, wrongly refers them to the jar mentioned before the women, and thus incorrectly interprets them.
81 *IG* V:2 514.

IV. Poseidon as 'Husband' and 'Father'

It is not to be supposed that god and bull were identical for the people of Pylos. On another tablet[82] is entered a *lectisternium* (*lechestroterion*) for Poseidon: *po-se-da-o-ne re-ke-to-ro-te-ri-jo*. A couch was provided for him as for a man and not for a bull. He was the divine husband in human form no less than in bull form. A *lectisternium* presupposes anthropomorphism, here alongside tauromorphism; this means not divine worship of the bull but only its tendance, in honor of Poseidon. In Pylos, indeed, we almost become witnesses of the change of symbol. It is natural for somebody who keeps a stallion, as we may read on one of the tablets, to have a special portion of land.[83] The coverer of mares, cited only as *i-qo*, *hippos*, "stallion,"[84] himself receives a special ration of aromatic *kypeiros* or *kypeiron*, a favorite herb of grazing animals in the Homeric poems.[85] This does not mean the stallion was kept as a god,[86] though it soon became the preferred epiphany of Poseidon.

In the cult document referred to, there follow the gifts assigned in their sanctuaries to three goddesses—a golden goblet and a woman each —and to Hermes, a golden bowl and a man. The trinity associated with Hermes seems to be of more modest rank, rather like that of Attic nymphs. Among them a place was found also for *di-u-ja*, the earlier

---

82   Pylos Fr 343 (plus 1213).

83   Pylos Eq 59.5, correctly interpreted by Ventris and Chadwick, *Documents in Mycenaean Greek*, p. 260.

84   Pylos Fa 16. If a demonic being were meant, a silenus would be a possibility: *si-ra-no* is a proper name in Knossos U 466.1. A stallion, it seems, is being transported over the sea on a seal impression from Knossos (reproduced in Palmer, *Mycenaeans and Minoans*, p. 175).

85   See, for example, the Homeric Hymn to Hermes 107; Iliad XXI 351; Odyssey IV 603. See also Liddell and Scott s.v. κύπειρος, κύπειρον.

86   This has been assumed because of an idea of Wilamowitz'; see above, ch. IV, note 22.

wife of Zeus. But the fact that after them gifts are listed for Zeus and Hera, too, and a son of Zeus,[87] all three with golden drinking bowls, the gods with a man each and Hera with a woman, is certainly not to be interpreted as meaning that their rank was lower than that of the others on the list. It was rather the case that at a festival of the Potnia and her retinue, gods of such high rank as Zeus and Hera and a son of Zeus must not be forgotten. They were remembered even in a month that did not in any way belong to them.

Nowhere in all the evidence is the Potnia corresponding to the Arcadian Despoina as the Great Goddess of the month placed so expressly in the foreground as in the document just discussed. The dead, denoted as *di-pi-si-jo, dipsioi*, the "thirsty ones," were closely connected with her, as one tablet attests.[88] The Despoina indeed had a secret name of her own, but Pausanias allows it to be seen that she could be more or less equated with the great underworld goddess of the Eleusinian mysteries, Persephone.[89] The wine taken to the palace is identified by the name of Dionysos—*di-wo-nu-so-jo* in the partitive genitive[90]—and was in all probability destined for the thirsty dead who in Attica in the same month on the day of the Pithoigia swarmed around the opened earthenware wine jars.[91] The *me-tu-wo ne-wo*, new wine, was celebrated together with a "divine mother" (*ma-te-re te-i-ja*, Matri

---

87   On the evidence in Pylos, see above, in ch. II. For the occurrence of *di-u-ja*, see Palmer, *Mycenaean Greek Texts*, pp. 261–63.

88   Pylos Fr 1240; cf. Fr 1231, 1232. The correct interpretation has been given by Palmer, *Mycenaean Greek Texts*, pp. 252–53, and by W. K. C. Guthrie there cited.

89   Pausanias VIII 37 9.

90   See Kerényi, "Möglicher Sinn von *di-wo-nu-so-jo* und *da-da-re-jo-de*," pp. 101–102.

91   See Kerényi, *Dionysos*, ch. VI, at note 91.

IV. Poseidon as 'Husband' and 'Father'

Theia),[92] a designation which could be attributed to Posidaeia in her capacity as Demeter, if it were certain that there was not yet another mother commemorated in this month, in connection with the wine for instance.

Among the shorter entries is one (listing oil allowances to the gods) that is worth some study as referring presumably to the same month as does the more detailed cult document we have been considering. That longer document called the month *po-ro-wi-to* but did not give the name of a festival. This shorter entry adds to the name of the month the festival name *wa-na-se-wi-ja*, "festival of the Wanassa (the Lady)." The festival could be the festival of the Potnia, the Lady already known to us, if it were not for the occurrence here of a different nomenclature. The meaning, however, may be the same. What occurs is the dual form *wa-na-so-i*, *Wanassoiin*, "to the two Ladies," as with the dual form "two goddesses"—*to theo*—in Eleusis. This use of the dual grammatical form accords with the mystery language of Eleusis and with that only. The Arcadian mysteries were in factual agreement with Eleusis; they had to do really with two goddesses. In Arcadia, in Lykosoura, however, as also in the detailed cult document from Pylos, the pair was enlarged to a trinity. Still, this very fact does not exclude the possibility that the *wa-na-so-i* (on the shorter entries found in Pylos) does refer to the Potnia and the Posidaeia. Poseidon himself is also named: *wa-na-so-i po-se-da-o-ne*, "to the two Ladies, to Poseidon."[93]

The most probable assumption is that in the shorter entries and in the longer document the same deities are referred to in two different languages, the language of a public festival in the longer document and the language used by a mystery cult in the shorter. The nomenclature

92 Pylos Fr 1202.   93 Pylos Fr 1219.

derived from the root *wanak-* was preserved in the name *anaktoron* given by Greek usage to the holy of holies of a mystery cult at Eleusis and Samothrace.[94] Public and secret rites of the same deity were possible[95] and are to be assumed in this case. Any other assumption would be to multiply hypotheses unnecessarily. The deities of the month would practically have to be doubled in number. In Corinth—the name occurs in the documents[96]—Poseidon himself is called, on votive objects of the archaic period, "Poseidon Wanax."[97] It is most probable that entries like *wa-na-so-i wa-na-ka-te*, "to the two Ladies, to the Lord," and *wa-na-ka-te wa-na-so-i* referred to him.[98] A second entry after the first of those quoted is *wa-na-so-i po-ti-ni-ja*. This may without doubt be regarded as tautologous. There is only slight difference of meaning between the words *wanassa* and *potnia*. The difference evidently was that *potnia* had a more general currency, like *despoina*. The tautological entry gave the deity prominence as the greater of the two goddesses of the cult association. We may translate it, "to the two Ladies, to the Great Lady." If Potnia had meant another goddess and not this same one, this Great Lady of Pylos, or if it had meant the same goddess in another place, a more precise identification would have been necessary. Here it was enough to give the cult association.

The significance of geographical identification has been dreadfully exaggerated. Especially in this case the geographical interpretation would be most unreasonable since it would put what was least transparent in the foreground, as for instance in the unclear compound

---

94 See Kerényi, *Eleusis*, pp. 88 ff.; also "Varro über Samothrake und Ambrakia," pp. 161–62; *Werke*, II, 151.

95 See, for example, the details of the Lenaia festival, in Kerényi, *Dionysos*, ch. VI, the section, "The Dionysian Festivals of the Athenians."

96 Corinth appears as *ko-ri-to* in Pylos tablet Ad 921.

97 *IG* IV 210.   98 Pylos Fr 1235 and 1227.

IV. *Poseidon as 'Husband' and 'Father'*

u-po-jo-po-ti-ni-ja.[99] Quite clear, on the other hand, are *a-ta-na-po-ti-ni-ja* on a tablet from Knossos, and *po-ti-ni-ja a-si-wi-ja* and *po-ti-ni-ja i-qe-ja* from Pylos.[100] The goddess Athena is meant, of whom the Athenian in Plato's *Laws* says that in the city named after her she is the Kore (Persephone) and Despoina.[101] She was also worshiped on the Kolonos Hippios with Poseidon as Athena Hippia. In Knossos, as we have just seen, the goddess' name is attested in combination with Potnia in a single word, as in the word *De-meter*. This is a definite fact which it would be pure folly to dispute. The *po-ti-ni-ja a-si-wi-ja* is confirmed in southern Lakonia as Athena Asia.[102] The *po-ti-ni-ja i-qe-ja* can only be an Athena Hippia, and this is evidence that this second Potnia of the people of Pylos adopted the new symbolic animal earlier than Poseidon himself did.

Poseidon received his name from the union of a god with a goddess. The union was present in Pylos about 1200 B.C. in the form of a cult association. This was not an association with Athena, who was the guardian of the patriarchal family,[103] but with another Lady. At least here we can discern the cultic framework in which Poseidon's mythical role of husband of a Great Goddess was conjured up and celebrated. Perhaps, too, there was not only a public but also a mystical framework. If, as is very probable, a bull was kept in the Posidaion of Pylos, this role of husband was indicated by the animal. What could not be so

---

99 Pylos Fn 187.8.

100 Knossos V 52; Pylos Fr 1206, and An 1281.1.

101 The root word from which the name of the city *Athenai* was formed is the name itself of the goddess (see W. Fauth, "Athena," col. 681). See also Plato, *Laws* VII 796 B: ἡ παρ' ἡμῖν Κόρη καὶ Δέσποινα.

102 For Athena Hippia, see Pausanias I 30 4; for Athena Asia, Pausanias III 24 7.

103 See Kerényi, *Die Jungfrau und Mutter*, pp. 19 ff.

clearly and surely grasped as the husband role was Poseidon's father role. The transition from bull to stallion as the form of expression of the same mythical content had not progressed so far that we can with certainty establish Poseidon's later hippomorphism in Pylos. Still, we can establish the condition that brought it about—the esteem for the stallion. It is quite possible that the stallion form and Poseidon's assumption of a father's dignity were a result of the same *general transformation*, the introduction of horse breeding and of the patriarchal family order.

This came about between 1200 and the Homeric history painting some four hundred years later. Poseidon's power widened its range and took in the sea, just as Zeus with his potentially omnipresent lighting up encompassed the whole Greek world. The expanding worship of Poseidon—in view of our limited horizon it can be suggested only tentatively, experimentally—would have moved outward from a circle drawn around Crete and the southern Peloponnese. Corinth, mentioned in the Pylian documents,[104] the city with two harbors, lay on a line from which sea routes radiated in all directions. According to the evidence of votive offerings in the ancient cult (mentioned earlier) in which Poseidon was still called Wanax, it was there that his cult association with Amphitrite was to be found, whether the weddings which he is supposed to have celebrated with her everywhere in Greek seas also originated there or not. Amphitrite in Homer is the female form of divine address for the sea itself. She has the waves and rears the wonderful animals of the deep.[105]

At the human pole of Poseidon worship there stood the seafarers and fishermen whose weapon of the chase, the trident, was to end up in the god's hand. On the mainland, worship of Poseidon spread

[104] See above, ch. IV, note 96. [105] Odyssey III 91, V 422.

IV. Poseidon as 'Husband' and 'Father'

among the peasants with the breeding of horses, which penetrated from the northeast. It was a conquest of the broad lands in which a Greekdom was forming in attachment to the soil. After the Peloponnese, of which a Greek historian[106] wrote that it had been the seat of Poseidon in ancient times, it could be stated also of Boeotia that it was all one holy land.[107] Thessalia, where the Cretan game of bull-catching persisted longer than anywhere else on purely Greek territory, was the most extensive scene of the transition from tauromorphism to hippomorphism in the Earthshaker's cult.[108]

The mountains of Arcadia, especially Mount Lykaion, were rather the scene of the cult's retreat and a territorial reserve for older cults. In Lykosoura, as we have seen, there persisted the worship of Poseidon Hippios in connection with the mystery cult of the Despoina.[109] A mutual assimilation, probably no more indeed than a mutual recognition, between this cult and the worship of the Eleusinian goddesses took place not only there but also in the still more remote valley of the river Ladon, north of Alpheios, in Thelpusa. There we encounter the myth—in its fully hippomorphic version—of the union of Poseidon with the goddess who was originally superior to him in rank, as to a husband. The story also takes in the myth of the rape of Persephone as passed on by Pausanias.[110] The two myths, the Arcadian one of Deme-

106 For this allusion by Ephoros, see Diodorus Siculus XV 49 4.
107 *Etymologicum Magnum*, p. 547.
108 The evidence collected by Paula Philippson, *Thessalische Mythologie*, pp. 25 ff., on the Thessalian cult of Poseidon is to be understood from this point of view. A "Zeus Posidan" did not exist in Thessaly, but a Zenoposeidon, with the native name Osogos, was a god of Asia Minor in Karia; see Farnell, *The Cults of the Greek States*, I, 149–50, note 41.
109 See above, in ch. IV, the section on the mysteries of Lykosoura; also Pausanias VIII 37 10.
110 Pausanias VIII 25 5. See also Kerényi, *The Gods of the Greeks*, p. 185 (Pelican edn., p. 163).

ter and the Eleusinian one of her daughter, belong together in meaning. In both the birth of a mysterious child is attributed to a dark, aggressive father. Demeter, according to the Thelpusa myth, was already searching for her abducted daughter when Poseidon began to pursue her with offers of love. The goddess transformed herself into a mare and mingled with the grazing horses of King Onkios. Poseidon detected the trick and covered Demeter in the form of a stallion. She bore him a daughter, whose name was not allowed to be spoken by anyone not initiated into the mysteries, and she also bore the stallion Arion. The same myth about Poseidon and Demeter was told, according to Pausanias, also in Phigalia, south of Mount Lykaion, with the sole difference that there Demeter bore only a daughter, no horse. This daughter of Demeter was the goddess whom the Arcadians called Despoina.[111]

These myths bear the same relation to the Arcadian mysteries as the myth of the rape of Persephone bears to the Eleusinian mysteries. That is, they are designed for public use to explain the mystery happening, beforehand. They give us the frame of reference in which Poseidon received the cult name "father." His role of husband enjoyed priority over his role of father. The husband role is spoken in the god's Mycenaean name and certainly is at the core of his Mycenaean myth. The Arcadian myths and cults do not add any extra feature to Poseidon's husband role, but they do to his husband image. The image is, to use an anthropological term, that of an exogamous husband, the originally foreign husband who intrudes from outside and is admitted into the matriarchal family. An altar of Poseidon Hippios stood above the sanctuary of the mysteries at Lykosoura and the sacred grove of

[111] Pausanias VIII 42 1–2.

IV. Poseidon as 'Husband' and 'Father'

the Despoina. In front of the Arcadian city of Megalopolis, where the two goddesses had their mystery cults under the name Great Goddesses, Poseidon with the epithet "Epoptes" had a temple,[112] as an initiated spectator—that is what *epoptes* means in Eleusis—or at any rate as one who came to the festival of the mysteries from outside. As the pursuer of the mother goddess, he also had to lie in wait outside the holy precinct before becoming her husband.[113]

Any account of Greek mythology must speak of Poseidon as the boisterous husband not merely of Amphitrite, but of many Nereids, Naiads, and heroines, and as the father of numerous sons who played their part in the heroic legend.[114] Poseidon's father image is a dark one, enclosing an animal husband image. His image is not a bestial one but it also is not a higher, let alone spiritual, one. Zeus's father image is exalted in the direction of what is higher and more spiritual. Zeus's quality, fluctuating between the natural and the supernatural, was to a certain extent prescribed by the fact that women in the matriarchal order, adapted as it was most profoundly to their nature, expected their children not from the bodily, Poseidonlike husband but from a wider environment, a "broader origin of life" that included the spirits of ancestors as well as the natural order. The Zeus image is not merely father image and nothing else. It is filled with archetypal content from

---

112 For the Great Goddesses, see Pausanias VIII 31 1; for Lykosoura, VIII 37 10. For Megalopolis and Poseidon Epoptes, see VIII 30 1.

113 One tauromorphic, exogamous divine husband on the mainland other than Poseidon was Acheloos, originally without doubt a greater god than a mere river god of western Greece; see H. P. Isler, *Acheloos*, pp. 109 ff. Isler observes (p. 117) that Acheloos was by no means always averse to a heroine, but that he is never an ancestor of hero families. It follows from this that Acheloos is to be regarded as a rudimentary figure surviving from matriarchal conditions.

114 See further Kerényi, *The Gods of the Greeks*, pp. 187–88 (Pelican edn., pp. 165–66).

two sources—first, from the image of the patriarchal father with which we have already become acquainted in the Olympian divine family, and second, from a husband image given by his union with Hera. And the discussion of Poseidon should have prepared us for a distinctive view of this Zeus Heraios, Zeus the husband.

V. ZEUS THE BROTHER-HUSBAND

THE SUPREME GOD of the Greeks, the event that became more present the more suddenly it broke through darkness—darkness of the sky, darkness of chaotic events among men—and thus deserved the epithet "Phanaios," "one who appears as light and brings light"[1]: this supreme god early on assumed a father image. Yet, this supreme power was not wholly comprised either in the father image or in the patriarchal father role in the Olympian divine family. It was more sublime than the father without actually being sublimated out of him. In no sense was it an "almighty god" sublimated out of the father. All that was derived from the father role was a greater power over gods and men than that of any other deity. The power that in any case was peculiar to the Phanaios was given concrete form by this role, in one particular direction, the moral one. In nature its power was given concrete form by the lightning in which it struck and was therefore called "Kataibates," "descending," "Kappotas," "down-falling," or actually "lightning," "Keraunos."[2] Yet, a historical dream shows us how even in this case the appearance of light was predominant. This is the dream of Xenophon's that induced him to take on the leadership of the Greeks.[3] He dreamed that

---

1 The epithetic expression Σύ μοι Ζεὺς ὁ φαναῖος is found in *Rhesus* 355, the tragedy ascribed to Euripides but composed perhaps by a later, fourth-century author.

2 See further "Keraunos," in H. Usener, *Kleine Schriften*, IV, 471 ff.

3 Xenophon, *Anabasis* III 1 11-12. In another historical dream (Plutarch, *Pyrrhus* XXIX 1) it is fire, the kindling of lightnings, that predominates, but this dream is not of good portent as Xenophon's was. Lightning strokes were of importance in the life of the Greeks because they did not know of any protection against them. Lightnings were regarded as "signs of Zeus" (see Cook, *Zeus*, II, 4 ff.), yet not absolutely or in every case; cf. Artemidoros, *Onirocritica* II 9.

lightning, with a great thunder, struck his home so that it appeared quite bathed in light. He explained the light spontaneously and immediately as the salvation that comes from Zeus, but it was also for him the sign of royal power. Absolute identification, in the sense of Zeus's being totally lightning, has never been proved. This possibility is indeed excluded by the name Zeus.

Nor was Zeus ever wholly comprised, either, in his husband role. The supreme god of the Greeks was never for them *posis Heras* and nothing more. Rather there was a limitation in this role itself. Before Hera was adopted into the divine side of the correlation "Zeus and the Greeks," he had had a goddess belonging to him, connected also linguistically, a *di-u-ja*. Such a completion was evidently demanded by the worshipers of Zeus as being the only way in which they could imagine a totality in the supreme position over them. Their demand may be called archetypal. It was human and leads us to the imaginary *i*, once more to the "husband archetype" as in the case of Poseidon,[4] yet not to a single archetype but to the archetypal couple whose two components belong to one another like the halves of a unity. This very close union is expressed by the fact that Zeus and Hera appear, if not as twins, nevertheless as a brother and sister couple.

Had Hera been for Homer only the consort of Zeus and not also his sister, the mythological wedlock of the two could have been understood with the usual simplification—that is, as the union of the boisterous father god of the immigrants on Mycenaean territory with the mighty female deity of the countryside, and in some sense his subordination to her. In the religion of the new people, the conquering god subdued

---

4 On *posis Heras*, see above, ch. III, note 47. / For the *di-u-ja*, see above, in ch. II. / The "husband archetype" and the mathematician's "i" are discussed above, in ch. IV.

v. Zeus the Brother-Husband

the native Great Goddess, but he in his turn was subdued by her. The oath formula of the king of Mycenae as quoted in the Iliad denotes this historical situation.[5] This is how that thrilling marriage came about, to be put to such rich use by Homer, and not to be forgotten by his predecessors. This interpretation, however, does only crude justice to the historical course of events.

It is rather Poseidon who appears in the role of a boisterous father god among the Greeks, and *he* mates with Demeter and with numerous other ladies—only not with Hera. The consequence is that Hera, too, gets a higher characterization. Her character or *Gestalt* would not necessarily exclude a subordinate *daimon*, a serving husband beside her. Zeus, however, according to the character sketch which I have attempted in the preceding chapters, could not have appeared in such a subordinate role beside Hera. The *two* unions of these deities, the conjugal union and the sibling union, are *more* than could have been motivated by the coming together of two religions. The unions must certainly have corresponded to possibilities stored up in the original character of each of the two deities. A brother and sister marriage would even have had to be shocking to Greek sensibilities if it had been specially invented and not already in existence as a mythological fact. Lucian's mocking remark that Zeus had married many women, last of all Hera, his sister, "according to the laws of the Persians and Assyrians," is a noteworthy reminder that the union of the supreme divine couple was certainly not according to the laws of historical Greece.[6]

If the union had at least accorded with the customs of the My-

---

5   Iliad VII 411, X 329, XIII 154, and XVI 88. See also above, in ch. III, the reference to the Mycenaean apparatus of titles.
6   Lucian, *De sacrificiis* 5.

cenaean kings, this would have meant that the Mycenaeans were following the customs of certain Oriental ruling dynasties (in historical times especially the Achaemenids of Persia).⁷ In view, however, of the legends attaching to the Atreids, the ruling house of Mycenae, a similar custom in Mycenaean Greece seems out of the question. In this house of Atreus, with its burden of terrible sins, incest with the daughter does, it is true, occur, but only with a special purpose. The avenger of the slaughtered sons of Thyestes had to be born of the same family on both sides as the victims were.⁸ No brother and sister marriage is ever even hinted at. In matriarchal circumstances such as those observed by Bronislaw Malinowski on the Trobriand Islands, incestuous relations between father and daughter, although considered bad enough, are not real incest. It is intercourse between brother and sister that is the truly horrible case of incest here.⁹ The ban on brother and sister marriages in historical Greece was evidently founded on matriarchal principles. Only the marriage of uterine siblings, *homogastrioi*, that is, a brother and sister having a common mother, was counted as incest, while that of the half-siblings, who only had a common father, was allowed.¹⁰ The marriage of Zeus with Hera was shocking enough and in matriarchal conditions must have been more shocking still. This divine brother and sister marriage is therefore to be explained hardly as an imitation of human customs, but by an older

7   See E. Kornemann, *Die Stellung der Frau in der vorgriechischen Mittelmeer-Kultur*, pp. 13 ff.

8   That is why Thyestes begets the avenger Aigisthos on his own daughter, Pelopia; see further Kerényi, *The Heroes of the Greeks*, p. 306. According to C. Robert, *Die griechische Heldensage*, I, 298, this legend bears the stamp of great antiquity for the very reason that matrilineal descent is also important in it.

9   B. Malinowski, *The Sexual Life of Savages in North-Western Melanesia*, pp. 153 ff., 448.

10   See Kornemann, *Die Stellung der Frau*, p. 37.

v. Zeus the Brother-Husband

mythologem, which ascribed to the gods the realization of a possibility completely forbidden among men.

Mythical genealogy is secondary to mythology. Mythology contains the mythologems, told in all their many variations, but does not arrange them in a system. Genealogy is a form of systematic arrangement, an activity of the mind turned more towards abstract thought than was the construction of the Olympian family. The principle, descent by begetting and bearing, is taken from nature. Genealogy is based on two different views of this process, the matriarchal and the patriarchal views. Both are in their fashion so close to the natural view, even independently of their institutional realizations, that neither the psychologist nor the historical investigator of mythology can leave either of them—as for instance the matriarchal—out of account. The brother and sister couple Zeus and Hera, as a mythological construct, presupposes at least the existence of a genealogy. On a matriarchal view this would start from a common mother, as in the case of the brother and sister pair Apollo and Artemis already discussed. On a patriarchal view there must have been a common father, even though he had to be taken over from another religion, as happened with Kronos.[11]

Father and mother in Hesiod's *Theogony* are Kronos and Rhea. The Homeric divine genealogy on this point[12] agrees with that of Hesiod. Where our two oldest authors diverge is that in Hesiod the trinity of Chaos, Gaia, and Eros, more of a philosophic than a mythological triad, forms the beginning of the genealogy, while in Homer, Okeanos and "mother Tethys," the former as the male "origin of the gods," the latter

---

11 On Apollo and Artemis, see above, in ch. III; for Kronos, see the end of ch. II.
12 Iliad XIV 194, 203.

Zeus and Hera

as his wife, do so.[13] According to a mythical genealogy preserved in prose, as also in Hesiod, a brother and sister pair are the mythological origin and beginning of everything. According to these evidences, the brother and sister marriage of Zeus and Hera—as, incidentally, all brother and sister marriages in Hesiod—would be the repetition of a pre-Hesiodic, purely mythological, cosmogonic theme. The theme is the basis of the oldest Greek divine genealogy known to us, the Homeric. Its genealogical consequences are comprehensible enough. The love story of Hera and her brother was one of its developments. In it Hera was certainly not the last wife of Zeus, as in Hesiod, but the first. Thus, this version represents not merely an earlier tradition attested by Homer, but probably the earliest of all after the first encounter of the two deities in history.

It is, however, difficult to suppose that Hera's wedding ever had a cosmogonic meaning inside the history of Greek religion. It was the results, the consequent posterity due to the wedding, that belonged to the cosmogonic theme. The theme of parthenogenesis is several times associated with Hera.[14] She did not need a husband to become fertile. Her union with Zeus was *not* an act of fertility. Homer's poetic account

13 Iliad XIV 201. / For the prose source, see Akusilaos, fr. 1, in Jacoby, *FGrHist*, I, p. 49 (2 F 1 1–14); cf. Hesiod, *Theogony* 133, 136. For the Hesiodic allusion to Hera, see *Theogony* 931.

14 Hera's fatherless sons are Hephaistos (Hesiod, *Theogony* 927), Typhaon (Homeric Hymn to Apollo 305 ff.), and Ares (Ovid, *Fasti* V 55 ff.). All of them are "misbegotten children"; see above, in ch. III. The goddesses conferred on Hera as daughters are her doubles. These "daughters" are Eileithyia, a wife goddess of the Minoan period whose place was taken by Hera (see ahead in the text, ch. VII, at note 85); and Hebe, a Hera double frozen at the age of puberty. (*Hebe* also means *pubes*.) Hebe in her eternal youthfulness represents her mother in relation to Herakles; see Kerényi, *The Heroes of the Greeks*, p. 204. The Roman Juno corresponds to Hera and her name is the translation of Hebe. See further Kerényi, *Bildtext einer italischen Vase in Giessen*, p. 348.

v. Zeus the Brother-Husband

of the repetition of this union, stage-managed solely by Hera, makes it possible to guess at its origins in the history of Greek religion. The possibility that Homer simply invented the love-making of the two deities can be ruled out. The subject *Dios kai Heras gamos* occurs elsewhere in the material that has come down to us.[15] Homer does not have to be held responsible for everything. His account in the fourteenth book of the Iliad is to be explained by a myth that preceded it both in time and, as a more original mythologem, logically. Yet, the account in Homer cannot be wholly attributed to the myth. One aspect that Homer invented was the help of Aphrodite, called in by Hera to make Hera irresistible to Zeus.[16] In all the more original mythologems Hera must have been the self-sufficient and yet not wholly self-sufficient female. She was not self-sufficient only insofar as she needed Zeus for the *gamos*, the act of marriage, again without consideration of fertility. In Attica, indeed, Zeus was called in this capacity "Zeus Heraios," "Hera's Zeus."[17]

It would not be right here to speak at once of the Hieros Gamos ("sacred marriage"), as is usual nowadays, without defining exactly what *hieros gamos* was for the Greeks. It is more correct to say that the *gamos*, the *consummatio matrimonii*, was performed in Hera's sense, that in it she preceded mortal women as an example and that there were also myths of it, a constantly repeated myth of marriage, in the *hieroi logoi* ("sacred stories"), as myths connected with the cult were usually called. It seems evident that the myth in this case was not a sacred story of the Zeus religion but a *hieros logos* of the Hera cult. A

---

15 For the wedding of Zeus near the ocean, independently of Homer, see Euripides, *Hippolytus* 745 ff.; also see Eratosthenes, *Catasterismorum reliquiae* III.
16 Iliad XIV 188, 198–99.
17 On the epithet "Heraios," see further in ch. V at note 45, below.

begetting father god—whether in the shape of Zeus or in that of Poseidon—had countless "marriages." Yet, no single marriage possesses in the life of a man the same meaning as one marriage in the life of a woman.

The minimal, but sure, definition that can be given of Hera, if only for these more general reasons, is that among the archetypal images of Greek religion Hera was *the wife*. The remark of an Abyssinian woman noted down by Leo Frobenius, "A good wife is before every love-making a girl but a mother afterwards," can be modified with reference to Hera.[18] She before every one of her periodically recurring weddings became a virgin, but afterwards she became once more that which is her most frequent epithet in the cult, "Teleia," "perfect one."[19] In marriage she attained perfection. Zeus in this connection was called "Teleios," "bringer to perfection."[20] For the wife, perfection does not mean merely, or necessarily, motherhood, which is rather something normal inside every perfection, a condition deserving respect for its own sake. Perfection means the whole essential life of woman, its fulfillment by the man. Therefore, the love-making, which gives her such life fulfillment, means incomparably more for the wife than for the husband. And whenever fulfillment is attained by it, it is again and again a wedding, before which the wife is a girl. A *hieros logos* only half kept secret, which we find in the Argive cult of Hera, told how the goddess each time became a virgin in her bridal bath, the spring Kanathos, before she celebrated her marriage with Zeus.[21]

18 See L. Frobenius, *Der Kopf als Schicksal*, p. 88.
19 For Τελεία, see Nilsson, *Geschichte*, I, 429.
20 Ibid., p. 430. See also O. Höfer, "Teleia, Teleios," cols. 254 ff., esp. col. 257. Zeus beside Hera Zygia (or Syzygia) is even called "Zygios," "marriage god"; see Höfer, "Syzygia," col. 1647.
21 On the bath of the goddess in the Kanathos spring, see further in the text, ch. VI, at notes 17 and 57.

v. Zeus the Brother-Husband

A pre-Homeric myth is quoted by Homer himself in his account in the Iliad. For it was certainly not his own invention to put the first lovemaking of Zeus and Hera back into that time when they had to love in secret, without their parents' knowledge.[22] Homer also hints that this was during the time of enmity between Kronos and Zeus. The brother and sister at that time were living with Okeanos and Tethys, hidden there by mother Rhea—a mythological tale of older style than Homer. A chance has revealed to us where a tale of this style, related to the life of the teller and his audience, could still be heard in Greece as late as Hellenistic times. Here it was still a genuine mythologem, a divine tale about which everybody could feel, *Somehow this concerns me*. In a conversation of women in Theokritos are the words, "Women know everything, even how Zeus took Hera. . . ."[23] It is reported that at exclusive women's festivals, to which men were not admitted, the participants said the most shocking things to one another. At the feast of the Haloa there were not only obscene mockeries but some very indecent behavior. The married women were led on by means of ritual play to things forbidden in marriage.[24] An appropriate story also found its way into the Homeric poems. The story of Aphrodite's adultery is recited in the Odyssey to the Phaiakians.[25] Virgil with a sure sense of style transposes the tale to a women's gathering; a water nymph tells her companions the story, together with the other love affairs of the gods "since Chaos."[26]

Although it is not a pure invention of Homer's, the account in the fourteenth book of the Iliad of the supreme divine couple's love-making

---

22 Iliad XIV 295–96. On the enmity between Kronos and Zeus, see Iliad XIV 203–204.
23 Theokritos XV 64.
24 See the scholium on Lucian, *Diologi meretricii* VII 4.
25 Odyssey VIII 266 ff.   26 Virgil, *Georgics* IV 346.

is an original piece of poetic writing, one of the boldest and greatest in all the world's literature. The ancient editors of Homer gave this book the heading "Dios apate," the "beguiling of Zeus." The distraction of Zeus from what was happening on the battlefield before Troy has its meaning in the context of the epic. Homer frees himself from tradition, however, to put the *gamos* of the divine couple to work in distracting Zeus. Zeus is sitting on the highest peak of Mount Ida watching the progress of events, which take place in accordance with the capacities and the *moirai* of the individual heroes. Hera would be unable to entice him away from this post. Consequently, she must seduce him there in the freedom of the natural scene, so that after love he may fall asleep in her arms, with the help of Hypnos, Sleep himself,[27] as is natural—for the natural in Homer's religion is the divine.

Yet open air love-making, however naturally it might occur in the sphere of Dionysos, was not allowed in the sphere of Hera. This is clearly stated when Hera, who has prepared everything for love in the open, pretends to resist it:

> . . . οὐκ ἂν ἔγω γε τεὸν πρὸς δῶμα νεοίμην
> ἐξ εὐνῆς ἀνστᾶσα, νεμεσσητὸν δέ κεν εἴη.
>
> . . . *I could not, not I, return to the house after
> rising from a bed of love* [*in the open*],
> *it would not be seemly.*[28]

Such a thing would be shameful, that is, in the view of the Hera religion, according to which love-making *belongs inside the house*.

Hera expressly names the *thalamos* of Zeus, *estin toi thalamos*, "you

---

27 See Iliad XIV 352–53, and 157–58.

28 Iliad XIV 335–36; translation mine. The *thalamos* of Zeus is referred to in line 338.

v. Zeus the Brother-Husband

do have your *thalamos.*" It was that room of the house which played such a large part in Greek wedding rites that it came to mean principally "bride chamber." It was the place of the *consummatio matrimonii* to which the bride was brought.[29] An essential part of the *thalamos*, its equivalent even, was the *pastos* or *pastas*, a tented alcove.[30] A Hellenistic poet actually speaks of the wedding of Hera on Olympos as if it had taken place behind such a curtain.[31] An equally essential requirement of the ritual performance of the action was the common bed. Theokritos gives this prominence in his "Encomium on Ptolemy," the Graeco-Egyptian ruler Ptolemy Philadelphos, who was married to his own sister and thus provided the occasion for the poet to evoke the brother and sister marriage of Zeus and Hera. And for the first time in our texts the expression *hieros gamos* is applied to a divine couple:

ὧδε καὶ ἀθανάτων ἱερὸς γάμος ἐξετελέσθη·

Thus too was consummated that sacred marriage of immortals.[32]

Thus too, as we soon shall see, was the *hieros gamos* of the mortals consummated. Only in Theokritos it was a servant goddess, Iris, who prepared the bed (*hen lechos*) for Zeus and Hera, each time with purified hands.

29 See V. Magnien, "Le mariage chez les Grecs anciens: L'Initiation nuptiale," p. 115.

30 See C. Vatin, *Recherches sur le mariage et la condition de la femme à l'époque hellénistique*, pp. 207 ff.

31 For the description by Poseidippos, see F. Lasserre, "Aux origines de l'Anthologie: I," p. 227:

χεύματι τῶιδ' ἄχρ]αντος ἐλούσατο παρθένος Ἥρ[η
ὡς τύχ' ἐπ' Οὐλ]ύμπωι παστὸν ὑπερχομένη.

32 Theokritos XVII 131; for Iris, see lines 133-34.

At Hera's seeming refusal to consummate marriage outside the *thalamos* and without a bed, Zeus in Homer answers that he will veil her in a great cloud, a golden cloud. Here we can recognize the traces of the myths attaching to mountain peaks, of which it was told that they had formerly belonged to Hera and later also to Zeus, and had been the scene of their meeting and love-making.[33] Homer's description, though it has something we tend to call "cosmic," was no doubt entirely the poet's own:

> *So speaking, the son of Kronos caught his wife in his arms. There*
> *underneath them the divine earth broke into young, fresh*
> *grass, and into dewy clover, crocus and hyacinth*
> *so thick and soft it held the hard ground deep away from them.*
> *There they lay down together and drew about them a golden*
> *wonderful cloud, and from it the glimmering dew descended.*
> *So the father slept unshaken on the peak of Gargaron*
> *with his wife in his arms, when sleep and passion had stilled him.*[34]

In the mythologem of the first love tryst quoted by Homer, it was *in the house* of Okeanos and Tethys that the divine child couple climbed into bed. The source of this was most probably a sacred story told or sung among women at a Hera festival. There is, however, yet another tradition, kept deliberately unclear, about a boys' song at some unidentified mysteries which may refer to the Hera cult at Argos.[35] We may

---

33 See Kerényi, *The Gods of the Greeks*, p. 97.

34 Iliad XIV 346–53 (tr. Lattimore). For the mythologem of the first love tryst, see Iliad XIV 201–204 plus 295–96.

35 For the reference to the mystic boys' song, see the passage from Dion Chrysostomos quoted in the text, and note 37, below.

v. Zeus the Brother-Husband

consider also the Stoic interpretation of Zeus as a loving god in Dion Chrysostomos (Dion of Prusa), an orator of the first century A.D., who attaches it to the myth of the Persian Magi about the ruler of the universe as a charioteer:[36] "He sends a complete lightning stroke, but not one of those irregular and unclean strokes he draws from the scudding clouds in stormy weather, no, a pure stroke of lightning without the smallest dark patch, and quick as thought he lightly changes shape. In thinking of Aphrodite and procreation, however, he tames and controls himself. Having quenched a great part of the light, he transforms himself into fiery air with a soft glow. Then he couples with Hera and in the most perfect enjoyment of intercourse—

μεταλαβὼν τοῦ τελειοτάτου λέχους

—he releases the whole of his sperm for the universe. That is the blessed marriage of Hera and Zeus, about which the sons of the wise sing their hymns in inexpressible secret rites—

τοῦτον ὑμνοῦσι παῖδες σοφῶν ἐν ἀρρήτοις τελεταῖς "Ηρας καὶ Διὸς εὐδαίμονα γάμον."[37]

With the greatest of ease the Stoic, for whom the world soul is fire and Hera is the air, casts back to the light-nature of Zeus, his lighting up, and is able without difficulty to combine it with the anthropomorphic happening of the *gamos*, which in the archaic and Classical periods had not yet dissolved into a physical process. The words "inexpressible secret rites" oblige us to assume that a ritual happening was meant, a

---

36 See Kerényi, "A világfogat," pp. 130-31.
37 Dion Chrysostomos, *Orationes* XXXVI 56. The English translation quoted here is based in part on the version of Winifred Elliger, in *Sämtliche Reden*.

wedding rite of the divine couple celebrated among men, the occasion for the recitation and singing of myths and hymns, which themselves had occasioned Homer's poetic narrative.

Not till the seventh century A.D. did a Christian writer call the Gamos a mystery of the ancient Greeks, and he no doubt was influenced by his view of marriage as a sacrament. What is definite is that there existed an old saying, originally in Sparta but also attested for Athens, which went *telos ho gamos*, "*telos* is the *gamos*."[38] *Telos* meant fulfillment, completion, also as the goal of initiation into mysteries, the goal of *telein*, of what went on in the Telesterion at Eleusis.[39] But there is no need to bring in the Eleusinian mysteries here. *Telos*, said of the *gamos*, is perfectly intelligible when brought into relationship with Hera Teleia and Zeus Teleios. In his quality of Teleios, Zeus no doubt brought many things to completion. The *telos* that Zeus in union with Hera as a divine pair attain for themselves and help human couples attain is—so far as human couples imitate the divine—the *gamos*. The word *gamos* as object of *telein* (*gamon telein*,[40] *telos gamoio*[41]) can be used quite generally. The correspondence between the legally performed Gamoi on earth and the Gamos of Zeus and Hera, as the goal for human couples, is attested in Athens with the utmost distinctness.

The feast at which earthly couples realized in themselves the com-

---

38 The Christian source is Maximus Confessor, *Ad Dionysi Areopagitae Epistulas* VIII 6, quoted by H. Bolkestein, Τέλος ὁ γάμος. For this and also the Spartan source, Areios Didymos, see Bolkestein, p. 2. For Athens, see Pollux III 38. Bolkestein, however, takes his criticism too far; no saying was ever coined to say nothing. See further Kerényi, *Hermes der Seelenführer*, p. 80.

39 See Kerényi, *Eleusis* s.v. *telos* in the index, p. 255.

40 For examples of the construction, see Kallimachos, *Hymnus in Apollinem* 14; Theokritos XVII 131 (quoted above in the text, at note 32). The married women of Kos were called τελεύμεναι; see W. Dittenberger, *Sylloge Inscriptionum Graecarum*, III, 1006.

41 *Odyssey* XX 74.

v. Zeus the Brother-Husband

pletion of the heavenly couple was celebrated in the winter month of Gamelion (about our January), on the 24th or probably as early as the 22nd.[42] Since the weddings of all young engaged couples in Athens were held at the same time,[43] a single day was hardly adequate for the festival of so many families related by blood or marriage. The month was sacred to Hera; her feast was the Gamelia.[44] This is to be understood as meaning that the goddess was celebrated through the Gamoi, since the completion signified by them was really the completion of Hera. Zeus for this reason bore the epithet "Heraios" and received a sacrifice.[45] For the divine wedding the feast was also called "Theogamia."[46] Otherwise the feast for that which happened between mortal couples, with the observance and completion of all the rites and ceremonies due to Hera, was called "Hieros Gamos." It was by this observance that the Gamos was sanctified; from these rites and ceremonies it got its epithet "sacred." Yet, this was wrongly understood even in late antiquity.

42   For evidence, see Menander, fr. 320. The end of the month, after which the weddings originally took place (see note 46, below), was evidently shifted further and further forward.

43   This follows from the actual calendar date of the yearly wedding day.

44   See Deubner, *Attische Feste*, p. 177; also Hesychios s.v. Γαμηλιών.

45   See Prott and Ziehen, *Leges graecorum sacrae*, I, No. 1, lines 20–22 (p. 4).

46   The name Theogamia turns up very late, and has been associated with Proklos (see his scholium on Hesiod's *Works and Days* 780, in T. Gaisford, ed., p. 430, line 19). To say that the festival was for this reason an invention of the Neoplatonists is an impossible idea of Nilsson's in his hypercritical observations on "Wedding Rites in Ancient Greece," p. 245. Hesiod in *Works and Days* 780, the passage referred to, advised against sowing the crops at full moon. Proklos in his scholium compared with this advice the timing of Athenian weddings in the days nearest to the *coniunctio* of sun and moon (new moon). The astrological view of this time may be due to him, so that the name Theogamia would be of late origin. Yet, the calendar dating—to which the dates given by Menander only approximately correspond—was certainly not a Neoplatonic invention.

With grammatical correctness the true state of affairs is defined in the *Lexicon rhetoricum Cantabrigiense*, under the phrase *hieros gamos*:

> οἱ γαμοῦντες ποιοῦσι τῶι Διὶ καὶ τῆι Ἥραι ἱεροὺς γάμους·
>
> Those who marry contract marriages sacred to Zeus and Hera.⁴⁷

The human act of Gamos could also be so contracted that the quality "sacred," which was associated with a definite date and the characteristic rites and ceremonies, did not attach to it. People spoke mockingly of *methemerinoi gamoi,* "marriages of a day," and meant by them the traffic with prostitutes.⁴⁸ *Hieroi gamoi* are mentioned in the literature for the first time by Socrates in Plato's *Republic*. He speaks of the Gamoi of the guardians of the state:

> γάμους . . . ποιήσομεν ἱεροὺς εἰς δύναμιν ὅτι μάλιστα·
>
> It is clear that we shall try to make our marriages as sacred as possible.⁴⁹

"Sacred marriages" for Socrates evidently still means no more than a completely right marriage, and he does not shrink from taking a biological view of rightness, as utility in producing good posterity. According to Plato's *Laws*, honorable wives come

> μετὰ θεῶν καὶ ἱερῶν γάμων ἐλθούσαις εἰς τὴν οἰκίαν
>
> with gods and sacred marriages into the home.

---

47 See Cook, *Zeus*, III, 1062, headnote.
48 See Demosthenes XVIII (*De corona*), 129.
49 Plato, *Republic* V 458 E. The passage in the *Laws*, quoted ahead in the text, is at VIII 841 D.

v. Zeus the Brother-Husband

But the people of Athens evidently wanted something else from the marriages—besides healthy couples and rightly consummated rites—before they could earn the title *hieros*. They wanted an approach to the divine couple in beauty. Anaxandrides, a poet of the Middle Comedy, says as much in the fourth century B.C.:

> ἂν μὲν γὰρ ἦι τις εὐπρεπής, ἱερὸν γάμον καλεῖτε·
> *It's Sacred Wedding if a man's good-looking.*[50]

While the weddings were being celebrated in Athens it was one long "sacred marriage."[51] The concrete realization of that for which Zeus and Hera set the example was invested with sanctity. It was not until all sense of this sanctity had been extinguished that the Neoplatonist Proklos explained Plato's words, which clearly referred to human marriages, as if the expression *hieros gamos* had originally had a place in certain "mystical stories" and been taken over from there:

> ἐκ τῶν μυστικῶν λόγων καὶ τῶν ἐν ἀπυρρήτων λεγομένων ἱερῶν γάμων.[52]

When Proklos lists several *hieroi gamoi* of the gods, he too puts that of Hera and Zeus first. Then come Ouranos and Ge, Kronos and Rhea, Zeus and Demeter, Zeus and Kore, and the unions of women with gods generally. Proklos, however, would hardly have spoken in this way if

---

50 Anaxandrides, fr. 34 (in Edmonds, *The Fragments of Attic Comedy*, II, 58–59).

51 In view of this situation, a new interpretation is needed of the rites, of which our knowledge is so fragmentary. We would welcome also a new interpretation of the wedding representations on Attic vases, despite the splendid account already given by Margarete Bieber, "Eros and Dionysos on Kerch Vases," pp. 31–38.

52 Proklos, *In Platonis Timaeum* 16 B. For Proklos' placing of Zeus and Hera first, see *In Platonis Parmenidem* 214.

a mystical Hera cult had not existed: the cult of Argos, which we shall investigate in the next chapter. The adoption of Proklos' generalization by all the modern literature on the subject testifies to a considerable remissness in regard to the human and concrete historical phenomenon that emerges so clearly from the sources.

The historical phenomenon is this. In Athens, a city that worshiped as its supreme goddess Pallas Athena—the virgin associated with the father and representing patriarchal ideas[53]—the contracting of marriage, apart from the legal aspects of the institution and those serving the increase of population,[54] was a sacred act owed to Hera and performed in her honor. This was completely determined by a way of thinking dominant in matriarchal societies, a way of thinking that Hera embodied. We know of a temple of Hera Teleia and Zeus Teleios that was probably outside the walls,[55] and certainly outside the Akropolis. The Olympian Zeus, the Zeus of Homer and the Zeus religion, also did not receive a worthy sanctuary except outside the city walls and that relatively late, under the Peisistratids, and it was Hadrian who first reconstructed it as a gigantic temple, the Olympieion.[56] The Zeus of the Athenians was originally one who lighted up in underworld darknesses, like the Zeus Meilichios who appeared in the form of a snake, a Minoan (and in Attica also Eleusinian) forerunner of the "Zeus of

---

53 Kerényi, *Die Jungfrau und Mutter*, pp. 14 ff. For Athena as the goddess of weddings, see ibid., p. 21.

54 This is where the Attic marriage formula ("for the plowing and sowing of legitimate children," in Menander, fr. 720) belongs, and the role of the priestess of Demeter who in Chaironeia communicated to newlyweds the marriage law of their ancestors (the *patrion thesmon*); see Plutarch, *Coniugalia praecepta* 138 B.

55 This would mean on the road from Phaleron to Athens; see Pausanias I 1 4 and X 35 2.

56 Deubner, *Attische Feste*, p. 177.

v. Zeus the Brother-Husband

all the Greeks," "Panhellenios." Hera belonged, however, to that first Zeus.

It may well be possible that during the Classical period, when the temple of the Teleia and Teleios stood as it had been burnt down by the Persians and unrestored,[57] the Hera cult, insofar as it was the cult of the Gamelia, was resettled in the sanctuary of a nymph at the foot of the Akropolis[58]—as if she had been the *nymphe Dios*, "bride of Zeus."[59] Homer's Hera, the queen of heaven of Argos, Samos, Olympia, Euboea, and Corinth with the sanctuary of Perachora across the bay, had a no less Panhellenic character than Zeus. She was exemplary for Athenian brides, whose patriarchal families saw to it that their Gamos was as "sacred" as possible, that is, assimilated to the Gamos of Hera. No Athenian bride was allowed to marry a *homogastrios*, a brother who had the same mother as herself. Such a marriage would have been contrary to the greatest matriarchal incest prohibition,[60] which only Hera was allowed to transgress. Of her it is said that she was the only sister allowed to have such a husband, the only one equal to her in birth.[61] So the Athenian girls who as brides came near to Hera could not be like her in every respect.

This privilege of marrying her own brother was reserved uniquely for Hera, and to her only as the future and actual monogamous wife

---

57 Pausanias I 1 5 and X 35 2.

58 The finds exhibited in a showcase in the Akropolis Museum have not yet been published as of this time. Among the finds, however, are vases with pictures that suggest this conclusion.

59 The phrase occurs in an epigram of the Samian poet Nikainetos, quoted in Athenaios XV 673 c. See also the new picture of Paestum in Kerényi, *Werke*, II, 237; and in the text, the end of ch. VII.

60 On the *homogastrioi*, see above in the text, ch. V, at note 10. On the incest prohibition, see the discussion of the matriarchal triangle in ch. III, above.

61 See the scholium on Iliad I 609: ἀδέλφη μόνη ἀνδρὸς ἔτυχε τοιούτου.

of Zeus, destined to it from all eternity. According to a myth about the Gamos of the divine couple, the goddess refused the god *dia ten metera*,[62] "because of the mother," that is to say, because they were *homogastrioi*. But she did then give herself to him as wedded wife, as the half become a whole with the rank of queen of the gods. This rank, the higher aspect of the female half in the union, was a thing Hera brought along with her from matriarchal conditions. Hera worship in her oldest cult sites, in Argos and Samos, undoubtedly goes back far enough for this to be possible.[63] In Athens her *myth* gave women the brilliant show of completion, the fulfillment of their totality, in a form unattainable and yet stored up in their woman's nature as *telos*, as a goal.

This aspect of the incestuous marriage so strictly forbidden in matriarchal conditions must not be ignored. The prohibition is only a negative way of expressing ambivalent behavior in face of a possibility that can be valued also quite positively. One highly positive valuation lay in the fact that brother and sister marriage persisted over wide areas which were no less matriarchally influenced than Greece—in Persia, Mesopotamia, Egypt, as a privilege of ruling dynasties. Even the higher aristocracy and the priestly class sometimes shared in this privilege.[64] Above all, among the rulers, the decisive reason was the imitation of the gods, the intentional repetition of mythological conditions. These were reflected even in a mythology that had become as conceptual as that of the religion of Zoroaster. The reason given for the brother and sister marriage of a Cappadocian ruling couple in the sec-

62 In the scholium to Theokritos XV 64, this is said following Aristokles the mythographer, who wrote about sanctuaries in Hermione.
63 On Argos, see ch. VI; on Samos, ch. VII.
64 See Kornemann, *Die Stellung der Frau in der vorgriechischen Mittelmeer-Kultur*, pp. 13 ff.

v. Zeus the Brother-Husband

ond century B.C., according to an Aramaic inscription in which Ahura Mazda occurs under the name Bel, was: "The Mazdaic Religion, the Queen, the Sister and Consort, spoke thus: 'I am the wife of Bel the King.' Whereupon Bel answered the Mazdaic Religion: 'My Sister, you are wise and more beautiful than goddesses, therefore have I taken you to wife!' "[65]

The ambivalence contained in the positive valuation can be clearly observed with reference to sibling incest in the purely matriarchal social order of the Trobriand Islanders. Everything that ought to occur in life appears in the mythology of the Trobriand Islanders as primordial happening, something performed as an example for future ages.[66] Among these happenings is also that most forbidden thing, incest between brother and sister. Malinowski limits himself in essence to noting this paradox and rightly rejects any external explanation.[67] He does not, for instance, attribute it to some unknown history of development. The ambivalence, the negative attitude to something that is at the same time valued very positively, and therefore feared, is explanation enough. Malinowski refers to one of the texts published by himself, the "story of the first love magic" and its very revealing expression of the tragic ambivalence. It is the mother who sends her daughter to the place where she falls victim to the love magic prepared by her brother for another.[68]

---

65 Ibid., p. 16.
66 See Malinowski, *Myth in Primitive Psychology*, pp. 21, 39.
67 See Malinowski, *The Sexual Life of Savages in North-Western Melanesia*, p. 453: "As we know, among all rules and taboos there is one which has a really strong hold over native imagination and moral sense; and yet this unmentionable crime is the subject of one of their sacred stories and the basis of love magic, and thus is directed, so to speak, into the full current of tribal life."
68 Malinowski, *Sexual Life*, p. 460: "Had she gone into the house herself and brought water to her daughter, the tragedy would never have occurred. She,

The love magic causes the scruples imposed on the brother and sister by the social order to disappear. The two—evidently because they are brother and sister, for otherwise the effect of the love magic would not be fatal—fall in love so passionately that they can neither eat nor drink and die of love. The further explanation that the Trobriand Island storyteller added was that this happened out of shame and remorse.[69] In the mythologem there is not a word of this. Love-making between brother and sister seems to be a thing that inherently exceeds the human norm. An inherent and internally motivated intensity—motivated by the powerful force of attraction of the nearest relative which can be balanced only by an equally great horror of incest, as is known in psychiatry[70]—qualifies the theme to serve a dual function. Thus, the theme serves to play a cosmogonic part as the procreative union of a "first couple" or else it serves to be developed mythologically as the love story of a Great Goddess, representing for ordinary mortals the most forbidden thing.

We have no sufficient reason to suppose that Homer incorporated in his account of the seduction of Zeus by Hera the theme of a powerful love spell from an ancient mythologem related to the Trobriand magic story. Hera borrows the magic from Aphrodite to whose natural range of influence the primordial magic of love belongs. Aphrodite is the goddess with whom bisexuality is associated in Greek mythology, a theme which can, so to speak, claim genetic priority over sibling

---

the very source of the matrilineal kinship bond, she from whose womb the two children sprang, she is also the involuntary cause of the tragedy."

69   Ibid., p. 457.

70   The case of a marriage of twins is reported in L. Szondi, *Schicksalsanalyse*, pp. 150 ff. Szondi's biological explanation is turned to account in what follows.

v. Zeus the Brother-Husband

unions.[71] The love of a brother and sister couple tends, more than normal love, to the restoration of a bisexual totality, which is presupposed by that powerful mutual attraction. This is where the much-feared dangers of the much-desired sibling love are to be found. They are on the frontier between reabsorption into the motionless unity of the primordial condition on the one hand, and forward movement by proliferation into children on the other. The union of siblings—for we may indeed state the deepest reason for the horror of this form of incest as follows—threatened the propagation of the human race. In myth the union of siblings was reserved for *gods* and was realized in Hera's Gamos, where the highest god of the Greeks joined her as *brother-husband*.

[71] On the "Mythos des Hermaphroditos," see Kerényi, *The Gods of the Greeks*, pp. 81, 171 ff. (Pelican edn., pp. 71, 151 ff.); and *Hermes der Seelenführer*, p. 97. Also see C. G. Jung and C. Kerényi, *Essays on a Science of Mythology*, p. 54.

VI. HERA CULTS IN THE PELOPONNESE, EUBOEA, AND BOEOTIA

IN THE HISTORY of Greek religion, before the time of Homer, Hera was already on the way to being sublimated into the pure image of the wife and consort. The content of her archetypal form was something the goddess brought with her from a more ancient time. About this period some sure inferences can be drawn from the Hera cult site on the mainland, in Argos. In this ancient correlation where Hera had occupied the divine side, the counterpole to a worship rendered above all by women, she was a more complex figure than that which she later became by sublimation and reduction. Homer contributed a great deal to the simplification of this great female deity. He stresses the possibility of some alienation between Zeus and Hera. After Homer, however, a separation from Zeus would have meant an intolerable situation for the goddess. For she would have become nothing but the powerless half of a whole needed by her and not by Zeus.[1]

Hera cannot originally have been like this! A figure as dependent as this could not have been the object of a cult. We should have been absolutely forced to assume some reduction and sublimation even if the goddess had not actually been called *panton genethla*, "origin of all things," by one of her worshipers.[2] In some unknown cosmogony she occupied a similar position to that occupied by Okeanos in yet another cosmogony, quoted by Homer, where Okeanos is called "*genesis for all.*"[3] The name Hera, or *Here*, tells us nothing about the original

---

1 See Iliad I 562–63.   2 Alkaios, fr. 24a 7, in Diehl, *Anth. lyr.*
3 Iliad XIV 201, 246.

VI. Hera Cults in the Peloponnese, Euboea, and Boeotia

character of the goddess. With Zeus and Poseidon, as we have seen, matters are otherwise. They were transparent Greek names, whereas with Hera it is not even certain in what language she was originally so called.[4] A hypothetical etymology, even if one of those hitherto proposed were probable, could not be the foundation of a historical account.[5] If the meaning, as was long assumed, were "Mistress" that would not take us any further. Only from her sanctuaries can we learn more about Hera.

Homer in listing Hera's favorite sites has her mention Argos.[6] For him she is "Argeie," "the one from Argos."[7] That she was connected not merely with the city of Argos but more truly and more originally with the whole land of Argos is proved by the situation of the Heraion, her sanctuary. Zeus was never given an important temple close by it as he was in the case of Olympia. When Homer lists Mycenae after Argos as a city dear to Hera,[8] he means there too the Heraion of Argos, which was equidistant from both cities. In Mycenae itself no temple of Hera has been either found or mentioned. The Heraion was for centuries the sanctuary of the whole country, originally in the same way as the temple at Jerusalem, for instance, was a unique temple of Israel. The position the Heraion occupied in the landscape was as if planted on a

---

4 On *e-ra* in the Mycenaean documents, see above, the beginning of ch. II.
5 Such accounts recently put forward include the following: F. R. Schröder, "Hera," pp. 64 ff.; A. J. Van Windekens, " "Ηρα '(die) junge Kuh, (die) Färse,' " pp. 309–311; W. Pötscher, "Hera und Heros," pp. 302 ff., and "Der Name der Göttin Hera," pp. 317 ff.
6 Iliad IV 51–52.
7 Iliad IV 8, V 908. On the association with Athena of Alalkomenai, see further in ch. VI at notes 119, 120.
8 Iliad IV 52. The third city Hera mentions among those dearest to her is Sparta, in another state–not in Argos but in Lakedaimon. In Sparta we know of several Hera temples, among them one of Hera Argeia, allegedly founded by the wife of Akrisios, primordial king of Argos; see Pausanias III 13 8.

balcony. This extremely important situating has been described most exactly by an eminent expert on the architecture of ancient temples.[9] He starts from the altar, the most essential structure in a Greek cult:

"Something of the nature of the altar can be learned perhaps even today in a sanctuary like the Argive Heraion, one of the oldest and most venerable in Greece. According to legend the oldest temple was built by Doros, the tribal ancestor of the Dorians.[10] It stood on the western slope of Mount Euboia, high over the plain which spread southward, on a rectangular terrace of which the retaining walls with their huge stones had been constructed probably as early as the eighth century. The earliest temple, of which nothing had been preserved, was replaced in the first half of the seventh century by a temple with ringed portico which occupied the whole terrace. So there was no room on it for an altar. When this temple was burnt down in the year 423,[11] the new one was built not in the same place but on a lower-lying terrace, at the north side of which halls for the reception of offerings had been standing since the end of the seventh century. From these it is clear that this terrace was the one on which the great cult performances and ceremonies took place as the climax of the festival processions from the city of Argos. This terrace was reached by a broad flight of steps only a few of which have been preserved. At the point where they reach the level of the cult terrace there stands the base of a square altar which both from the style of its stonework and the archaic pottery fragments found on the spot must be of earlier date than the new temple of the fifth century. It must be at least as early as the halls on the north side. But it may be older than they are, for between the halls on the

9 H. Kähler, *Der griechische Tempel*, pp. 8–9.
10 See Vitruvius, *De architectura* IV 1 84.
11 For confirmation of this detail, see Thukydides IV 133.

VI. Hera Cults in the Peloponnese, Euboea, and Boeotia 117

north side there is a gap, through which it is possible that, originally, the way led up to the old temple on the highest terrace. Before this altar, which is pushed right forward to the extreme southern edge of the cult place, the broad plain stretches away, ringed by the ancient sites of which this sanctuary was the center, Mycenae, Argos, Tiryns, and Midea. Right across to the mountains under which Argos lies, the view from the altar extends over the flat countryside through which the solemn procession once advanced, after the games in the stadium, to sacrifice to the goddess who was the mistress of the plain and its cities. The altar is the beginning of the sanctuary."

When Homer had Hera list her favorite sites, in the ninth or eighth century, at least this altar must have already been standing. Those who sacrificed at the altar must also have had their facing partner. Thus, the Pylians,[12] for instance, or the Milesians, who sacrificed at the huge Poseidon altar, a notable example of the cult without a temple,[13] had as their facing partner the *sea*, in its incalculable mobility, rest and unrest. The sky, a scene of events, could also form such a vis-à-vis. A plain, in all its passivity, however luxuriant, could hardly do so. If sacrifices had been performed there to Ge, to mother earth, the altars would have had to be differently constructed. Some concrete appearance—at least as concrete as that of Zeus in his lighting up—if not on earth, then in heaven, is required as a possible, if not regular, facing partner *by the logic* of this cult installation. The historian of Greek religion must here dispense with the kind of logic unknown to this religion, the logic of one-to-one nomenclature. Since the moon in certain

---

12 On the performance of the great sacrifice by the Pylians, see above, in ch. IV.

13 See in T. Wiegand, ed., *Königliche Museen zu Berlin. Milet*, the volume by A. von Gerkan, *Der Poseidonaltar bei Kap Monodendri*.

mythological tales is called Selene and since it has its own special myths, it might be thought that it could not also be a manifestation of Hera, that the waxing and waning of moonlight could not be Hera's happenings. But they could. No other facing partner for the worshipers at the Heraion of Argos is conceivable.

The terrace of the Argive Heraion, and the precinct below and behind it, must be regarded as an immense cult stage. The cult performed there may be called a mystical one. This does not mean, however, that initiations occurred here, as in Eleusis, in a closed building; there is no basis in the texts for postulating a "Telesterion."[14] The cult was mystical insofar as a part of the rites and the myths attached to them were not accessible to everyone. There is mention of a brook with the name "freeing water" (*Eleutherion hudor*) which must be crossed by those who came from Mycenae. The women employed in the sanctuary and on the mystical rites (*ton thysion es tas aporrhetous*) purified themselves in it.[15] The designation "freeing water" entitles us to suppose that the women ministrants once actually had to be declared free as long as they were performing the ceremonies in the sanctuary. They must have belonged originally to the population subjected by the Greeks and were now continuing an ancient Hera cult of their own.

Pausanias does not disclose the "more secret myth" (*aporrheteros logos*) that referred to the pomegranate in the hand of Hera enthroned, Polykleitos' cult statue. It was a fairly transparent piece of symbolism which we can unravel.[16] For once Pausanias does reveal a "secret tale"

14 The East Building was designated as the Telesterion by C. Waldstein, *The Argive Heraeum*, I, 9, fig. 2:IV; also by G. Gruben, *Die Tempel der Griechen*, p. 99, fig. 92:7, who dates the "Telesterion" to the middle of the fifth century B.C.
15 See Pausanias II 17 1.   16 Ibid., par. 4.

VI. *Hera Cults in the Peloponnese, Euboea, and Boeotia*

(*logos ton aporrheton*) about the spring Kanathos, in which every year Hera bathed—that is to say, her statue was bathed—in order to regain her virginity.[17] The spring is by the convent Agia Moni at Nauplion and would be visible from the Heraion if the terrain in this direction were not so hilly. It is conceivable that there was a procession there to bathe the goddess, although the festival could also be celebrated in the closer surroundings of the temple, and certainly was so celebrated. We can put it down to the mystical character of the myths and rites of the Heraion that Pausanias disguises the cult names borne by Hera in them.

The disguise is very transparent. The closer surroundings comprised three strips of countryside which had the names Euboia, Prosymna, and Akraia. These, according to Pausanias, were the names of three daughters of the river god Asterion (a bigger stream than the "freeing water") who were the nurses of Hera.[18] But they were certainly the Great Goddess herself in her three local manifestations. Akraia can only have been Hera Akraia, "she of the mountain ledge," as she was also called in Corinth[19] and at her residence in Perachora, across the bay from Corinth.[20] Under this name she belonged to the mountain

17 Ibid., II 38 2-3.   18 Ibid., II 17 1.
19 The epithet "Akraia" occurs in Euripides, *Medea* 1379 (and see Scholium 237); also H. Payne, *Perachora*, pp. 19–20. "Hera Bunaia" (attested for Corinth; see Pausanias II 4 7) is another name for "Hera Akraia." See the commentary on the passage in H. Hitzig and H. Bluemner, *Pausaniae Graeciae descriptio*, I:2, 509–510.
20 A visit to Perachora in 1956 did not convince me that the remains of inscriptions which, according to Payne, *Perachora*, p. 78, were found "in the votive deposit over the Agora," with the letters KPAI, AK, and AKPA, must refer to the temples (three successive buildings) standing in the city. The attribution of the temple down on the small bay to Hera Limenia cannot be doubted. Hera Akraia could have had her residence where the lighthouse stands today; the remains of inscriptions could have slid down from there. Between the Limenia and the Akraia, Hera had her main cult place in the middle, where Payne would

opposite the Heraion which Pausanias calls by this name[21] and is today the site of the chapel of Elias Berbatiotikos. It is a long narrow mountain ridge, 2,300 feet at its highest point.[22] The high point of the goddess' epiphanies was undoubtedly connected with it. Of Prosymna Pausanias says that it was the name of a place (*chora*) *below* the Heraion.[23] According to Strabo this place, which has not yet been located, had a Hera shrine that in his time was no longer inhabited.[24] Prosymna is a name which as a divine epithet is suited to a low-lying situation, in the way that Akraia was suited to the highest. In the middle lay the domain in which the Heraion itself was situated on a low rise, a natural terrace. Here, between the highest region of the Akraia and the lowest of the Prosymna (with its smaller sanctuary), the goddess—and also the mountain on which the buildings of the great sanctuary stood—was called "Euboia," "she who is rich in cattle."[25]

The name of the river god, father to the three daughters, Asterion, as the brook was called that rose at the back of the mountains in

---

have placed the temple of the Akraia. Here at the main cult place Hera probably had the epithet "Leukolenos"; see Payne, pp. 111, 258. The site is not an *akra* but rather to be compared with the Euboia in the Heraion of Argos. The cult of sacrifice took place at the so-called "triglyph altar." A parallel to the situation of the Limenia is provided near the Sele estuary; see further, in ch. VII, the discussion of Paestum.

21 Pausanias II 17 2.
22 See V. Steffen, *Karten von Mykenai*, text p. 40.
23 Pausanias II 17 2.
24 Strabo VIII 6 11. Axel W. Persson looked for the place behind the mount of Elias Berbatiotikos, near the village of Berbati, which was renamed Prosimni in accordance with this opinion. Gösta Säflund more correctly calls the excavations that he carried out there *Excavations at Berbati*, without giving them an ancient name.
25 Carl W. Blegen transferred Prosymna to this more central region, equally without sufficient reason. See the published account of his excavations in *Prosymna. The Helladic Settlement Preceding the Argive Heraeum*.

VI. Hera Cults in the Peloponnese, Euboea, and Boeotia

Berbati, was also transparent in its reference to Hera. "Asterion," "river of stars," points to the sky. The *asterion*, according to Pausanias, also was a plant that grew by the brook.[26] Wreaths for the goddess were plaited from its leaves—from a "sort of aster," as Heinrich Schliemann wrote,[27] meaning a "starflower" which has since been botanically identified.[28] A father and a wreath alluding to the stars befitted the queen of heaven. And that is who Hera was here, in three manifestations—high, middle, and low.

The thirty-day month and its division into three was usual among the Greeks.[29] The moon for them could have three faces, a waxing, a full, and a waning sign of a divine presence in the sky. This inference can be drawn from the moon's mythology without begging any questions.[30] At every step we encounter *three* goddesses, and, what is more, of the kind that form not only a chance group of three persons, at most three sisters, but female trinities, of which any one member is almost no more than a single threefold goddess. Without qualification Hera was a goddess of this type, expressly designated as a single goddess in three phases, for example, at Stymphalos, about which we shall come to speak.[31] It is not a limitation to phases of the moon that is insisted on here, but rather the extension of the moon's phases into a new dimension, that of a divine womanly form which for the goddess' worshipers

26 Pausanias II 17 2.
27 See H. Schliemann, *Mykenae*, p. 29.
28 See further A. Frickenhaus, *Tiryns*, I, 121–25.
29 W. Sontheimer, "Monat," cols. 44–74.
30 See Kerényi, *The Gods of the Greeks*, p. 31 (Pelican edn., p. 27), and *Niobe*, pp. 26 ff., for the ancient and the astronomical figures. It is unscientific superstition to want to rule out the entire possibility of a "moon mythology" among the Greeks.
31 On the three Hera temples in Stymphalos, see further in ch. VI at note 67, below.

Zeus and Hera

was visible in the moon's light. This view would be fully justified by the data from the Heraion at Argos even if it could not be corroborated from other cult places.

If we sought to read off the characteristics of the goddess from the plain before the Argive Heraion, on the analogy of the similar fertile flatlands on which the Hera temples of Samos and Paestum stand, we should at once be defeated by the Akraia on the peak of Elias Berbatiotikos. It is, of course, difficult to imagine a phase of ceremonial cult proceedings in places of such difficult access as this mountain ridge or the peak of Mount Oche on the island of Euboea.[32] And yet in such high places we can glimpse, if not a cult site, at least a place of mythical pre-eminence in the sacred tales—a high spot in the goddess' myth, reached by her as Hera Teleia. "Akraia" means the same in topography as "Teleia" means in myth and in the sky during full moon. In Hermione, on the east coast of Argolis, there stood on a low hill a temple of Hera, who was worshiped there as "Parthenos," "virgin,"[33] but on a higher hill outside the town there stood the temple of Hera Teleia and Zeus, who seduced her there.[34] The time of full moon is not indicated for these rites, but it was customary in Greece—though not uniformly and not everywhere—to hold weddings at full moon.[35] In this case they were certainly celebrated as a festival of Hera Teleia.

For a definite reason it is not probable that in the Heraion at Argos a celebration of the Gamos was associated with the Akraia and the full moon. The mountain with the temple of Hera Teleia at Hermione had

32 On the association with Mount Oche, see further in ch. VI at notes 110, 111, below.

33 See Stephen of Byzantium s.v. Ἑρμιών; also Pausanias II 36 2.

34 See note 36, below.

35 This was emphasized, without regard to such an important example to the contrary as the Athenian, and with his usual one-sidedness, by M. P. Nilsson, *Die Entstehung und religiöse Bedeutung des griechischen Kalenders*, p. 41.

VI. Hera Cults in the Peloponnese, Euboea, and Boeotia 123

expressive names. "Kokkyx" or "Kokkygion," "cuckoo" or "Mount Cuckoo,"[36] was a name undoubtedly associated only with this peak. It displaced the older name "Thronax" or "Thornax," "footstool," and was based on the myth of the seduction of Hera by Zeus just alluded to.[37] The seduction myth implies the use of this older name, meaning the "throne footstool" under Hera's feet. For *she* was enthroned there. The cuckoo into which Zeus transformed himself needed neither throne nor footstool. The story goes that Hera had become separated from the other gods and goddesses—a theme that is better motivated elsewhere in her cult—and thus got caught in the thunderstorm let loose by Zeus upon the mountain which in fact belonged to Hera. She sat there, where her temple was later to be situated, allowed the half-frozen cuckoo to alight on her knees, and covered it with her robe. Then Zeus revealed himself as her suitor. At first Hera appealed to the mother because of *her* ban on love-making between sister and brother;[38] but then she became Zeus's wife. The whole tale shows Zeus as the intruder in the matriarchal domain in which Hera was here enthroned as ruler. The Greeks were well acquainted with the cuckoo's underhand trick of laying eggs in other birds' nests.[39] By this unique mythological creation Zeus is *precisely fitted into the history of the Hera religion of Argos*. In Hermione, not far from Argos, there was also a living tradition that Zeus and Hera first landed there on coming from Crete.[40] This, too, may have been a reflection of the historical course of events in regard to Zeus.

36 See the scholium to Theokritos XV 64.
37 On Thornax and the Cuckoo Mountain, see also Pausanias II 36 1–2.
38 On the matriarchal incest prohibition, see above in the text, the end of ch. V.
39 See further O. Keller, *Die antike Tierwelt*, II, 64–65.
40 Stephen of Byzantium s.v. Ἑρμιών.

In the Heraion of Argos there were allusions to the cuckoo wedding, but they associated the actual wedding itself with the Hermione countryside. This makes it improbable that a full-moon Gamos of the Akraia was celebrated at Argos. The cuckoo was a theme of the marble decoration of the Classical temple built there after 423 B.C.[41] And the same bird sat on the scepter of Hera enthroned, the gold and ivory cult statue created for the temple by Polykleitos. The story told was that Hera had chased the cuckoo and caught Zeus.[42] To infer from this that there was a corresponding cult performance on Mount Akraia would be an unnecessary step; the Cuckoo Mountain in Hermione lies close enough. The connection of the worship of Akraia with the full moon—monthly for small ceremonies, yearly for great ones—has its own justification independently of any further assumptions. The same goes for the association of the low point in the Hera myth with Prosymna and the new moon.

Homer knows about this low point. Zeus in the Iliad is alluding to a voluntary withdrawal of Hera's when he calls out to her:

> ... *And for you and your anger*
> *I care not; not if you stray apart to the undermost limits*
> *of earth and sea, where Iapetos and Kronos seated*
> *have no shining of the sun god Hyperion to delight them*
> *nor winds' delight, but Tartaros stands deeply about them;*
> *not even if you reach that place in your wandering shall I*
> *care for your sulks; since there is nothing more shameless*
>   *than you are.*[43]

41 This is reproduced in Waldstein, *The Argive Heraeum*, I, 124, fig. 61.
42 Pausanias II 17 4.
43 Iliad VIII 477–83 (tr. Lattimore).

vi. Hera Cults in the Peloponnese, Euboea, and Boeotia

The allusion here is to a voluntary journey of Hera through the underworld. It is echoed in the *Aeneid* by a verse that Virgil (without mentioning Hera's journey itself) puts into the mouth of his Juno, the queen of the gods, who is so extensively modeled on Hera:

> *flectere si nequeo superos, Acheronta movebo.*
> *If I cannot bend the gods to my will, I shall move the underworld.*[44]

In his description of Aeneas' underworld journey, Virgil dares to call Proserpina, the Greek Persephone, "Iuno inferna,"[45] and thus to put the queen of the dead beside the queen of the gods. He can do this probably because he knows all about the Hera religion of Argos, as his "Iuno Argiva" shows.[46] The pomegranate in the hand of Polykleitos' enthroned Hera[47] plainly characterized the goddess as a second Persephone, like this Juno.[48] The secret tale mentioned by Pausanias gave more particulars.[49] Virgil's allusions, which have not been understood by his interpreters, are connected with the Prosymna cult. And this epithet itself, "Prosymna," points in the same direction, the underworld aspect of Hera.

Prosymnos is the name of Dionysos' guide to the underworld from Lerna,[50] an entrance to Hades through the waters of the swamp. "Pro-

---

44 Virgil, *Aeneid* VII 312.
45 For the epithet, see *Aeneid* VI 138. Eduard Norden, in his commentary, would have it that this was a bold invention of Virgil's, a *hapax legomenon*.
46 *Aeneid* III 547.
47 Pausanias II 17 4.
48 See Kerényi, *Eleusis*, pp. 134–38.
49 Pausanias II 17 4.
50 Pausanias II 37 1. See also Clement of Alexandria, *Protrepticus* II 34; Kerényi, *The Gods of the Greeks*, p. 259 (Pelican edn., p. 228).

symne" was the epithet of Demeter in the same underworld domain,[51] which was part of the Argos countryside. A translation of the ancient cult name Prosymnos is given as "Polymnos" or "Polyymnos"[52]—a very clear explanation, because a being connected with the underworld was "sung to" at certain festivals with hymns. In the person of Prosymnos it was a phallic being,[53] or when female a goddess, who was summoned and accompanied with songs. In like manner the new moon was summoned by choruses at the time when it lingered invisible in the darkness. This has been handed down in Athens in regard to Pallas Athena, the "Kore of the Athenians," who was born with the new moon.[54] The same can be assumed of Hera as Prosymna, at new moon, in her small sanctuary, below the great one, the Heraion of Argos.

The continuation of the ceremony, it may be assumed, was that Prosymna was conducted from the place of her reappearance to the bath, in a procession of "freed" women.[55] The goddess would have been in the form of a wooden figure, like the wooden statue in Samos which was "found again" in the thicket of *lygos* bushes.[56] This ceremony of the bath happened once a year.[57] From the internal logic of the event that restored Hera to Zeus, the bath in which the goddess had her virginity restored, according to the "secret story" of the Kanathos spring, must have been a purification and bridal bath. The mystic boys' song about the early union of Zeus and Hera referred to by Dion Chrysosto-

51 Pausanias II 37 1.
52 On the name, see O. Höfer, "Polymnos," cols. 2657-61.
53 See Kerényi, *Dionysos*, ch. VI, at notes 123, 124.
54 Euripides, *Heraclidae* 777-83. See also Kerényi, *Die Jungfrau und Mutter*, p. 42.
55 See above, ch. VI, at note 15, the discussion of "freeing water."
56 On the *lygos*, see further, in ch. VII, the section on Samos.
57 Pausanias II 38 2.

VI. Hera Cults in the Peloponnese, Euboea, and Boeotia

mos[58] may have come afterwards, at the wedding of the divine couple. This wedding occurred in the Heraion shortly after the appearance of the new moon. The ceremony was called *lecherna*, for the bed (*lechos*).[59] In the antechamber of the Heraion Pausanias saw "Hera's bed,"[60] an article of the cult, which may also have been brought as an offering. The models of houses in temples of Hera[61] were other offerings alluding to the Gamos as the goddess liked it, that is, in the house.[62]

After passing the low point of Hera's periodic being, the cult proceedings took place in the middle region, called Euboia, just as the goddess herself was called Euboia for the greater part of her cult year. The queen of heaven took pleasure in her favorite animals, which were sacrificed to her in hecatombs.[63] In earlier times these were sacrifices by the people in substitution for itself, but afterwards they were meals of the goddess shared in common with her subjects. As a result of prehistorical and early historical research in territories adjoining Greece, we are told that the "use of cattle is intimately connected with the cult of the moon goddess, and in the very oldest cult performances of the Asian Near East they were her sacred animal."[64] The horns of cattle, according to this observation, became the symbol of the crescent moon.

---

58 See above, in ch. V, the passage quoted from Dion Chrysostomos; see there also note 37.
59 Hesychios s.v. Λεχέρνα.
60 Pausanias II 17 3: κλίνη τῆς Ἥρας.
61 For those in the Heraion of Argos, see the reconstruction drawing in Erika Simon, *Die Götter der Griechen*, p. 39, fig. 27. See also Payne, *Perachora*, pp. 34 ff., 42 ff., and pl. 9.
62 See above in the text, ch. V, at notes 28, 29.
63 Scholium on Pindar, *Olympia* VII 152 A: τὰ Ἥραια . . . καὶ Ἑκατόμβαια λέγεται διὰ τὸ πλῆθος τῶν θυομένων βοῶν. For the significance of the hecatomb, see above, in ch. IV.
64 See E. Orth, "Stier," col. 2497. / For the Homeric formula *bo-opis potnia Here*, see, for example, Iliad I 551 and 568.

The Minoan horns of consecration are the most obvious example. The eyes of *bo-opis potnia Here*, the "cow-eyed Mistress Hera," expressed—more discreetly than horns would—her moon nature. Yet, above all Hera was in her great part-secret, part-public cult the *woman and wife as goddess*, even in her transformations according to the moon's phases.

There can scarcely have been a place where Hera could better unfold her moon nature than in the spellbinding moonlight of Greece,[65] across great surfaces of water like those of the swampy Lake Stymphalos. This swamp was not entirely overgrown with vegetation and a thicket of marsh plants served as a convenient refuge for the goddess at her low point. The ruins of the town of Stymphalos lie on a moderate, elongated rise at the northern end of the lake, which today is largely dried out. The excavations have not created such a clear situation here as in the Heraion of Argos.[66] We are still entirely dependent on Pausanias. He speaks of three Hera temples in Stymphalos.[67] He says they were founded by Temenos, son of Pelasgos, an aboriginal inhabitant of the land of Arcadia who here reared the goddess and gave her the three epithets usual in Stymphalos. As long as she was the

65 It was the archaeologist Karl Lehmann who prepared me for the experience of the moon in Samothrace, and he could not be accused of any sympathy with romantic mythology. The reality surpassed expectations. The full moon is a concrete, existential experience in the grounds of the Samothracian sanctuary and not only there but throughout the whole geographical area of Greek religion.

66 This was my impression on a visit to Stymphalos in 1970. The identification of a "god throne," perhaps a throne of Hera, by H. Lattermann and F. Hiller von Gaertringen, "Stymphalos," p. 76, fig. 3, was undoubtedly mistaken. The "throne" belongs to a veritable burial chamber in the tomb area. In *Praktika . . . 1929*, see p. 29 for the report that A. K. Orlandos has finally established from the inscription ΠΟΛΙΑΔΟΣ that the temple on the Akropolis belonged to Hera! As sole evidence, however, this is not worth much.

67 See Pausanias VIII 22 2.

VI. Hera Cults in the Peloponnese, Euboea, and Boeotia 129

virgin, Parthenos—elsewhere that was her name in this phase[68]—she was called "Pais"; after marrying Zeus, she was called "Teleia"; but after she "fell out with Zeus and had returned to Stymphalos," that is, returned to the lake, she was called "Chera," "widow." It follows from this text that the temple of Hera Teleia was to be looked for on one of the higher mountains surrounding the lake, the temple of the Pais probably in the town, and that of the Chera close by the lake.

Parthenos and Pais, "virgin" and "girl," in the Hera myth by no means had the simple meaning of being without a man, without the brother-husband! Rather these names meant secret love-making with him, such as Homer knew about[69] and was the subject of a special tradition in Samos. There it was related that this condition lasted for three hundred years.[70] In Hera the *woman and wife* was always present from the beginning, in all the forms of a woman's loving fancy, without her thereby becoming polygamous.[71] It is only the designation "Chera,"

---

68 The epithet "Parthenos" is attested for Hermione (see the reference to the sanctuaries of Hermione above, in ch. V, note 62) and for the island of Euboea; see the scholium to Pindar, *Olympia* VI 149 E. Pindar himself calls her Parthenia, her name also in Samos; see further in ch. VII, at notes 43, 46.

69 See above in the text, ch. V, at note 22.

70 Kallimachos, fr. 48; see also the scholium to Iliad I 609.

71 See the Homeric Hymn to Apollo 328 for Hera's monogamous remark before, in union with the underworld, she conceives Typhaon. In connection with a further son of Hera, Prometheus, who in Athens was a second Hephaistos, the Hellenistic poet Euphorion named an underworld lover of Hera, the giant Eurymedon. By him Hera is said to have become the mother of this son who so well fitted her hostile phase; see J. U. Powell, *Collectanea Alexandrina*, p. 48, fr. 99, and Kerényi, *Prometheus*, pp. 35, 59. Hera's epithet "Pynna" (see Hesychios s.v. Πύηνα), which stamped the goddess as a boyish playmate of Zeus, also belonged to the ancient myth (see S. Eitrem, "Hera," col. 392). The goddess' mouth play revealed on a votive tablet allegedly set up in the Heraion of Argos or Samos (a feature which has become notorious through Chrysippos' interpretation in terms of natural philosophy; see H. von Arnim, ed., *Stoicorum veterum fragmenta*, II, 1071–74), was probably a reference to the games of the

"widow," that requires us to assume a low point without a man in the round dance of the three phases handed down to us so clearly in Stymphalos in relation to the life of women. And yet this most natural explanation of the lowest point, which in the literal meaning of widowhood would not be justified in the case of the wife of Zeus, is the very thing that leads us to the moon's course. The Romans openly assigned the periodicity measured by the lunar month to the woman's nature—*provinciam fluorum menstruorum*—of their Juno.[72] They speak of a "Iuno Fluonia,"[73] and even recognize a period of the "abstinence of Juppiter," "castus Iovis,"[74] which becomes intelligible only in this context—as abstinence by the married couple, Juppiter and Juno. Their anthropomorphism in this case even goes beyond that of the archetypal couple Zeus and Hera. This can hardly be explained except by the supposition that the supreme divine couple of the Romans came about historically in imitation of the Greek divine couple and actually exceeded it. The myth about the abstinence of the couple followed from the archetypal data in the most natural fashion.

In Greece, plant mythology[75] and medical literature supply further points of reference. Here a more general observation must suffice. It appears that under archaic conditions the periodicity of women not only corresponded in general to the periodicity of the moon but also followed the moon's phases more closely. That this was the case among Greek women or at least was with some reason believed to be so is

---

divine couple, if it in fact referred to the divine couple at all. What is remarkable is that such an erotic memorial was possible in a Hera sanctuary.

72 An allusion to this is found in Varro, cited by Augustine in *De civitate Dei* VII 2; in Dombart, ed., II, 274.
73 See Festus (Paulus) 92 65; in Lindsay, ed., p. 82, lines 4–5.
74 *CIL* I 1² 360 and 361a.
75 See W. H. Roscher, *Juno und Hera*, pp. 38 ff.

VI. *Hera Cults in the Peloponnese, Euboea, and Boeotia*   131

attested by Empedokles, Aristotle, and the doctor Diokles.[76] According to them the *katamenia* ("monthlies"), as they were called in Greek, occurred with the waning moon, according to Aristotle even at new moon. Later gynecologists, like Soranus, disputed this. The circumstance that the weddings of couples in one city *could be* held on one definite day, or over a short period, is evidence for a fixed common time for the *katamenia* so as to make the common weddings possible. The choice of the time was not an individual concern.

In Athens this time fell in the month of Gamelion, originally after new moon.[77] The same time was worked out for the celebration of the wedding of Hera in Argos. Since the large unit of time in the life of nature and also in the world of Greek man was the solar year, that dark moon time of women, like the union of women and men in wedlock, was only once a year linked up with the state community and celebrated as a festival. The sign was probably given by the appearance of the newborn moon in the sky. Hera, who was both woman and heavenly being, rose from her bath of purification a virgin once more, for her wedding. I should think the temple of Hera Chera in Stymphalos was in all probability situated at the waterside. This would have been the obvious location for carrying out the bathing ceremony. The temple of Hera Limenia, "harbor Hera," was found in a similar location in Perachora.[78]

76 Aristotle, *Historia animalium* VII 2 582a 34; Soranus, *Gynaecia* IV 21 (in Rose, ed., p. 185); Empedokles, in Diels, *Die Fragmente der Vorsokratiker*, 31 [21] A 80 32–37 (vol. I, p. 299). On the relationship between Aristotle and his pupil Diokles, see W. Jaeger, *Diokles von Karystos*, pp. 16 ff.

77 See above, ch. V, notes 42 and 46.

78 See Payne, *Perachora*, pp. 14, 110 ff., for evidence from the middle of the eighth century. / The Hera cult in the middle area, the temple of the Leukolenos (see above, ch. VI, note 20), dates back to the late ninth century.

The excavations in the Argive Heraion and its neighborhood[79] have turned up a number of those prehistoric female figurines that are widely distributed elsewhere and also may have represented a universal wife goddess, the moon goddess. I cannot see why this latter designation should be ruled out now that we know it as an evident characteristic, though not an exclusive one, of Hera. One type of these stylized figures is the "crescent figurine"; another is more like the shape of the full moon.[80] The sources themselves are evidence that we have the traces here of a prehistoric moon religion which, as an outline filled with female human content, became the Hera religion. The Middle Helladic period, from about 2000 B.C. on, does not seem too early a date to assign for its beginnings.

On the Greek mainland it is Olympia in the Peloponnese and Boeotia outside it that have further substantial contributions to make to the Hera religion. The plain of Olympia about the river Alpheios, the inhabitants of which were probably mentioned even in Mycenaean Pylos,[81] was appropriated by Zeus. The region is dominated by a hill known as the Hill of Kronos, which makes it easy to understand the take-over. As on Mount Lykaion, the ruling deity here was identical with El, the god of the West Semites. The priests of the ancient inhabitants of Olympia descended from a pre-Greek royal race and were

79 On the excavations in the neighborhood of the Argive Heraion, see Blegen, *Prosymna*. A fine example of the crescent type is reproduced in L. Drees, *Olympia*, pl. 2b, which shows a clay figurine associated with the cult of the "Mycenaean Hera as moon goddess" at Tiryns. Drees's tendency, however, to trace the sanctity of Olympia back to fertility cults is totally mistaken.

80 For examples of the two types of terracotta figurines, crescent and full moon, see the illustrations in Blegen, *Prosymna*, II, 148, fig. 612; p. 149, fig. 611.

81 See H. Mühlestein, *Die oka-Tafeln von Pylos*, pp. 20–21. The reference to Olympia on the Alpheios River seems to be confirmed by our present knowledge of the Pylos region.

VI. Hera Cults in the Peloponnese, Euboea, and Boeotia

called "Basilai," a name they had inherited from queens.[82] Even Kronos seems to have displaced a female sovereignty here—and how much more so did Zeus.

Hera appears beside Zeus in a position which is more exalted than that of a completely subordinate goddess and yet does show subjection. The victorious superiority of the Zeus religion in Olympia is an outstanding phenomenon of Greek religious history which we must accept as a decisive historical fact. The Zeus religion of Olympia was in all its ingredients, from the endless cattle sacrifices and the competitive games to the building of the temple and the erecting of the admired statue of Pheidias, exclusively the business of men. It did not require the myth of a divine *couple*. And yet even in Olympia this myth, in its Homeric form, may be assumed.

It is inconceivable that the Zeus religion should have brought the Hera religion in its train only to put it in the shade. The religion of Hera was not even the earliest woman-religion in Olympia. With Kronos went Rhea, the mother of the gods. And it was not in fact the Hera priestess but the priestess of Demeter Chamaine, the goddess linked with the soil, who was the only woman allowed to watch the contests of naked men, probably because of a neighbor situation in which the competing men were later arrivals and had taken the ground for the stadium away from Demeter. Later on Hera was given an altar in the stadium, and was there called "Hippia," beside Poseidon Hippios.[83] The probable reason for this altar was that from time immemorial there had been races for Hera among the women. Later she was also to have a share in the chariot races of the men.

[82] On the derivation of *basilai*, see above, in ch. III. On the most ancient cults in Olympia, see H.-V. Herrmann, "Zur ältesten Geschichte von Olympia," pp. 3 ff.

[83] Pausanias V 15 5.

It was to Hera, however, that the first temple in Olympia was dedicated, much earlier than the one to Zeus. In the form in which it has been excavated, but originally built with wooden pillars, the temple of Hera dates from the second half of the seventh century.[84] A still earlier date for a temple structure is given, which puts the first temple of Hera at about 1000 B.C.[85] The goddess' preference for her house[86] makes this tradition plausible. Only with reference to the form must a limitation be made, to the extent that the "Doric temple" was invented for the Heraion of Argos and not transferred to Olympia until a temple of Hera had already been standing there for three hundred years. A *house*—perhaps one of those excavated in the neighborhood of the Hera temple and today regarded as prehistoric dwelling houses—could have belonged to her earlier, like the altar on which sacrifices had been performed to her from time immemorial. Zeus with his altar of ashes growing into the hillside could have been left without a temple forever if this expression of worship, the temple as a gift to the deity, had not reached Olympia with the Hera religion.

For internal reasons it is probable that the girls' races held every four years at the feast of the Heraia were more ancient than the men's contests at Olympia.[87] The race still possessed its original meaning in the domain of the moon goddess Hera. The girls in this fashion celebrated the almost visible course of the moon in the sky. They ran in *three* age groups, which was not the case with the boys' races, a contest

---

84 For the dating, see Kähler, *Der griechische Tempel*, pp. 31-32.

85 The date is based on Pausanias V 16 1; the temple was founded, Pausanias says, about eight years after Oxylos came to power in Elis.

86 On the *thalamos* inside the house, see above in the text, ch. V, at notes 28, 29.

87 This is the well-founded view of L. Weniger, "Das Hochfest des Zeus in Olympia," p. 30.

VI. Hera Cults in the Peloponnese, Euboea, and Boeotia

first introduced in the seventh century. The races themselves always formed an important part of the games,[88] if not their core. The hair of the girl runners was let down. Their dresses reached to just above the knee and left the right shoulder bare as far as the breast. The prize was an olive wreath and a share of the cow sacrificed to Hera.[89] The winners proved themselves worthiest of the goddess, resembling her most closely.

The most probable supposition is that the Hera religion reached Olympia sooner than the Zeus religion.[90] This is corroborated clearly and unambiguously by the circumstance that in the Hera temple the goddess was represented on her throne, with Zeus *standing beside her*.[91] She had here adopted Zeus as the only consort worthy of her. Otherwise that standing image would not have so clearly expressed the subordinate position of the supreme god of Olympia beside the goddess.[92] Pausanias describes the standing Zeus beside the seated Hera as a helmeted and bearded man. Unbearded, helmeted statues, however, among the bronze finds at Olympia from the eighth and seventh centuries, must also be considered as possible representations of this Zeus. The archaic view in this case was that the queen of heaven had chosen a beautiful young husband in her Zeus. The myth of Hera's early choice of a husband, in Homer and in very ancient hymns of the Argive cult, may have contributed to the effect. In Olympia it was not

88 See L. Ziehen, "Olympia," cols. 17–18.
89 Pausanias V 16 2–3.
90 This supposition and what follows is contrary to the view of Herrmann, "Zur ältesten Geschichte von Olympia," pp. 13 ff., who attributes the oldest votive statues to Kronos.
91 Pausanias V 17 1.
92 The situation was correctly interpreted by Emil Kunze, "Zeusbilder in Olympia," p. 102, note 15. For the unbearded representations of Zeus, see Kunze's figs. 5–13, and his accompanying commentary.

only the consciousness of Greek men that was mightily enhanced but also the consciousness of the female sex, which recognized itself in Hera as in a higher image of itself and, enhanced by the goddess, enhanced her too. It was such women who inspired the creator of the regal form of Queen Sterope in the east pediment of the temple of Zeus.[93]

The series, extending for centuries, of votive statues in clay and bronze may be used as a concrete groundwork for the cult history of Olympia, as a conducted tour of the period *before* the temples were built. In this series of votive statues, Zeus appears as a thunderbolt-waving bearded figure from the beginning of the fifth century, by no means as early as Wilamowitz apparently thought from the first finds.[94] With regard to the helmeted unbearded statues from the first half of the eighth and into the seventh century, it is more precise to speak of Hera's cult associate. The epithet "Parastates," "one who stands beside," was brought to Olympia not by Zeus—he was an actual "bystander"—but by Herakles. There were two altars dedicated to him (although, considering that he was the reputed founder of the Olympic games these must seem too few.)[95] At one altar he was worshiped as Herakles Parastates and as an Idaean Daktyl (Pausanias repeats the epithet "Parastates"). At the other altar Herakles was worshiped in the company of Kouretes, who were also understood as Idaean Daktyls in the guise of young warriors.[96] Were Herakles' role as Parastates not so

---

93 On the pediment, see the summarizing (and in its interpretation forward-looking) work of Marie-Louise Säflund, *The East Pediment of the Temple of Zeus at Olympia*.

94 For these early votive figures of Zeus, see Kunze, "Zeusbilder in Olympia," figs. 14–17. For Wilamowitz' view, see his "Zeus," p. 2.

95 Ziehen, "Olympia," col. 65.

96 For the altar to Herakles Parastates, see Pausanias V 14 7; cf. V 8 1, VI 23 3. For the second altar, see esp. V 14 9 and V 7 6.

VI. Hera Cults in the Peloponnese, Euboea, and Boeotia

emphatically connected with his quality of an Idaean Daktyl, we might with more justification identify the helmeted unbearded figurines with Herakles than with Zeus.

Herakles, the hero of the twelve labors, was a servant of the goddess and bore her name in his own. Herakles means the one who won fame through Hera. Under this name he originally belonged to her in Tiryns, a citadel of the Mycenaean kingdom in the neighborhood of the Heraion of Argos. In Homer Hera does not mention Tiryns among her favorite sites. Her temple there was one of the most venerable in Argolis and to some extent competed with the Heraion of Argos,[97] but it was not built until after 750 B.C., after Homer, that is. The Herakles cult is attested for Tiryns;[98] the cult association follows from the hero's name. His closest association with the goddess was retained by Herakles in the form of persecution by Hera, after he had been made a son of Zeus and Alkmene in the hero mythology and translated to Thebes.[99]

In their original form the Idaean Daktyls were anonymous phalli produced by Rhea, the mother of the gods, for her personal service.[100] Their number, five, corresponding to the fingers (*daktyloi*) of one hand, betrays their oldest form, in which they accompanied the Mother

---

97 The evidence is to be found in Frickenhaus, *Tiryns*, I, 20 ff. He himself would favor the priority of the Hera cult in Tiryns. Against this is to be set the fact that Homer knows the Heraion of Argos, but does not apparently know Tiryns as a city of Hera. On the chronology of the Hera temple at Tiryns, see G. Karo, "Tiryns," col. 1465.

98 See Frickenhaus, *Tiryns*, I, 19. A search was made in vain for a *special* Herakleion in Tiryns; see ibid., p. 126. A. B. Cook, in his essay "Who was the Wife of Zeus?" pp. 365-78, 416-19, spoke for the great likelihood of an original cult association of Herakles and Hera. This was opposed by Frickenhaus, p. 43, note 4.

99 See Kerényi, *The Heroes of the Greeks*, pp. 128 ff.

100 On the Idaean Daktyls, see below, ch. VII, note 86, and Kerényi, *The Gods of the Greeks*, pp. 83-84 (Pelican edn., p. 73).

Goddess to Olympia. They had their cult place in the neighborhood of the Hera temple. The mythographers have been at pains to find the different individual names given for them by Pausanias together with Herakles Parastates. It is a significant fact that the Hera-Servant Herakles could fit so well into the company of the servants of Rhea and that his name could be given to one of the Daktyls. From this we can draw conclusions about Herakles' original nature, which he never lost even in his heroic development.

Clay and bronze figurines from the eighth and seventh centuries and even earlier times[101] represent an emphatically male being, not ithyphallic, but still crudely phallic, more or less in the attitude with raised hands that in Minoan art expressed both epiphany and worship at the same time. The Parastates was more a worshiper than an appearer. Not till the middle of the eighth century at the earliest did Zeus take his place in the series which began with these rudely masculine representations. Indeed, it is possible that Zeus only did so by displacing the Kourete-like young god, Hera's original cult associate, who took time to achieve this promotion. It is possible, too, that a bearded Zeus was substituted for the Herakles standing beside the enthroned goddess, particularly when Zeus's nature began to change in this direction.

A "Daktylic Herakles" was the partner of the great moon goddess Hera in Olympia almost to the middle of the eighth century. At this time it was that Homer's poetry made its contribution to the final shaping of the two religions, the Hera cult and the Zeus religion. The great god

---

101 Kunze, "Zeusbilder," figs. 1–4. See also Kunze, *Berichte über die Ausgrabungen in Olympia*, VII, 138 ff.; and Herrmann, "Zur ältesten Geschichte von Olympia," pls. 2–3. The earliest date for the bronze figures, according to Kunze, *Berichte*, VII, 141, would be the first half of the ninth century. The oldest clay figurine (see Herrmann, pl. 2:1–2) so far has not been dated more closely than to say that it could be earlier than the first half of the ninth century.

VI. Hera Cults in the Peloponnese, Euboea, and Boeotia

of the men, to whose moral content above all the consciousness of the community of all Hellenes belonged,[102] was gladly accepted by the worshipers of Hera in place of the mere Parastates, who was only a servant of women. The foundation of the Olympic games was attributed in the higher poetry to "Theban" Herakles.[103] Alongside this, however, the story was preserved that Herakles organized the first race with his brother Daktyls and crowned the victor with a branch of wild olive, and that this was the founding of the Olympic games.[104] It is nowhere suggested that Herakles was a son or servant of Rhea. The foundation story in which Hera's own Daktyl played the part of the first organizer testifies to the claims of this goddess. Hera as the real mistress of the Olympic games was not allowed to be forgotten.

It would also have been difficult not to remember her. The high point of the festival period was the great sacrifice to Zeus. At his altar, earlier without a temple, later in front of his temple, the common devotions of the Panhellenes took place. Hecatombs were offered to the male deity who stamped these peoples as Hellenes and continued to hold them together; the contests were held; and the sacrificial animals were feasted upon by the worshipers in community with one another and with the highest of their gods. But this had to happen each time, that is, in every fourth year in the prescribed month, either Apollonios or Parthenios, on the day that after the fulfillment of the goddess in heaven was the true day of full moon.[105]

Outside the Peloponnese I have already mentioned Boeotia as the mainland territory where Hera had her special domain of sovereignty.

102 See above in the text, the concluding section of ch. I.
103 Pindar, *Olympia* II 3, VI 68–70.
104 Pausanias V 7 7; also see Diodorus Siculus V 64 6.
105 Ziehen, "Olympia," col. 18.

The great island that lies off Attica and Boeotia must also not be forgotten. It was called Euboea and was in a special way Hera's property[106] —from its name, just like the ground on which the Heraion of Argos was built. Allegedly the island also had the unfestive name "Makris," "the long."[107] *Euboia* must for Greek ears have had a festive sound, not only because of its wealth of cattle, the sacrificial animals, but also because of the goddess who, as we know, had this epithet. It is certainly no exaggeration to maintain that at the feast of the Heraia the whole island was more or less an entire cult stage on which processions marched and hecatombs were slaughtered and devoured. All four of Euboea's landward-facing harbors, Aidepsos, Chalkis, Eretria, and Karystos, must be regarded as Hera cult sites.[108] In addition, Sophokles called a small island off Euboea "Nymphikon Elymnion," "bridal Elymnion," because the Gamos of Zeus and Hera took place there.[109]

The goddess' name was associated with the two highest of the island's peaks: with Mount Dirphys she was associated as "Dirphya," and with the almost equally high (1,500 feet) Mount Oche—a name also of the island itself—through the myth interpreting the word *oche* as *ocheia*, "mating."[110] How much further the myth went into the crude details of the Gamos and whether it was accompanied by a ritual representation is not known. A stone house with a low roof, one door, and two windows which has been preserved from antiquity at a giddy height just below the peak of Mount Oche is perhaps to be identified with the cult building. It was believed after its discovery to be the oldest temple

---

106 See the scholium on Apollonius Rhodius, *Argonautica* IV 1138: ἡ δὲ Εὔβοια ἱερά ἐστι τῆι Ἥραι.
107 Several islands were so called; see L. Buerchner, "Macris," col. 814.
108 For confirmation, see Eitrem, "Hera," col. 371.
109 See the scholium to Aristophanes, *Peace* 1126.
110 Stephen of Byzantium s.v. Κάρυστος, and Δίρφυς.

VI. *Hera Cults in the Peloponnese, Euboea, and Boeotia* 141

of Hera, but this was also disputed. From the stone work it has been dated to the sixth century B.C.[111] Yet the style of building does not stand out at all surprisingly from the timeless slate buildings of the neighborhood and the nearby islands, Tenos and especially Andros.[112] The Mount Oche structure, with its difficulty of access, its panoramic views, and atmosphere of almost constant gales could have served for the observation of approaching ships. Or again such a house might have been pleasing to Hera as a place where her statue could be kept for ritual purposes. On a little platform immediately below this house stands a chapel of St. Elias, no different from the profane slate buildings of the district. Shepherds, so one of them told me, until recently used to climb up there to celebrate the *paniyiris*, the festival of the chapel, once a year—doubtless with a *choros*, the round dance which in the end replaced all pagan open-air observances in Greece.

"One must have seen how the clouds attracted by such mountain peaks enfold them in their arms—in order to understand the outlook of the people," wrote Welcker, who, however, regarded Hera as the goddess Earth.[113] As a traveler in Greece he grasped the natural atmosphere in which the rites of the Gamos took place, as they have been handed down to us from Boeotia, geographically almost joined to Euboea.

111 It was T. Wiegand, "Der angebliche Urtempel auf der Ocha," pp. 11–17, who put it in the sixth century B.C.
112 See F. P. Johnson, "The 'Dragon-Houses' of Southern Euboea," pp. 398–412, and figs. 1–11. Fig. 11 shows the chapel of St. Elias (see Johnson, pp. 405–406) which I discuss here in the text. Too little attention has been paid to the fact that much of the style of building here is determined by the material—slate. The dating is difficult, consequently, and often irrelevant. The slate buildings can seem quite new and yet reach back into prehistory; see Kerényi and Sichtermann, "Zeitlose Schieferbauten der Insel Andros," pp. 25–36, and also Kerényi, "Die andriotische Säule," in *Werke*, III, 408 ff.
113 F. G. Welcker, *Griechische Götterlehre*, I, 364.

There was a wedding festival of Hera celebrated with great pomp on the peak of Mount Kithairon in Boeotia, certainly the end product of a story uniting several different layers of the cult. The real festival, which compounded and crowned the smaller celebrations and was called the "Great Daidala," took place only in every sixtieth year. The "Little Daidala," on the other hand, was every seventh year, reckoned in old-fashioned lunar years. This complicated method of reckoning was discovered more than a century ago and since then no better method has been found to take its place.[114] For a description of the festival proceedings we have eyewitness accounts from Plutarch and Pausanias,[115] and we have also gained additional points of view enabling us to discriminate among the different layers.

The first act was the choosing of the tree from which Hera's wooden substitute was to be manufactured, probably both for the Little Daidala, which was celebrated only by the inhabitants of Plataia, and also for the Great Daidala celebrated throughout the whole of Boeotia. The difference between the festivals no doubt consisted in the number of participating cities and sacrificed animals. Every city contributed one cow and one bull. The fourteen wooden statues, the *xoana*, of which Pausanias says that they were already there from the Little Daidala, "manufactured annually" (in which case two must have been produced yearly), cannot possibly have represented Hera.[116] Their number was too large. Rather we may recall the "twice seven" beautiful nymphs attributed to Juno by Virgil.[117] Further, there is the agreement

---

114 See K. O. Müller, *Geschichten Hellenischer Stämme und Städte*, I, 216 ff.

115 For Plutarch, see Eusebios, *Praeparatio Evangelica* III 1; the Pausanias passage is at IX 3 1-8.

116 On the fourteen statues, see Pausanias IX 3 5.

117 *Aeneid* I 71.

VI. Hera Cults in the Peloponnese, Euboea, and Boeotia

of this number with the days of a half month, and finally the fact that in Plutarch's description it was nymphs who carried the water of Hera's bridal bath in the wedding procession, while the Boeotians provided the escort. These were the Tritonian nymphs, named after the Triton River near Alalkomenai, on which according to Boeotian tradition Pallas Athena was born. These nymphs therefore belonged also to the goddess who, like Hera before her bath, is associated with the dark time of new moon.[118] The scene for the first act of the festival, the choosing of the tree, was set in the domain of Athena of Alalkomenai.

The tree for Hera was sought out in an oak wood, a dark wood for the Greeks. The Plataians for this purpose repaired to a region rather distant from Mount Kithairon, the scene of the wedding. A further association with the domain of Pallas Athena is given by the fact that, according to Plutarch, on the first occasion when once upon a time the festival had been *founded by Zeus himself*, the Primal Man of Alalkomenai, Alalkomeneus, gave a hand and advised the "stratagem" which follows. The crafty Primal Man Alalkomeneus was known in Boeotia as the tutor of Pallas Athena[119] and is comparable with Temenos in Arcadia and Asterion in Argos in their relationship to Hera. Odysseus according to Plutarch was said to have been born in the Boeotian Alalkomenion.[120] He too was an "Alalkomeneus" and was on excellent terms with Athena. The "stratagem" recommended to Zeus by the Boeotian Primal Man was designed to arouse the jealousy of Hera, who had withdrawn herself, and thus win her back. A "false Hera" was to be manufactured of wood and a pretense wedding celebrated with the statue. This was the rationalization of the festival at the time of

118 See Kerényi, *Die Jungfrau und Mutter*, pp. 41 ff.
119 Pausanias IX 33 5-7.
120 Plutarch, *Quaestiones graecae* 301 D.

Plutarch and Pausanias. Originally in the cult, the "Hera" manufactured for this cult use was not "false" but the statue of the goddess, which could be carried.

The procedure for choosing the tree for the wooden statue was to lay down bits of meat for the ravens in the oak wood. These birds did not occur everywhere in Greece in antiquity, any more than they do today, but here they were certainly the black birds in a dark region. It was observed upon which tree the bird that ate the meat alighted after feeding. This was an oracle rendered by a creature symbolic of the dark of the moon.[121] A *xoanon* was made of the oak and this act of choice and portraiture was repeated each time the festival was held. Neither the maypole nor those straw dolls that were made and burnt at certain folk celebrations in northern Europe can be regarded as analogous to this.[122] The importance of the portraiture is emphasized by the very name of the festival. "Daidala," that is, works of art, are also the fourteen *xoana* which accompany the chief statue, the bride Hera, on Mount Kithairon, to be burnt with her. She, according to Plutarch, was called "Daidale."

It is evident how far the Hera cult, which spread from Euboea, had come into contact in this region of Boeotia with the sphere of another goddess, the Athena of Alalkomenai, and had so to speak overlaid it. The crossing from the great neighboring island is expressly confirmed by two of the three versions of the mythological rationalization of the cult proceedings described by Plutarch and Pausanias. One version contains only the theme of the withdrawal of Hera. According to Plutarch, she hid herself, and only after Zeus at Alalkomeneus' advice had led

---

[121] On the fable of the raven or crow, see Kerényi, *Asklepios*, p. 93.

[122] The northern European folk celebrations were brought in by Nilsson, *Griechische Feste*, p. 55.

around the "false Hera" in the wedding procession did the true Hera rush down from Kithairon. Coming near she saw through the deception and herself, reconciled, became the bride of the ritual mock marriage. According to Pausanias, Hera had withdrawn herself to Euboea.[123] So it was from there that she had to come to the festival in Boeotia. In Plutarch's version Zeus eloped with Hera to the Gamos on Mount Kithairon when she was still living in the care of her nurse Makris (another name for the island, as we have seen) on Euboea. This version in addition testifies to a contact of the Hera cult on Kithairon with the worship of another goddess—Leto. Makris, it said, while looking for Hera was put off the scent by the mountain god Kithairon with the lie that Zeus was resting there with Leto in a hiding place. That was why Hera, Plutarch added, had a common altar with Leto and why sacrifices were made first to this goddess under the name "Leto Mychia" (thus called after the hiding place, *mychos*) or "Leto Nychia," "nocturnal Leto." According to a tradition from the likewise adjoining Attica, it was Pallas Athena who conducted Leto from Cape Sounion over the islands to Delos, where she gave birth to Apollo.[124] The cult circles of the three goddesses intersect in the region of Kithairon (to say nothing of the role of this mountain in the religion of Dionysos) and this circumstance had its effect on the shaping of the myth of the Daidala festival.

The next act in the festival proceedings took place farther down, at the river Asopos, on the plain of the city of Plataia, where the procession started from the temple of Hera. The "false Hera" was also given out to be Plataia, a daughter of Asopos. She represented the bridal aspect of the goddess, who was worshiped by the Plataians in their Hera temple as "Nympheuomene," "she who marries," and as Teleia. Plu-

123 Pausanias IX 3 1.
124 See Hypereides, Delian fr. 70.

tarch spoke of the Tritonian nymphs who in the role of *loutrophoroi*, carriers of the water for the bridal bath, accompanied the procession. The possibility has already been mentioned that the fourteen accompanying *xoana* were thus referred to. The symbolical bath was certainly not missing from the ceremony, but it may have been a bath in the river. The heavily veiled statue of the "bride" was set on a cart drawn by cows. With her a woman rode as bridal escort. On other carts the rest of the statues (*daidala*) stood. The procession marched, with an accompaniment of flute music, to Mount Kithairon. People from all over Boeotia followed with enthusiasm. Up on the peak an altar had been built, in the style of a stone house, but constructed actually of wood lined with brushwood. It was, so to speak, a "nuptial chamber," to quote L. R. Farnell's summary of the total impression made by the structure.[125] Here the sacrifice was performed and, to conclude, the false stone house together with all the *xoana* were set on fire.

This great Boeotian Hera festival was based on a complicated time-reckoning and was itself a complicated affair. Its noteworthy feature was that throughout the whole wedding procession the bridegroom was missing.[126] Up above, however, on Mount Kithairon, he was no longer missing. For the mountain belonged to Zeus in the same sense as so many peaks in Greece did where Zeus's lighting up was experienced.[127] At him blazed out the mighty sacrificial fire of the bridal chamber, the greatest and most widely visible fiery glow, according to Pausanias, to

---

125 Farnell, *The Cults of the Greek States*, I, 190.

126 Because of the absence of the bridegroom, Nilsson wanted to reduce the wedding character of the feast, transmitted and elaborated in ritual, to a "celebration of the year" (like that which is customary in northern Europe), thus doing violence to the transmission in a manner that seemed dubious even to him; see his *Geschichte der griechischen Religion*, I (1941 edn.), 404, note 2.

127 See p. 29, above. Zeus Kithaironios is mentioned in Pausanias IX 2 4 at the wrong point of his text, but in its substance quite correctly.

be seen anywhere. The inference is inescapable. Hera was the supreme goddess of a religion that still used portable idols for its rites; Zeus, on the contrary, was a supreme god who *even in the world of nature had a spiritual character of his own,* a character that he had as lighting up, an ever-near invisible presence with which he stood ready to break in.

VII. THE GREAT GODDESS OF SAMOS AND PAESTUM

SAMOS in the east and Paestum in the west, with their temples, testify to the power of the Hera religion in a manner deserving of the closest attention from students of human history. In the fundamental correlation to which every religion can be reduced, and in this special case the correlation between the Great Goddess Hera and those who actually *needed* her religion, there have been not only sacrificers on the human side but also builders—communities that channeled the economic strength at their disposal into a remarkable flow of building activity. Who was the partner at the receiving end of this sacrificial and building activity? This question has already been answered in the previous chapter and in what follows will be answered even more emphatically.

However much the cult and building of temples may have been intensified by ideas of representation and pride of state, the temples themselves were not intended for some indeterminate thing, a being devised or imagined for the fulfillment of every kind of wish, but were intended for a goddess with a definite content who seemed worthy of such costly forms of worship. Worship is at least affirmation, even when it takes the form of fear. The correlation "religion" admits of fear. It presupposes affirmation, the recognition of an essence, even if only an imagined one. On one side is Hera in her essence as woman, in her manifestation as waxing and waning moonlight; on the other side are temple buildings, on the scale of Samos and Paestum. From a human point of view this is a remarkable historical phenomenon.

This structure—the outline, so to speak, of the Hera religion—

VII. *The Great Goddess of Samos and Paestum*   149

emerges from everything that has been said so far. There it stands, unique, full of significance, but perhaps it may still appear rather shadowy. The Samian findings confirm this structure and are for their part made intelligible by it. Individual traits of the Samian cult give it concrete form and this concrete form acquires meaning. We achieve the concrete effect by concentrating both study and reflection on that which has been recovered from the past and stands before our eyes, on every trace of myth or ritual preserved, on all the remains handed down or excavated, on everything relating to the goddess and her cult. It cannot be denied that a similar concentration has been attempted before. Yet it was never consistent enough and did not confine itself to the actual data of antiquity, which were self-explanatory without the help of general ideas imported from outside. A "miraculous image" was prematurely offered as the clue. A found object of miraculous origin and influence was the supposed nucleus of a religion that was after all responsible for the building by the tyrant Polykrates, in the middle of the sixth century, of a temple never exceeded in size by any other in Greece!

"How many sanctuaries of ancient and modern times, down to the very latest, owe their existence to the finding of the image! How strongly such a find must have affected people who as yet made no line of demarcation between 'image' and 'imagined being,' between 'original' and 'portrait.' We cannot do other than trust to the legend of the finding even when it has come down to us in distorted form." General notions like these were taken as the starting point by Ernst Buschor, to whose investigations of the sanctuary of Samos we are otherwise so greatly indebted.[1] Equally fallacious was another gen-

---

1   E. Buschor, "Heraion von Samos: frühe Bauten." The definition, "miraculous image," appears on p. 2.

eralization with which the great archaeologist himself, as it were, demolished his "miraculous image" theory. "Anyone who wants to get close to the true germ cell, the effective center, of a Greek sanctuary will turn first of all not to the temple building, nor to the cult statue, not even to the sacrificial altar, but to the so-called 'cult objects,' the traces of the most bodily presence of the deity worshiped there."[2]

The theory of a "miraculous image," together with the thesis about "cult objects," was refuted in the case of Hera by the fact that both in the Heraion of Argos[3] and in Olympia the "true germ cell, the effective center" of the sanctuary was found to be the sacrificial altar—in Olympia a sacrificial altar for Hera and another larger one for Zeus.[4] The same is the case in the Heraion of Samos. "On the altar site it was possible to discern very early versions of the altar of burnt offering."[5] As early as the beginning of the first millennium a simple stone altar was laid down (about 8 feet by 4). This was the germ cell of more and more imposing altars, which in the course of the eighth, seventh, and sixth centuries encased this nucleus. "The seventh altar, the 'Rhoikos Altar' erected about 550 B.C., in its immense size (at about 120 feet by 54 it covered two hundred times the area of Altar I) and in the splendor of its sculptured and decorated ornamentation was the most important monument of its kind, until it was overshadowed in turn by the Hellenistic altar at Pergamon. The simple form of the altar of burnt offering, a table with flanged windguards on three sides and with a platform at the open west side for the priest to stand on, is here enlarged

2 See Buschor, "Imbrasos," p. 1.
3 On the ancient altar of burnt offering in the Argive Heraion, see above, ch. VI, at notes 9 ff.
4 On the ancient sacrificial altar to Hera in Olympia and the larger one to Zeus there on the hillside, see above, ch. VI, at notes 83 ff.
5 See Buschor, "Samos 1952–57," p. 200.

to giant size, the windguards loaded with sculptured friezes of animals, colored strings of leaves and loops of flowers. On the actual 'sacrificial table' the ashes of centuries had piled themselves up in a great cone."[6]

An altar like this, facing away from the temple and so also from the alleged "miraculous image," cannot be thought of—even in its earliest nuclear form—in relation to a cult statue inside the temple. Its orientation, at first here in Samos to the southeast,[7] then to the east, can be explained by a certain point of the sky, never by an object located on the earth's surface, least of all by a "miraculous image," which among the Greeks was never the object of an altar cult of this kind with its related building activity. It would be absurd to think of it. (Where magnificent buildings have been put up around a miraculous image, it was a dogmatic system—and the church supported by it—that guaranteed the "miracle of grace" expected of the image.) An assumed, or even experienced, "magical" effect would never have been sufficient for an altar cult and its activity. There is no tradition of the *finding* of an image or the basing of a cult upon it, let alone any record in a credible ancient text.

The text to which the miracle image theory appeals is by the Samian author Menodotos, who lived about 200 B.C.[8] He told a story—not a myth, not even a *hieros logos*, but a miracle story in the style of the

---

6   G. Gruben, *Die Tempel der Griechen*, p. 317.

7   The exact astronomical determination of this orientation has still to be made. It could, however, be directed towards Sirius, as is supposed by Hans Walter, *Das griechische Heiligtum*, p. 22. This orientation comprised–together with the rise of the full moon in the east—yet another rising possibly as important for the calendar as the early rising of Sirius was in the Minoan period; see Kerényi, "Licht, Wein, Honig," pp. 206 ff.

8   For the text, see Menodotos of Samos, in Jacoby, *FGrHist*, III, B, pp. 524-26 (541 F 1 4 ff.).

Hellenistic aretalogies[9]—which was supposed to explain to festival visitors a piece of ritual at the Heraia.[10] This ritual was performed in the region of the Imbrasos estuary, which was overgrown with chaste tree (*Vitex agnus-castus*; in Greek, the *lygos*). Every year the primitive statue of the goddess vanished from the temple and was found again in the estuary, appeased with purifications and sacrificial cakes, and brought back to its pedestal (which has been excavated).[11] This ceremonial procedure had to be explained to a Hellenistic public that no longer understood that the disappearance of the statue, manipulated by the temple staff, represented the mythical flight of the goddess. Some eight hundred years separated the Hellenistic public from the archaic rite, which possibly dated back to the time of the Ionian migration and had been brought by it to Samos from Argos.[12] The new public had a taste of its own for divine epiphanies, pirate stories, and miracles. Besides this, the Samian Menodotos was not well disposed towards the people of Argos, who possessed the *other* great Hera sanctuary. Still, the transference of the cult from Argos to Samos was part of the temple tradition, in the form that the Argonauts had brought a Hera statue onto the island[13]—the usual method of missionary activity among the Greeks.

So the Samian related that a sanctuary of Hera had been founded by the mythical aborigines, Leleges and nymphs,[14] and had already

---

9 For the aretalogies, see R. Reitzenstein, *Hellenistische Wundererzählungen*, pp. 1 ff.
10 Athenaios XV 671 F–674 A; Jacoby, *FGrHist*, III, B, p. 524, lines 15 ff.
11 See D. Ohly, "Die Göttin und ihre Basis," pp. 25 ff.
12 On the Ionian migration, see Buschor, "Heraion von Samos," p. 3.
13 Pausanias VII 4 4.
14 The reading νυμφῶν in Athenaios' Menodotos quotation (see Athenaios XV 672 B) is most easily to be understood as Νυμφῶν. If Menodotos regarded the

VII. *The Great Goddess of Samos and Paestum*   153

been standing on the island when Admete, Eurystheus' daughter (she for whom Herakles had to fetch the girdle of the Amazon),[15] was driven out of Argos and came to Samos. Hera, whose priestess she was,[16] had rescued her. The goddess in person, in an epiphany, put Admete in charge of her Samian sanctuary, so Menodotos continues. But the Argives tried to have the cult statue stolen, so that the Samians would punish their priestess for negligence. They hired Tyrrhenian pirates, who loaded the cult image from its open temple onto their ship. Then the miracle occurred. They could not move their ship from its place. So the sea robbers put the statue back on the beach and there offered it sacrificial cakes. The Samians, who were still barbarian, believed it was the goddess who had fled, so set her up beside a *lygos* hedge (*lygou thorakion*) and bound her fast with *lygos* branches. Admete freed the goddess, bathed her, and put her back on her pedestal.

In the rest of his story, too, Menodotos has a good deal to say about the *lygos*. So it is all the more remarkable that he does not mention the *lygos* tree which played a part in the story of Hera's birth and also was searched for by archaeologists in the belief that it was the "cult object" by which the altar of the sanctuary was oriented.[17] They found it at last in the form of a 15-inch-thick tree stump, with its top encased in stone,

---

Leleges as aborigines, they must have had nymphs as womenfolk. For the nymphs on Lemnos, see further Kerényi, *The Gods of the Greeks*, p. 211 (Pelican edn., p. 187). The historical non-Greek inhabitants of Samos were, for Menodotos, the Karians.

15 On Admete and Herakles, see further Kerényi, *The Heroes of the Greeks*, pp. 159–60.

16 Georgius Syncellus, *Chronographia* 172 A.

17 See Ohly, "Die Göttin und ihre Basis," p. 27, where, however, the wrong view of the altar is described insofar as the sacrificing priest could not have stood so as to turn his back on the *lygos* if this represented the goddess as cult object.

southeast of the altar, at a deep level of the altar place.[18] Pausanias, who lived about three hundred years later than Menodotos, saw this *lygos* tree. He records for us the Samian myth that Hera was born under it.[19] The tree, a rarity because the *lygos* normally grows only as a shrub, was regarded by Pausanias as the world's oldest living tree.[20] Menodotos had no reason not to mention this mythical plant—had it been there. In his time, it seems, there was no *lygos* standing by the altar. The one that Pausanias saw was planted only later and grown on into one of the sights of the temple. Properly pruned, the *lygos* shrub does grow into a tall tree.[21]

Buschor regarded this tree in the sanctuary at Samos as a sort of "cult object," but he expressed himself cautiously. According to him, the chaste tree thicket formed, near the Imbrasos estuary, the center point of the cult required by his general theories.[22] Buschor's fellow excavator, Richard Eilmann, describes this vegetation in its colorful splendor. *Lygos* bushes push out their blue and white and pale red candles far and wide over the beach flats, in countless numbers.[23] A sacred precinct, a second *temenos* for Hera, was carved out of this vegetation beside the grounds of the Heraion. Only this much, and nothing resembling a cult object, can safely be presumed.

18 For details of the find, see E. Homann-Wedeking, "Samos 1963," col. 225; for an illustration, see Walter, *Das griechische Heiligtum*, p. 15, fig. 8. The *lygos* was found southeast and not northwest of the altar, as Buschor and Ohly had expected—not in the position, that is, where it should have stood as "cult object" if this cult object hypothesis had been correct.

19 Pausanias VII 4 4.   20 Pausanias VIII 23 5.

21 See R. Eilmann, "Frühe griechische Keramik im Samischen Heraion," pp. 123–24, note 2. A picture of the *lygos* tree in Aigina is featured as the frontispiece in the 1933 volume of the *Athenischen Mitteilungen* (in which Eilmann's article appeared).

22 Buschor, "Imbrasos," p. 1.

23 Eilmann, "Frühe griechische Keramik," p. 123.

VII. *The Great Goddess of Samos and Paestum*   155

    The myth, a birth myth of Hera which is otherwise unknown and has not been handed down in any of the divine genealogies, deserves more serious consideration here than merely to be linked with a definite tree. For this tree could also have been planted artificially, and although it was perhaps some hundreds of years old, it could hardly have been a thousand-year-old tree. The myth was the prior condition for the planting or the replacement of an earlier tree. It was the lasting element that so to speak floated over the vegetation and settled on it. The myth, which was transported to Samos about 1000 B.C. with the Hera cult, can hardly have been confined to the mere pronunciation of the name "Hera"; that would have been a minimal myth. The theme of the birth of a deity under a tree is known to us not only in association with Hera. According to a Boeotian myth, Hermes was born under a wild strawberry tree, *komaros—andrachnos* in Pausanias[24]—a shrub (*Arbutus unedo*) that more readily grows into a tree than the *lygos*. Whether associated with a tree, or without a tree, what can be assumed as the sure content of the Samian myth is that Hera was born in a thicket by the river Imbrasos, where the *lygos* grew and flowered abundantly.[25] The Heraion of Argos *possessed* the myth which, *mutatis mutandis*, corresponded to this.

    The common fundamental theme is the birth by a river and the association with a flowering plant that grows just there. This association is attested by the cult name "Hera Antheia" borne by the goddess in the city of Argos and elsewhere too.[26] *Antheia* means "flowering one." Indeed, from a purely linguistic point of view, as a feminine form for

    24 Pausanias IX 22 2.
    25 See U. von Wilamowitz-Moellendorff, "Hephaistos," p. 24, note 4.
    26 The epithet "Antheia" appears, for example, in Pausanias II 22 1, and on an inscription in T. Wiegand, ed., *Königliche Museen zu Berlin. Milet*, in the volume *Das Delphinion*, No. 31(a), line 5.

anthos (flower), "Hera Antheia" may actually be translated "Hera the Flower." At the Heraion of Argos the river was the Asterion, with its transparent Greek name. In one mystificatory tale Hera's place is taken by the three aspects of the Great Goddess personified as daughters of the river god.[27] Originally, no doubt, the story was that Hera was born in that spot, in the vegetation which grew there and provided the wreath of "starflowers" the cult image was adorned with. In Samos the river preserved its pre-Greek name Imbrasos, but because of its close association with the goddess it was also called Parthenios, which was given out as its earlier name.[28] The island itself had the poetic name "Parthenia," "island of the virgin," also with the false claim of being the original name of Samos.[29] Another name of the island is supposed to have been "Anthemous" or "Anthemoussa," "rich in flowers,"[30] applications of the Greek myth to Samos, which itself had a pre-Greek name and kept it. The Greek Hera myth had appropriated to itself the vegetation by the Imbrasos, especially as the *lygos* there flowered in three colors.

In the river and flower name Asterion there was a subtle allusion, probably a Hellenization of something that in Argos too had been pre-Greek. Connected with the vegetation by the Imbrasos was a highly archaic experience, supposed or genuine, but at any rate one that was repeatedly and clearly expressed. Too little was known about the *lygos*, even as early as the time of Menodotos, at least in literary circles.[31]

27   See above, in ch. VI, the section on the river god Asterion.
28   Kallimachos, fr. 599. The matter is correctly stated in the scholium on Apollonius Rhodius, *Argonautica* I 185–86.
29   Aristotle, fr. 570 (in Rose, ed.); Kallimachos, *Hymni* IV 49.
30   For these occurrences, see in Aristotle, *Fragmenta*, Rose's commentary to fr. 570.
31   This is why so much was written about the *lygos*, following the Anakreon verses alluded to here in the text (and further in note 33). Also see E. Diehl, "Nikainetos," col. 245.

VII. The Great Goddess of Samos and Paestum

Nikainetos, the Samian poet of the third century B.C., would like to wear the *lygos* wreath of the ancient Karians, historically the aboriginal inhabitants of Samos, and thus get drunk singing songs to Zeus's famous bride (*nymphe*), the Mistress of the island.[32] Anakreon, a contemporary of Polykrates, knew better. He sang of a man, Megistes by name, who for ten months *afterwards*—it must have been a great debauch—wore the *lygos* wreath and drank only sweet must.[33] Anakreon, at the time when the biggest temple was being built, knew more about the *lygos*.

Lygos meant: to withdraw into the sphere of sobriety. The *lygos* checked the sexual urge, so we learn from ancient medical writings.[34] On the other hand, it stimulated women's *katamenia*.[35] The name handed down by Dioskorides, *amiktomiainos*, combines both effects, abstinence (*amiktos*) and the *katamenia* or "monthlies" (*miainos*). The women strewed *lygos* branches on their couches during their days of abstinence at the feast of the Thesmophoria, or else they used the branches themselves to make a bower.[36] The men were kept away from the women's places of retreat by the threat of cruel punishments.[37]

The Thesmophoria were nothing else but the periods of the Greek women elevated to an annual festival, accommodated with this name in the sphere of Demeter Thesmophoros. This did not mean that it was exclusively allocated to Demeter. There was no exclusiveness of sphere between one Great Goddess and another. In the *lygos* bushland by the

---

32 The epigram of Nikainetos is quoted in Athenaios XV 673 BC.
33 For the verses, see Anakreon, fr. 21, in Diehl, *Anth. lyr.*
34 See further E. Fehrle, *Die kultische Keuschheit im Altertum*, pp. 139 ff.
35 Pliny, *Natural History* XXIV 59; Dioskorides, *De materia medica* I 134.
36 Aelian, *De natura animalium* IX 26.
37 *Suidas Lexicon* s.v. Σφάκτριαι (in Adler, ed., IV, 484), and Θεσμοφόρος (II, 710). Men were expressly forbidden to watch; see Aristophanes, *Thesmophoriazusae* 1150–51.

Imbrasos there was a hedge against which the portable cult image of Hera was leaned.[38] Thus, a concrete sphere of sobriety and abstinence, associated with the *lygos*, was set apart. As a parallel we may quote the corresponding custom among the Wemale of West Ceram in Indonesia.[39] Here instead of the *lygos* hedge there are special huts. An older woman friend furnishes one of these provisional huts for the adolescent girl just before her first menstrual period and withdraws into the hut with her, generally in the company of a second older woman. The women stay at least three days in the hut. They take extra special care that no man sees the girl.

A woman in this society is not allowed, either on this first occasion or later on when she has made her monthly withdrawal into the general menstruation house of the village, to speak to a man nor any man to her. Carelessness in this regard counts as an offense that has serious consequences for the offending man and woman. The whole families of both must submit to a ceremony of expiation, at which a cock or a young pig or even a full-grown pig is sacrificed. The first provisional menstruation hut is left standing untouched after the women have returned to the village—it was outside of course, in the bush. It is left to rot or else is burnt. Evidently it is regarded as unclean. We learn, however, that the occurrence of menstruation among the Wemale is anchored in their mythology. There is a tale which expressly states that the moon woman withdraws herself for the same reason as other women. That is why she cannot be seen for three days, and that is why the Wemale woman in this situation must remain *invisible*. They are said to have their periods mostly at full moon or new moon.[40]

38 See above in the text, at the beginning of ch. VII, the resumé of Menodotos' narrative.
39 On the Wemale, see further A. E. Jensen, "Die drei Ströme," pp. 138 ff., 146–47.
40 Ibid., p. 140.

VII. *The Great Goddess of Samos and Paestum*   159

We cannot exclude the possibility that for the Karian women, too, some similar retreat was hidden in the *lygos* bush before the Greeks arrived in Samos about 1000 B.C. with their Hera cult. More than that cannot be asserted. The little we know of Samian myth and ritual would agree with this hypothetical view. The significance of the isolation of the women during the time of their *katamenia* was not the promotion of fertility. The religion of a whole people or tribe was never concerned with an individual woman who happened to be unfertile. So long as the women had their periods, experience proved that they possessed fertility. It was in the spirit of the Demeter religion—not of the Hera religion—that they were able, during these days especially, to do something for the fertility of the earth, because they were sure of their own fertility.[41] In the Hera religion, on the contrary, the isolation of the women is to be understood entirely and absolutely with reference to their men. In the archetypal image of Hera it is this reference and not fertility that is important. Like the moon and the goddess this reference too can have its phases.

Apart from the birth by the river Imbrasos, which took place more as a coming into bloom than under the shade of a tree, there was a paradoxical element in the Samian Hera myth. Hera in Samos, diverging somewhat from her manifestations elsewhere, was the "Imbrasia," "Imbrasian one,"[42] and "Parthenia"[43]—not in one phase a *parthenos* (maiden), as elsewhere, but among her different aspects displaying particularly the one in which she came nearest to being a virgin goddess, an Artemis. Paradoxically, however, the Samian myth gave a

41   A rite of the Thesmophoria is interpreted in late antiquity as a "fertility rite"; see the scholium on Lucian, *Dialogi meretricii* II 1. Evidently the rite served the fertility of the earth, and the application to human fertility was secondary in this case too.
42   Apollonius Rhodius, *Argonautica* I 187-88.
43   In the scholium on Pindar, *Olympia* VI 149 B, she is the "Samian."

special place to Zeus beside her as the husband of the Parthenia. The two of them, according to the Samians, were for three hundred years a loving couple.⁴⁴ This myth would exclude the two certain elements of the ritual that we know about—the disappearance of the goddess and her retrieval for the wedding—if it was not in fact the prior condition for them. It was a half-secret *hieros logos*, like the content of the hymn about the early love-making of the divine couple that was probably sung in the Heraion of Argos. This story was well known and was also imitated in the wedding customs of some of the islands.⁴⁵

The scene of this love story, the *eratizein* of Zeus with Hera, had also been moved to the Imbrasos. In one of the river's ancient courses that had been filled in with earth, a block of stone has been found with an inscription of greeting to three holy persons:

> Ἴμβρασος ἱερός
>
> Παρθενίη ἱερή Παρθένιος ἱερός.⁴⁶

Call holy: the river god, and the goddess Parthenia (Hera who was born there), and a male deity who cannot be Imbrasos, because he has already been called, but only the one who has here been adopted by the Parthenia as her companion: Zeus as Parthenios, as yet nothing more than the playmate of the small Parthenos.

44 See above in the text, ch. VI, at note 70.

45 An initiation is attested for Naxos (see Scholium T on Iliad XIV 296), and probably for Samos, since Kallimachos alludes to Hera's love-making with Zeus. It was evidently regarded as bringing luck if the bride passed the night before the actual wedding night with a lucky boy—such, for example, as a *pais amphithales*, a boy who had both parents alive—as the queen of the gods had done with the king of the gods. The allusion to the only-half-secret story is in Kallimachos, fr. 75, lines 4–5.

46 See Buschor, "Imbrasos," p. 4. Buschor, incomprehensibly, thought that the Parthenia was to be understood here as a "nymph of the locality," and that the male deity was Imbrasos.

VII. The Great Goddess of Samos and Paestum

The rite, which we infer from Menodotos, took place over a somewhat more extended stage—between the altar and the sea, along the Imbrasos.[47] From the eighth century on, the goddess possessed at her altar place, as a special gift from her worshipers, a building many times larger than the small open shrines in which her cult image had stood till then. As with the hecatombs the number one hundred was used in this building. This structure, which may be seen as the nucleus of an Ionic temple, was a hundred feet long. It was a "space between two parallel walls, obstructed by the supporting pillars along the central axis, narrow, confined, undivided, overlong, only illuminated by the door."[48] Thus, while a cult image could be accommodated there, the room was not designed for it. Rather, the cult image would have to be set up against the back wall, unsymmetrically, which proves that for this temple the cult image was not the main thing. Indeed in early times the cult image was only a board (sanis),[49] subordinate to the ritual happening which it served. People came to it through the temple, through a long corridor, clothed it, and fetched it to be set up outside, for the ritual performance in which it was a "property." It was very far removed from being a "miraculous image" or even an "image." It had first to be clothed, with beautiful robes, like those of which we possess an inventory on a marble stele.[50] Not till it was clothed did it begin to look like the goddess as imagined by those who wanted to please her with the clothing. The only way they could do this at first was by the

---

47 For a conjecture about the time, see Eilmann, "Frühe griechische Keramik," p. 123, and Walter, *Das griechische Heiligtum*, p. 22. The end of July is probable.

48 Kähler, *Der griechische Tempel*, p. 27.

49 Kallimachos, fr. 100.

50 For this epigraphical evidence, see C. Michel, *Recueil d'Inscriptions grecques*, No. 832.

use of a clothes-wearing board. Its place was later taken by the clothed dolls and the first rounded sculptures, statues which were carved and worked by sculptors but were to be regarded in principle as clothed boards. The *daidala* of the Hera cult on Mount Kithairon prove that this assessment of the cult images of the Heraion of Samos is the only correct one. In the giant temple begun by Polykrates, at the period of the stele inventory referred to, in the fourth century B.C., a more simply clothed reserved statue was kept and cited as "The Goddess Behind,"[51] while "The Goddess," richly clothed, was more accessible to the temple visitors. Of the greatest significance for the cult was a drum-shaped block of stone, which was found outside the temple and could have supported a 43-inch-high statue or a still higher unworked board.[52]

The story told by Menodotos starts from this foundation. The place was found empty, the goddess was gone, the search for her began. Hera's disappearance was doubtless tied to a point of time when she herself was invisible. The same happening must be performed with the board or the image that *played her part*. If the goddess was already united with her Zeus, the separation now began. The sky at new moon showed a similar disappearance. Searching and fetching back were necessary. But this would have been impossible to reconcile with the myth of the undisturbed love of the young divine couple—a condition which was forbidden for mortal sisters and brothers—if this very myth had not provided the explanation. It took the form that Hera at a cer-

---

51 See Ohly, "Die Göttin und ihre Basis," pp. 33 ff. On the *daidala* of the Mount Kithairon cult, see Ohly, pp. 39 ff.

52 See further E. Buschor and H. Schleif, "Heraion von Samos: Der Altarplatz der Frühzeit," p. 161, and the drawing on p. 158, fig. 9. / My thanks for having drawn my attention to these technological considerations are due to my son-in-law, Dr. Hans Peter Isler, a member of the excavation team at the Heraion of Samos, with whom I also had conversations on the spot.

VII. *The Great Goddess of Samos and Paestum* 163

tain moment had resolved to set a divine example for the periodicity of mortal women. She went before them into that secluded spot in the *lygos* bushes where the women of Samos originally had to pass the time of their *katamenia*.

This supposition, and with it the proposed reconstruction of the whole myth that formed the basis of the Samian ritual, rests on the well-attested belief in the effect of the chaste tree and on the analogy of the archaic custom observed among the women of a primitive people. What is not yet explained, however, are the goddess' bonds from which her priestess freed her. The binding and tying up of a goddess was a ceremony so archaic that its meaning had been completely lost among the Greeks of historical times. Besides Hera, it was carried out also on Artemis, who in Sparta bore the epithets "Orthia," "she who arouses," and "Lygodesma," "she who is bound with *lygos*." The explanatory tale was that the goddess was found in a *lygos* bush where her statue stood bound with *lygos* withes.[53] The two epithets characterized, in this case as well, a goddess associated with moonlight, and in two opposite senses, the one who stimulated the sexual organ and the one who curbed it. In the Asia Minor city of Erythraia, the sitting image of Artemis was bound and we are given the explanation that she was bound because it was believed that the images of the gods were unsettled and often moved from one place to another.[54] Such is the language used about things that were not understood.

Yet in 1959 we found ourselves suddenly face to face with a bound Artemis statue. It was found in the Piraeus. I noted my impressions: "The small figure has her arms folded under her robe, behind a cross-binding coming down from the neck in front to the girdle at the back,

53 Pausanias III 16 10.
54 See Polemon, in the scholium to Pindar, *Olympia* VII 95 A.

then to the front again where it is knotted and hangs down—all ingeniously emphasizing the folding of the arms with hands hidden. An aspect of the goddess—probably carried by a priest of the cult and displayed—'So may you remain!' The features sweet, almost imploring. Not at all suitable for a terrible deity who had to be 'tamed' in this fashion. At any rate a feminine cult clothing of a kind not previously known."[55] Such was the contradictory effect of the sculptural representation of a highly archaic ritual some five hundred years later than the Samian origins, in the fourth century B.C.

It was no doubt in her most dangerous aspect that Hera, like Artemis, was bound. This would be the aspect that became effective at new moon in the seclusion of the *lygos* bushes and had to be curbed in its power. It was the Prosymna and "Iuno inferna" aspect[56] in a quite archaic form and treatment. A special name has been handed down from the great Hera festival, the Heraia of Samos; it is "Tonea," no doubt correctly spelled Toneia[57] or Tonaia. This must be derived from *tonos* (cord, rope) and probably refers to this most striking feature of the ritual, the tying up of the statue of the goddess, followed by her being untied and bathed. Four cult bathing places of the seventh century have been discovered.[58] So in this relatively late period it was not the sea that served for purification and at the same time for the bridal bath before the wedding, the last act of the ceremonies.

Only a few very summary allusions refer to this last act. On the inventory stele there is the name "Euangelis," "she who is the messen-

55 See further Kerényi, *Werke*, III, 305; also the illustration in *BCH*, LXXXIV (1960), p. 653, fig. 8.
56 See above in the text, ch. VI, at note 45.
57 This spelling is correctly given by Wilamowitz, "Hephaistos," p. 24, note 4.
58 Buschor, "Samos 1952–57," p. 200.

VII. *The Great Goddess of Samos and Paestum* 165

ger of good tidings," evidently the official name of the priestess of Hera.[59] From this priestess came the proclamation that the goddess had been found again and that her wedding could be celebrated. It is hardly to be supposed that anyone but the priestess led the bathing ceremony and the "bringing back" procession. About the wedding as it happens, we are told only by one Roman source, which describes it as *nuptiae*, as an act performed with the ritual of the *gamos* and celebrated as an annual feast of the goddess. M. Terentius Varro, who as a Roman admiral in the Pirate War visited Samothrace for the celebration of the mysteries, gives what is probably an eyewitness account, albeit somewhat summary, of the Heraia in Samos: "Insulam prius Partheniam nominatam, quod ibi Iuno adolevit ibique etiam Iovi nupserit. Itaque nobilissimum et antiquissimum templum eius est Sami et simulacrum in habitu nubentis figuratum et sacra eius anniversaria nuptiarum ritu colebatur." ("The island was formerly called Parthenia, because Hera grew up there and also married Zeus there. That is why her most famous and ancient temple is in Samos, and a statue in the costume of a bride was worshiped and her yearly festival celebrated with the rites of marriage.")[60]

The Christian author who quotes this passage had a very crude idea about the wedding rites.[61] It is certain and is clearly stated that the ritual was centered on a statue clothed as a bride. The same rites were performed with the statue as when a bride became a wife. Whether the cult statue or another doll was used for this purpose is irrelevant. No further details have come down to us. We know that in the Heraion of

59 See Michel, *Recueil*, No. 832, line 22.
60 See Kerényi, "Varro über Samothrake und Ambrakia," p. 157. In the quotation given above in the text, I attribute to Varro not only the first sentence; see G. Funaioli, *Grammaticae romanae fragmenta*, p. 351, fr. 399.
61 L. Caelius Firmianus Lactantius, *Divinae institutiones* I 17 8.

Argos a "bed of Hera" stood in the entrance hall of the temple[62]—except, of course, during the period of the ceremony—and from the Heraion of Samos good fortune has preserved a wooden relief from a bed donated to Hera.

As early as the 1930s a small terracotta relief had been found among the remains of sacrificial gifts. It represented the divine couple in Samos. Hera is seen as a naked standing woman. Zeus, a bearded figure, fondles her with one hand and grasps her by the hand with the other.[63] The background of this terracotta relief seems to be vegetation and the scene, the banks of the Imbrasos[64]—a mythological illustration rather than a picture of actual rites. The wooden relief came to light at the beginning of the fifties, when at the levels reached then by the excavations wooden remains were found preserved in the wet sand of the Imbrasos. The relief itself had evidently been attached to one of the four posts of a wooden *kline* (bed) of the seventh century. It depicted Zeus and Hera standing but in a position and with gestures that appear at the same time erotic and ritual. Zeus is grasping Hera's right breast (the goddess shows both her breasts bared) and is embracing her. At the same time he is making a step towards her. Between the two there hovers the stylized but clearly recognizable image of an eagle.[65] Zeus's arrival for the wedding was expected like that of an eagle.

On the grounds of the Samian sanctuary, the altar and temple grew to an enormous size. The space for the ceremonies of seeking and

62 See Pausanias II 17 3; also see above, in ch. VI, the section on the *lecherna* ceremony.

63 For a reproduction of the relief, see *AA*, XLVIII (1933), p. 255, fig. 16.

64 See Eilmann, "Frühe griechische Keramik," p. 123, fig. 69, and note 2.

65 This bird is certainly not the cuckoo of Hermione. For the wooden relief, see Ohly, "Holz," pp. 77–83, pls. 13–15, 18–19. As for the four-poster itself, this wonderful piece seems not to have been preserved.

VII. The Great Goddess of Samos and Paestum

finding, the bath and the bringing home, between the temple and the sea, was limited to a few hundred square yards and in relation to the giant building apparently became still smaller with time. Both the temple and the place for the ceremonies by the Imbrasos, so to speak, only a square in front of the temple, belonged to the goddess in the two phases that in the Heraion of Argos were called Euboia and Prosymna and in Stymphalos, Pais and Chera. A separate cult of the Teleia as Akraia on a more distant mountain spur or peak is conceivable, but it is also conceivable that the unique great sanctuary in Samos served all the goddess' aspects.

At the opposite pole to this concentrated installation we have the scatter of the Hera cult in Paestum, on the Gulf of Salerno, from the temples in the city to those at the estuary of the Silaros River (the Sele of today), five and a half miles away. Such was the distance the processions had to cover to get from one sanctuary belonging to the goddess to another.[66] The distance is great enough to demand an explanation of why the two cult sites were set up so far from one another, and yet not great enough to justify the assumption that there were two Hera cults existing here independently of one another, one at the sea and river, the other in the city.

The explanation can only lie in that characteristic of the goddess' nature which we encountered in Argos and Samos—her two aspects. One required the cult near a river, as in Samos the Imbrasos estuary. At Argos, the site of the Prosymna cult has not yet been identified, but it certainly lay lower than the cult site of Hera Euboia, probably in swamp land. The other aspect required a situation just like that of Paestum,

---

66 For the possible route taken, see P. C. Sestieri, "Ricerche Posidoniati," p. 37.

on firm ground, here some sixty feet above sea level. The excavations at Paestum have now yielded the surprising result that not only the two larger of the three temples standing in the city but a dozen smaller temples or cult buildings as well were dedicated to Hera.[67] Thus, Paestum itself is stamped as a city of the queen of the gods—irrespective of the city's Greek name, Poseidonia[68]—and we must therefore ask, Why does Strabo confine himself to mentioning only a "sanctuary of Hera" by the Silaros?[69] Evidently the cult down there in the swamp land was connected with that in the city, so that while Hera dominated the landscape from the Monti Alburni to the sea, only the sacred precinct at the Sele estuary was ruled *by her alone*.

The question where the cult came from is answered by Pliny the Elder.[70] It was the Hera of Argos whose worship had moved eastward to conquer Samos about 1000 B.C. and afterwards reached the coasts of Italy. The legend that it was brought there by Jason and the Argonauts only proves that the religion which could create for itself such cult places as the Heraion of Argos and that of Samos is not to be understood as a *peculiar* cult, a so-called tribal cult, brought by a distinct tribe. In the case of Samos, too, it was the Argonauts who figured as cult disseminators, although equally in that case the connection with the Heraion of Argos was well established. It is only through the two older and most famous Hera temples that those in Paestum and at the

67 Ibid., pp. 40 ff. Also see Paola Zancani Montuoro, "Paestum," p. 833.
68 The Poseidon sanctuary probably stood on the Akropolis, which must be looked for in the Agropoli of today; see Zancani Montuoro, "Il Poseidonion di Poseidonia," pp. 165–83.
69 Strabo VI 1 1. The epithet Ἀργονίας in the text of Strabo is wrong, and so is the "correction" Ἀργώιας, since a "Hera of the Argo," which would imply that the ship Argo was a cult place, certainly did not exist. The correct reading is Ἀργείας, which would agree with Pliny (see below, note 70).
70 See Pliny, *Natural History* III 70, for the phrasing "Iunonis Argivae."

VII. *The Great Goddess of Samos and Paestum*

Sele estuary become intelligible. On the way taken by the Hera religion from Greece to the Sele estuary lay another sanctuary of the goddess, though today only one pillar of it is standing. This sanctuary was on the promontory of Lakinion near Kroton, a city founded by the Achaians. For the dissemination of the Hera worship in a westerly direction accompanied the Greek colonization movement of the eighth to seventh centuries, at a time when it was already in its first flowering in Samos.

The picture sketched by Livy of the sanctuary of Kroton, on what is today Cape Colonne, corresponds to the state of affairs at the time of the Punic Wars but it does contain the nucleus and starting point of the cult. Livy wrote that "six miles from this famous place [the citadel of Kroton] there was a temple dedicated to Lacinian Juno, a building more famous even than the city itself and held in reverence by all the peoples of the neighbourhood. It had an enclosure surrounded by dense woodland, with lofty firs, and, in the centre, rich grassland where cattle of all kinds, sacred to the goddess, grazed without any shepherd to attend them. At night the various flocks and herds used to return each to their own stalls, unharmed by lurking beasts of prey or marauding men. Thus a great deal of money was made out of these cattle, and from the profits a column of solid gold was dedicated to the goddess. The temple, too, was as famous for its wealth as for its sanctity, and, as often happens with well-known places, stories of supernatural things are connected with it: for instance, it is said that in the entrance court there is an altar on which the ashes are never stirred by the wind."[71]

This altar of burnt offering is attested as similar to those known to us as nucleus and centerpoint of the oldest Hera cults, in Olympia and Sa-

---

71 Livy XXIV 3 3–7 (Penguin edn., p. 234); see also Pliny, *Natural History* II 111, 240. The profits from the herds referred to by Livy is understood to mean profits from the skins of the animals and the cheese.

mos, and the similarity must be assumed also for the Heraion of Argos.[72] (The primeval ash heap was pronounced miraculous by the temple guide.) The importance of the altar in the sacred precinct by the Sele estuary even led to its duplication. At a short distance from the temple, which was not built till the beginning of the fifth century B.C., one large altar has been excavated. It is not quite aligned with the temple.[73] That it was abundantly used for animal sacrifices the bone remains show. Beside it and parallel stands a smaller altar, without sacrificial remains.[74] We could say that it is almost only a symbolic altar, erected in the fifth century when the earlier altar of burnt offering that perhaps stood here was removed. The general archaeological picture makes all this plausible.[75]

Other buildings—a hall and the temple with the astonishing metope relief—began to accumulate from the first half of the sixth century, and small figurine-type offerings to Hera date from as early as the seventh century. There is nothing, however, that could be called Greek from an

---

[72] On the ancient sacrificial altar in the Heraion of Argos, see above in ch. VI, at notes 9 ff.

[73] See B. D'Agostino, "Heraion del Sele," p. 167.

[74] The smaller altar is shown on the plan supplied by Paola Zancani Montuoro for her contribution to *Santuari di Magna Grecia*, p. 206, fig. 12.

[75] I venture this conjecture with some hesitation since the excavator herself, Paola Zancani Montuoro, to whom I am indebted for the particulars of this second altar (see *Santuari di Magna Grecia*, p. 6), only hazarded a conjecture: "Si potrebbe credere l'ara maggiore riservata ai sacrifici cruenti e l'altra ai riti preliminari, complementari o meno solenni, come libagioni, offerte d'incenso e simili." ("We could say that the main altar was reserved for the bloody sacrifices and the other for the preliminary rites, supplementary or at least solemn, such as libations, offerings of incense, and so on.") For such an arrangement, however, parallels would have to be found, whereas there is no lack of parallels for an earlier altar of burnt offering. The excavators had enough ashes to bother with, in fact, but needed little persuading to regard them as volcanic ash from Vesuvius. *Non liquet!*

VII. *The Great Goddess of Samos and Paestum* 171

earlier period.⁷⁶ An altar of the seventh century, with which the Hera cult might have started, is conspicuous by its absence.⁷⁷ In the city region of Paestum itself the goddess received an unusual Doric temple, at about the same date as the oldest buildings by the Sele estuary.⁷⁸ This temple in Paestum was the so-called "Basilica," the structure of which is entirely based on the number nine (3 x 3) and is just as little adapted to a cult image as was the oldest, Ionic, temple in Samos. The Paestum temple is Doric, with nine pillars in front, eighteen at the sides, and three between the antae. The cella is divided in two lengthways. We may well say that, as in Samos, this too is a building that stands on its own, among those devoted to Hera. A Classical temple close by was put up to Hera in the city, as in her precinct down by the river, in the fifth century.

For as in Samos, Hera had two sacred precincts in Paestum, the lower of which clearly exhibits her connections with the underworld. Besides the altar—ultimately two altars—there were in this lower precinct down at the estuary *bothroi*, trenches designed for sacrifices to the gods of the underworld.⁷⁹ These trenches have yielded us a great

76 The exception to this is a sub-Mycenaean piece that was found beside a piece from the late seventh century; see P. Zancani Montuoro and U. Zanotti-Bianco, *Heraion alla foce del Sele*, I, 25. / For the accumulation of the sixth-century evidence, see *Heraion*, I, 28 ff.

77 The excavators had always assumed a smaller temple from the sixth century (ibid., I, 28-29), but they were finally forced to the conclusion that the building with the metopes was not a treasure house but a temple. This is in agreement with the opinion of Zancani Montuoro, *Santuari di Magna Grecia*, p. 205, that the building was "constructed in the first half of the sixth century, probably for the worship of the goddess in a particular one of her many aspects." It is extremely improbable that there was no great altar belonging to this temple. The altar in question may have been the old altar of burnt offering.

78 Kähler, *Der griechische Tempel*, p. 21. / For the comparison to the Ionic structure at Samos, see above, ch. VII, at note 48.

79 Paola Zancani Montuoro and U. Zanotti-Bianco, "Capaccio. Heraion alla foce del Sele," pp. 299 ff.

number of votive offerings alluding to Hera's association with the earth as a place of the dead and of growth, emphasizing her nature as "Iuno inferna." This underworld nature was not only negative; it was associated also with the return from the dead, for which the goddess herself set the example.

The increased religious valuation of the lowest phase seems to have been characteristic of the west. The oldest statuette (from the end of the seventh century) found in this region shows the facets of this underworld phase. Flat as a board the goddess is represented, yet she holds a child by the left hand, a pomegranate in the right.[80] The number of terracotta pomegranates found is large, of flowers still larger.[81] Characteristic of this cult were small terracotta busts of the goddess, emerging as far as her bare breasts from leaves and wearing on her head a large, lilylike flower, as if she were herself a flower. This composition served for smoke offerings, from a small fire in the flower.[82] The epiphany of the goddess as a flower was at the same time a flaming up, an appearance of light. Votive statuettes show Hera as ruler of the underworld enthroned, two sphinxes on her shoulders.[83] These representations were balanced by motherly images. The representations of the goddess as a nursing mother is doubtless an assimilation to an ancient Italian goddess, later also identification with Kybele, the Great

80 Ibid., pp. 219 ff., and figs. 5–6.
81 For one example among many, showing fruits (apples, figs, almonds) and birds, popular gifts, see ibid., p. 224, fig. 8. For an example showing flowers, see p. 225, fig. 9.
82 J. M. W. Stoop, *Floral Figurines from South Italy*; also L. von Matt and U. Zanotti-Bianco, *Grossgriechenland*, figs. 43–44.
83 See "Abenteuer mit Monumenten (Wandlungen in Paestum)," in Kerényi, *Werke*, III, 406. I have to discuss these objects according to my own ideas because too little has been published about them.

VII. *The Great Goddess of Samos and Paestum* 173

Mother of the gods.[84] The function of the great pre-Greek wife goddess, Eileithyia, whose sphere of influence had been reduced to helping in childbirth, was taken over by Hera in Argos; she performed the same function also as "Iuno Lucina" in Italy. And she did so at Paestum, too, represented in a kneeling position as though she herself were giving birth.[85] Even this position was adopted here by Hera as the universal woman goddess. The two male figures who support her belong to the Great Mother of the gods, while the dove she holds refers to the love goddess Aphrodite.[86]

    84 See P. C. Sestieri, "Iconographie et culte d'Héra à Paestum," pp. 149–58.
    85 See von Matt and Zanotti-Bianco, *Grossgriechenland*, fig. 46.
    86 The Great Mother of the gods had not only twice five Daktyls corresponding to her fingers (hence the five Daktyls of Olympia; see above in the text, ch. VI, the section on Olympia), but instead of them also two male helpers. These two give her support and remain as her coadjutors (*paredroi daimones*); see Apollonius Rhodius, *Argonautica* I 1125 ff., and Kerényi, *The Gods of the Greeks*, p. 85 (Pelican edn., p. 75). They also observe her while she gives birth, as is written in an oracle of the Klarian Apollo (*CIG* 3538, lines 17–19). In this case they are more likely called Kabeiroi or Korybantes, in Crete Kouretes; see E. Ohlemutz, *Die Kulte und Heiligtümer der Götter in Pergamon*, pp. 192 ff. These two figures may also be inimically disposed towards the child; see Kerényi, *The Gods of the Greeks*, pp. 86 ff. (Pelican edn., pp. 76 ff.). As obstetricians they appear beside the goddess as she gives birth; and she can be either the Great Mother or else Eileithyia on a well-known statue in the Museum of Sparta. As observers through a hole the two figures lie on the roof of a shrine of the Great Goddess. This little shrine, dated to the eleventh century B.C., is in the Archaeological Museum in Heraklion. (The catlike animal on the roof beside the two figures is the animal of the Great Mother.) As obstetricians the two figures wait upon the goddess on a relief pithos of the early seventh century from Thebes; behind them there are two lions, which makes the attribution to the Great Mother certain. These two male figures were arbitrarily associated with Hera by Erika Simon, *Die Götter der Griechen*, p. 57, fig. 51, and p. 62, fig. 57, as were a clay seal impression and the Lion Gate of Mycenae (Simon, p. 63, fig. 58). See fur-

The strength of the association with the underworld of the goddess by the Sele estuary—at the time of the greatest prosperity of this cult place, in the sixth century—is best shown by a unique find during re-examination of the site in the year 1959. In none of the series of metope images that once adorned Greek cult buildings is there, so far as my knowledge goes, a representation of anything in the underworld—except here! Among the scenes from hero mythology and the Hera myth adorning the metopes of the sixth-century temple (which the excavators at first took for a *thesauros*, a treasure house) is one of the punishment of Sisyphos in Hades.[87] The sinner is rolling his stone uphill, all the while a winged demon of the underworld, such as has not been found anywhere else, goads him on in case he should tire.

The three temples that are still standing in the city region of Paestum today—to say nothing of the so-called "Italic" temple, the Corinthian Doric building in the forum of which the ruins have been preserved[88]—testify not to the sole sovereignty of Hera in Paestum but to her predominance, and this becomes even more impressive when we take in the buildings down near the Silaros as well. In chronological order, the "Basilica" was the first big building and at the same time the first temple of Hera in the city of Paestum.[89] Afterwards, at the turn of the sixth to fifth centuries, Athena received the second great temple

---

ther Kerényi and Sichtermann, "Zeitlose Schieferbauten der Insel Andros," p. 31; also P. Aström and B. Blomé, "A Reconstruction of the Lion Relief at Mycenae," pp. 159 ff.

87 The find and the reconstruction of the metope relief were the work of Paola Zancani Montuoro; see her "Heraion alla foce di Sele," pp. 57 ff. See also Kerényi, "Abenteuer mit Monumenten," in *Werke*, III, 406. / On the identification of the building as a temple, see above, ch. VII, note 77.

88 For publication of this building, see F. Krauss and R. Herbig, *Der korinthisch-dorische Tempel am Forum von Paestum*.

89 For the Doric "Basilica" in Paestum, see above in the text, ch. VII, at note 78.

VII. *The Great Goddess of Samos and Paestum* 175

of the city, the so-called "Temple of Ceres." And on a larger scale—*oktostylos* against *hexastylos*—but in a similar style, Hera her new temple by the river.[90] The third great Hera temple (the second dedicated to her in the city itself) was the Classical building, long regarded as a temple of Poseidon, the "Tempio di Nettuno." The temple was erected, about the middle of the fifth century, with a great altar of its own and a bath of the goddess.[91] This gift to the goddess, which surpassed all others in beauty, was a renewed confession of her power, a confirmation of the fact that the inhabited region in the city, just as much as that carved out of the swamp lands by the river, belonged to Hera above all. The temple was also marked by the name *Paistos* or *Paiston* and *Paestum*. This stamped the city, a narrower region than the whole great area that stretched from the Akropolis (modern Agropoli) to the Silaros, as a second particular precinct of Hera. No historian can ignore this evident meaning of a Greek city name formed on regular phonetic principles, *Paistos* from *Paid-tos*.[92] Since the beginning of the nineteenth century an inscription on a silver plate has been known[93] which was found in a Paestan grave and attests Παῖς as an epithet of "The Goddess" for Paestum:

Τᾶς θεῶ τ(ᾶ)ς Παιδός ἠμί.

A dead woman, probably a priestess of Hera, is announcing herself to the deities of the underworld: "To the Goddess, to the Pais I belong." The epithet "Pais" has already been taken as evidence that Hera was

90 On the contrast, see F. Krauss, "Paestum, Basilika. Der Entwurf des Grundrisses," pp. 102–103.
91 See Kähler, *Der griechische Tempel*, pl. 12.
92 The linguistic discovery of Franz Altheim's came to my attention in oral communication.
93 See the exchange of letters between the Neapolitan scholar Francesco M. Avellino and F. G. Welcker, in *Rheinisches Museum*, III (1835), 581–87.

"The Goddess."[94] Now this inference must be drawn since we know that in fact Hera, like no other, was *the* Goddess in the Paestan region. The material, silver—instead of gold, which was the material of the passes for the dead among the Orphics of southern Italy and Crete[95]—occurs also in the form of a silver disc with a votive inscription in Paestum.[96] The meaning of the second inscription refers to Hera as the guardian goddess of warriors, a quality attested for her, though less characteristic than the metal which suggests silver moonlight.

It was in her higher precinct, the city region of Paestum, that Hera bore the epithet "Pais," as was probably also the case in Stymphalos. From Pais she became a bride, the "Nymphe of Zeus," as she is called by the Samian poet.[97] Zeus is attested in Paestum on a monumental scale as husband and cult associate of Hera. A seated statue of Zeus in terracotta, the mature work of a master of the second half of the sixth century, was found in a pit near the Classical Hera temple.[98] It is probable that he received worship in the "Basilica," the oldest great temple of Hera, which while not arranged for any *single* cult image,[99] could accommodate two—one in each of its "naves." Thus, Zeus now sits enthroned, reconstructed from many fragments, in the Museum of

94 For the inscription itself as well as this reading, see H. Collitz, *Sammlung der griechischen Dialekt-inschriften*, II, 158, No. 1648; see also the similar reading of Wilamowitz in the note to *IG* XIV 665 (p. 179).

95 See O. Kern, ed., *Orphicorum fragmenta*, fr. 32.

96 See Margherita Guarducci, "Dedica arcaica alla Hera di Posidonia," pp. 145 ff.

97 For Stymphalos, see above in the text, ch. VI, at note 67. For Nikainetos, the Samian poet, see above in the text, ch. VII, at note 32.

98 For the statue of Zeus, see P. C. Sestieri, "Statua fittile di Posidonia," pp. 193 ff.

99 On the absence of adaptation to a single cult image in the "Basilika," see above in the text, ch. VII, at note 78; for the similar structure in Samos, see the text at notes 48, 49.

VII. *The Great Goddess of Samos and Paestum* 177

Paestum, a memorial of the archaic supremacy of the supreme male deity.[100]

Towards the end of the sixth century a little house of cleanly fitted freestones was built, half underground, in what was just about the center of the city, in a small sacred precinct.[101] No other divine being but Hera, neither god nor hero, can lay claim to this building, if only because of its house form. Neither the building nor its precinct carry any inscription, as Greek temples usually do. On a *heroön* one would be more likely to read the hero's name. Among the broken vessels, offerings to the building's owner, found round about, however, was an *amphoriskos* (a miniature amphora) with a picture of a bursting lily-like flower between two marsh birds, an immediately intelligible allusion to the Hera Antheia of the swamp lands at the Sele estuary. Under it was written, moreover,

>Τᾶς νύνφας ἐμὶ ἱα[ρόν
>
>*To the nymph I am sacred—*

property of the proprietor of the small sanctuary.[102]

Hera, the nymph of Zeus, also had a bed in this partly underground house. In the middle of the cleanly plastered inner room, into which one descends today after lifting up one of the big roof tiles, there lay on two square stone blocks five iron rods, and over them the remains

---

100 See Sestieri, "Statua fittile di Posidonia," pl. II.
101 Sestieri, "Il sacello-heroon Posidoniate," pp. 53 ff. On the discussion about the identification of the building, see Sestieri, "Il sacello ipogeico di Paestum," pp. 25 ff. Sestieri was the discoverer of the building, and it was his idea that it had been erected for the "hierogamia" of Zeus and Hera. "Hierogamia" is not an ancient word, but the finds have borne him out.
102 For the inscription, see Sestieri, "Il sacello-heroon Posidoniate," p. 55. For an illustration of the amphora itself, see ibid., p. 57, fig. 9.

of some sort of basketwork and some textile, evidently a blanket.[103] For human use it would be too short a bed, yet it was certainly a couch (such as we know from the picture of an Etruscan loving couple only half reclining). Beside the couch in Paestum stood nine large and splendid jars, hydrias and amphoras of bronze, and two painted amphoras from Attica. In the bronze jars were found remains of honey, which was what they had contained, while the Attic amphoras doubtless contained wine. All this is in contrast with what the *lygos* signified in Samos, in the country of the "fugitive Hera"—sobriety.[104] The pictures on the Attic jars found in Paestum were also far removed from sobriety.[105] One shows Herakles' journey to Olympos; the other shows the dance of maenads and satyrs around Dionysos. Both these sons of Zeus, Herakles and Dionysos, had aroused the anger of the queen of the gods in well-known legends. Yet these splendid vases were chosen, because everything here was an offering to a contented and rejoicing Hera, after her underworld phase.

After this had all been set up, the entrance, which never had a proper door, was carefully walled up with big blocks of stone. The house with its bed—and its sources of jollity, both sweetness and intoxication, in the jars—was a gift to Hera, like the model house in the sanctuary of Argos and in Perachora. The fountainlike basin, with stairs for the cult bath, that belongs on the square of sacramental buildings beside the Classical temple in Paestum is evidence that the ceremony of the wedding of the divine couple was celebrated here in one of the great

---

103 These remains are illustrated in M. Napoli, *Il Museo di Paestum*, p. 69.

104 On the *lygos* as signifying sobriety, see above in the text, ch. VII, at notes 33 and 34.

105 See the illustration in M. Napoli, *Paestum*, p. 43, fig. 56; also *Il Museo di Paestum*, pls. XIII, XIV.

VII. *The Great Goddess of Samos and Paestum* 179

temples, and since Classical times in the region's finest temple of Hera.[106]

The very concrete wedding ceremonies, carried out with bed and wooden bride in Samos and Paestum, on Mount Kithairon, and probably also in the Heraion of Argos, bring to view indirectly but none the less clearly the spiritual nature of Zeus the *invisible* bridegroom and husband. The history of Greek religion made it possible for Hera to be replaced by an artificial substitute. For Zeus in the rites of the Zeus and Hera cult no substitute was possible. There existed for the Greeks, ever since they had had this religion, the god himself—a spiritual he who happened—apprehended in the cosmos or in the life of men, acted in their ceremonies.

106 For the "afterlife" of the Hera festivals in the Madonna cult—the cult of the Madonna del Melagrano in Capaccio Vecchio, the hill town in the Monti Alburni, and the cult of the Annunziata in Paestum itself—see Zancani Montuoro and Zanotti-Bianco in their great work *Heraion alla foce del Sele*, I, 18–19. See also the record of my experiences and thoughts in "Das neue Bild von Paestum," in Kerényi, *Werke*, II, 233 ff.; also "Abenteuer mit Monumenten," in *Werke*, III, 400 ff., and in the index s.v. Paestum.

LIST OF WORKS CITED

ABBREVIATIONS

These are used in the footnotes and in the List of Works Cited. Shortened titles readily identified in the List of Works Cited are not included.

AA *Archäologischer Anzeiger* (Supplement to *Jahrbuch des deutschen archäologischen Instituts*). Berlin. (References are to columns, not pages.)

AJA *American Journal of Archaeology*. Princeton, New Jersey.

AM *Athenische Mitteilungen* (*Mitteilungen des deutschen archäologischen Instituts, Athenische Abteilung*). Berlin.

ARW *Archiv für Religionswissenschaft*. Freiburg im Breisgau and Berlin.

BCH *Bulletin de correspondance hellénique*. Athens.

CIG *Corpus inscriptionum graecarum*. Edited by August Boeckh et al. Berlin, 1828-77. 5 vols.

CIL *Corpus inscriptionum latinarum*. Berlin.

CSEL Corpus scriptorum ecclesiasticorum latinorum.

Diehl, *Anth. lyr. Anthologia lyrica graeca*. Edited by Ernst Diehl. 3d edn. Leipzig, 1949-54.

GCS Die griechischen christlichen Schriftsteller der ersten drei Jahrhunderte. Leipzig.

IG *Inscriptiones Graecae*. Berlin.

Jacoby, *FGrHist Die Fragmente der griechischen Historiker*. Edited by Felix Jacoby. Berlin and Leiden, 1923-59.

LCL Loeb Classical Library. London and Cambridge, Mass.

Nauck, *TGF Tragicorum graecorum fragmenta*. Edited by August Nauck. 2d edn. Leipzig, 1889.

OCT Oxford Classical Texts.

Praktika Πρακτικὰ τῆς ἐν ᾿Αρχαιολογικῆς ῾Εταιρείας. Athens.

RE Georg Wissowa et al. (eds.). *Paulys Real-Encyclopädie der classischen Altertumswissenschaft*. Stuttgart, 1894- . (References are to columns, not pages.)

Roscher, *Lexikon* W. H. Roscher (ed.). *Ausführliches Lexikon der griechischen und römischen Mythologie*. Leipzig, 1884-1937. 6 vols. in 9 parts with 2 supplements. (References are to columns, not pages.)

TAPA *Transactions of the American Philological Association*. Cleveland, Ohio.

LIST OF WORKS CITED

In general, classical texts are unlisted except when an edition or translation has been cited. Unless noted to the contrary, English versions of quoted passages are the author's and translator's own.

AELIAN. *De natura animalium.* Edited by Rudolf Hercher. Leipzig, 1864–66. 2 vols.

AISCHYLOS. *Supplementum* [Fragments]. In: METTE, HANS J. (ed.), q.v.

ALTHEIM, FRANZ. *Griechische Götter im alten Rom.* Giessen, 1930.

ANTONINUS LIBERALIS. Μεταμορφώσεων συναγωγή. In: *Mythographi Graeci,* II:1. Edited by Edgar Martini. Leipzig, 1896.

APOLLONIUS RHODIUS. *Scholia in Apollonium Rhodium vetera.* Edited by Carl Wendel. Berlin, 1935.

ARISTOPHANES. *Scholia graeca in Aristophanem.* Edited by Friedrich Dübner. Paris, 1842.

ARISTOTLE. *Fragmenta.* Edited by Valentino Rose. 3d edn. Leipzig, 1886.

ARNIM, HANS VON (ed.). *Stoicorum veterum fragmenta.* Leipzig, 1903. 2 vols.

ÅSTRÖM, PAUL, and BÖRJE BLOMÉ. "A Reconstruction of the Lion Relief at Mycenae." *Opuscula Atheniensia,* V (1965).

ATHENAIOS. *The Deipnosophists.* With an English translation by Charles Burton Gulick. (LCL.) 1927–41. 7 vols.

AUGUSTINE. *Augustinus: De civitate Dei.* Edited by Bernard Dombart. Leipzig, 1892. 2 vols.

BÉRARD, VICTOR. *De l'origine des cultes arcadiens.* (Bibliothèque des écoles françaises d'Athènes et de Rome.) Paris, 1894.

BIEBER, MARGARETE. "Eros and Dionysos on Kerch Vases." *Hesperia,* Supplement 8. Athens, 1949.

BISCHOFF, ERNST. "Kalender." *RE,* X:2.

BLEGEN, CARL W. *Prosymna. The Helladic Settlement Preceding the Argive Heraeum.* Cambridge, 1937. 2 vols.

BOLKESTEIN, H. Τέλος ὁ γάμος. (Mededelingen der Koninklijke Nederlandse Akademie van Wetenschappen. Afdeling Letterkunde, LXXVI:2, Ser. B.) Amsterdam, 1933.

BOSSHARDT, ERNST. *Die Nomina auf -ευς. Ein Beitrag zur Wortbildung der griechischen Sprache.* Zurich, 1942.

BOWRA, C. M. (ed.). See under PINDAR.

BRITISH MUSEUM. *Catalogue of the Greek Coins: Thessaly to Aetolia.* Edited by P. Gardner. London, 1883.

BRUCHMANN, KARL FRIEDRICH HEINRICH. *Epitheta Deorum.* Leipzig, 1893.

BRUGMANN, KARL. "Die Syntax des einfachen Satzes im Indogermanischen." *Zeitschrift für vergleichende Sprachforschung,* Supplement 43. Göttingen, 1925.

BUBER, MARTIN. *Israel and Palestine: The History of an Idea.* Translated by S. Godman. London, 1952.

BUERCHNER, L. "Macris." *RE,* XIV:1.

BUSCHOR, ERNST. "Heraion von Samos: frühe Bauten." *AM,* LV (1930).

——. "Imbrasos." *AM,* LXVIII (1953).

——. "Samos 1952–57." In: *Neue deutsche Ausgrabungen im Mittelmeergebiet und im vorderen Orient.* Berlin, 1959.

——, and H. SCHLEIF. "Heraion von Samos: Der Altarplatz der Frühzeit." *AM,* LVIII (1933).

CALHOUN, G. M. "Zeus the Father in Homer." *TAPA,* LXVI (1935).

COLLITZ, HERMANN. *Sammlung der griechischen Dialekt-inschriften,* II. Göttingen, 1899.

COOK, ARTHUR BERNARD. "Who was the Wife of Zeus?" *Classical Review,* XX (1906).

——. *Zeus: A Study in Ancient Religion.* Cambridge, 1914–40. 3 vols. in 5.

D'AGOSTINO, BRUNO. "Heraion del Sele." In: *Enciclopedia dell'Arte Antica Classica e Orientale,* VII. Rome, 1966.

DEUBNER, LUDWIG. *Attische Feste.* Berlin, 1932.

DIEHL, ERNST. *Anth. lyr.* See the abbreviations preceding this List of Works Cited.

——. "Nikainetos." *RE,* XVII:1.

DIELS, HERMANN. *Die Fragmente der Vorsokratiker.* 6th edn. edited by Walther Kranz. Berlin, 1951–52. 3 vols.

——. "Zeus." *ARW,* XXII (1923–24).

DION CHRYSOSTOMOS. *Dio Chrysostom,* III. With an English translation by J. W. Cohoon and H. Lamar Crosby. (LCL.) 1940.

DIOSKORIDES. *De materia medica.* Edited by M. Wellmann. Berlin, 1906–1914. 3 vols.

DITTENBERGER, WILHELM. *Sylloge Inscriptionum Graecarum*, III. 3d edn. Leipzig, 1920.

DREES, LUDWIG. *Olympia.* New York, 1968.

EDMONDS, JOHN MAXWELL (ed.). *The Fragments of Attic Comedy.* Leiden, 1957–61. 3 vols. in 4.

EILMANN, RICHARD. "Frühe griechische Keramik im Samischen Heraion." *AM*, LVIII (1933).

EISSFELDT, OTTO. *Molk als Opferbegriff im Punischen und Hebräischen, und das Ende des Gottes Moloch.* (Beiträge zur Religionsgeschichte des Altertums, 3.) Halle, 1935.

EITREM, SAMSON. "Hera." *RE*, VIII:1.

ELLIGER, W. (ed.). *Dio Chrysostomus: Sämtliche Reden.* (Bibliothek der Alten Welt.) Zurich, 1967.

ENNIUS. *Ennianae poesis reliquiae.* Edited by Johannes Vahlen. 3d edn. Leipzig, 1928. (Including *Annales.*)

ERATOSTHENES. *Eratosthenis Catasterismorum reliquiae.* Edited by Carl Robert. Berlin, 1878.

Etymologicum Magnum. Edited by Thomas Gaisford. Oxford, 1848.

EURIPIDES. *Scholia in Euripidem.* Edited by E. Schwartz. Berlin, 1887–91. 2 vols.

EUSEBIOS. *Praeparatio Evangelica.* Edited by Karl Mras. (GCS.) Berlin, 1954–56. 2 vols.

FARNELL, LEWIS RICHARD. *The Cults of the Greek States.* Oxford, 1896–1909. 5 vols.

FAURE, PAUL. *Fonctions des cavernes crétoises.* (École française d'Athènes.) Paris, 1964.

———. "Nouvelles recherches de spéléologie et de topographie Crétoises." *BCH*, LXXXIV (1960).

FAUTH, WOLFGANG. "Athena." In: *Der kleine Pauly*, I. Edited by K. Ziegler and W. Sontheimer. Stuttgart, 1964.

———. "El." In: *Der kleine Pauly*, II. Stuttgart, 1967.

———. "Kronos." In: *Der kleine Pauly*, III. Stuttgart, 1969.

FEHRLE, EUGEN. *Die kultische Keuschheit im Altertum.* Giessen, 1910.

FEHRLE, EUGEN. "Zeus." In: Roscher, *Lexikon*, VI.

FESTUS. *Sexti Pompei Festi. De verborum significatu quae supersunt cum Pauli epitome*. Edited by Wallace M. Lindsay. Leipzig, 1913.

FRAZER, JAMES GEORGE. See under PAUSANIAS.

FRICKENHAUS, AUGUST. *Tiryns*. Part I, *Die Hera von Tiryns*. Berlin, 1912.

FRIEDRICH, JOHANNES. *Hethitisches Wörterbuch*. Heidelberg, 1952.

FRISK, HJALMAR. *Griechisches etymologisches Wörterbuch*, I. Heidelberg, 1960.

FROBENIUS, LEO. *Der Kopf als Schicksal*. Munich, 1924.

FUNAIOLI, GINO. *Grammaticae romanae fragmenta*. Leipzig, 1907.

GALLAVOTTI, CARLO. *Documenti e struttura del greco nell'età micenea*. Rome, 1956.

———. "La triade lesbia in un testo miceneo." *Rivista di filologia*, N.S., XXXIV (1956).

GEORGIEV, VLADIMIR. "Mycénien et homérique: le problème du digamma." In: *Proceedings of the Cambridge Colloquium on Mycenaean Studies*. Edited by L. R. Palmer and J. Chadwick. Cambridge, 1966.

GEORGIUS SYNCELLUS. *G. Syncellus et Nicephorus*. (Corpus Scriptorum Historia Byzantinae, 7.) Edited by Wilhelm Dindorf. Bonn, 1829. 2 vols.

GÉRARD-ROUSSEAU, MONIQUE. *Les mentions religieuses dans les tablettes mycéniennes*. Rome, 1968.

GERKAN, ARMIN VON. See under WIEGAND, THEODOR (ed.).

GRUBEN, GOTTFRIED. *Die Tempel der Griechen*. Munich, 1966.

GUARDUCCI, MARGHERITA. "Dedica arcaica alla Hera di Posidonia." *Archeologia Classica*, IV (1952).

HAMP, ERIC P. "The Name of Demeter." *Minos*, IX (1968).

HAVERS, W. "Primitive Weltanschauung und Witterungsimpersonalia." *Wörter und Sachen*, XI (1928).

HEDEN, ERIK. *Homerische Götterstudien*. Uppsala, 1912.

HEISENBERG, WERNER. *Der Teil und das Ganze*. Munich, 1969.

HERRMANN, HANS-VOLKMAR. "Zur ältesten Geschichte von Olympia." *AM*, LXXVII (1962).

HESIOD. *Fragmenta Hesiodea*. Edited by Reinhold Merkelbach and M. L. West. Oxford, 1967.

———. *Hesiodi Carmina*. Edited by Aloisius Rzach. 3d edn. Leipzig, 1913.

———. Scholia. See under PROKLOS.

———. *Theogony*. Edited by M. L. West. Oxford, 1966.

HESYCHIOS. *Hesychii Alexandrini Lexicon post Joannen Albertum*. Edited by Moritz Schmidt. Jena, 1858–68. 5 vols.

HEUBECK, ALFRED. "Griechisch βασιλεύς und das Zeichen Nr. 16 in Linear B." *Indogermanische Forschungen*, LXIII (1957–58).

HITZIG, H., and H. BLUEMNER. *Pausaniae Graeciae descriptio*. Leipzig, 1896–1910. 3 vols. in 6.

HÖFER, O. "Polymnos." In: Roscher, *Lexikon*, III:2.

———. "Syzygia." In: Roscher, *Lexikon*, IV:2.

———. "Teleia, Teleios." In: Roscher, *Lexikon*, V.

HÖLDERLIN, FRIEDRICH. *Hölderlins Werke*. Edited by Anton Brieger. Salzburg, [1966].

HOFMANNSTHAL, HUGO VON. Preface to *Griechenland*, by Hans Holdt. Berlin, 1922.

HOMANN-WEDEKING, ERNST. "Samos 1963." *AA*, LXXIX (1964).

HOMER. *The Iliad of Homer*. Translated by Richmond Lattimore. (Phoenix Books.) Chicago, 1961.

———. *The Odyssey of Homer*. Translated by Richmond Lattimore. (Harper Torchbooks.) New York, 1968.

———. *Scholia graeca in Homeri Iliadem*. Edited by W. Dindorf and E. Maass. Oxford, 1874–88. 6 vols.

Homeric Hymns, The. Edited by Thomas W. Allen et al. 2d edn. Oxford, 1936.

HYPEREIDES. *Hyperidis Orationes sex cum ceterarum fragmentis*. Edited by F. Blass. 3d edn. Leipzig, 1894.

ILIEVSKI, P. H. "Two Notes on the FR-Tablets." *Minos*, VII (1961).

IMMERWAHR, WALTER. *Die Kulte und Mythen Arkadiens*, I. Leipzig, 1891.

ISLER, HANS PETER. *Acheloos. Eine Monographie*. Bern, 1970.

JACOBY, *FGrHist*. See the abbreviations preceding this List of Works Cited.

JAEGER, WERNER. *Diokles von Karystos*. 2d edn. Berlin, 1963.

JENSEN, ADOLF ELLEGARD. "Die drei Ströme." In: *Ergebnisse der Frobenius-Expedition 1937–38*, II. Edited by A. E. Jensen and H. Niggemeyer. Leipzig, 1948.

JÖRGENSEN, O. "Das Auftreten der Götter in den Büchern ι–μ der Odyssee." *Hermes*, XXXIX (1904).

JOHNSON, FRANKLIN P. "The 'Dragon-Houses' of Southern Euboea." *AJA*, XXIX (1925).

JUNG, C. G., and C. KERÉNYI. *Essays on a Science of Mythology: The Myth of the Divine Child and the Mysteries of Eleusis*. Translated by R. F. C. Hull. (Bollingen Series XXII.) New York, 1950. Princeton / Bollingen Paperback, 1969. (London, 1951; titled *Introduction to a Science of Mythology*.)

KÄHLER, HEINZ. *Der griechische Tempel: Wesen und Gestalt*. Berlin, 1964.

KALLIMACHOS. *Callimachus*. Edited by Rudolf Pfeiffer. Oxford, 1949–53. 2 vols. (Including the scholia.)

KARO, GEORG. "Tiryns." *RE* (2d Ser.), VI:2.

KAZANTZAKIS, NIKOS. *Report to Greco*. Translated by P. A. Bien. New York, 1965.

KELLER, OTTO. *Die antike Tierwelt*, II. Leipzig, 1913.

KERÉNYI, CARL (in some publications KARL). "Aidos und Themis." In: *Pro Regno, pro Sanctuario. Een Bundel Studies . . . voor Gerardus Van der Leeuw*. Edited by W. J. Kooiman and J. M. van Veen. Nijkerk, 1950.

——. *Die antike Religion*. 3d edn. Düsseldorf, 1952.

——. *Apollon: Studien über antike Religion und Humanität*. 3d edn. Düsseldorf, 1953.

——. *Asklepios: Archetypal Image of the Physician's Existence*. Translated by Ralph Manheim. New York (Bollingen Series LXV.3) and London, 1959. (Originally published in German as *Der göttliche Arzt*, 1947.)

——. *Bildtext einer italischen Vase in Giessen*. (Collection Latomus, 70.) Brussels, 1964.

——. *Dionysos: Archetypal Image of Indestructible Life*. Translated by Ralph Manheim. Princeton (Bollingen Series LXV.2) and London, 1976.

——. *Eleusis: Archetypal Image of Mother and Daughter*. Translated by Ralph Manheim. New York (Bollingen Series LXV.4) and London, 1967.

——. "Die Entstehung der olympischen Götterfamilie." *Paideuma*, IV (1950).

——. *The Gods of the Greeks*. Translated by Norman Cameron. London and New York, 1951. (Published simultaneously in German as *Die Mythologie der Griechen*; English version reprinted with different pagination in Pelican Books, Harmondsworth, 1958.)

——. *Griechische Grundbegriffe*. (Albae Vigiliae, N.S., XIX.) Zurich, 1964.

——. *Hermes der Seelenführer.* (Albae Vigiliae, N.S., I.) Zurich, 1944.

——. *The Heroes of the Greeks.* Translated by H. J. Rose. London, 1959; and New York, 1960. (Originally published in German as *Die Heroen der Griechen,* 1958.)

——. *Die Jungfrau und Mutter in der griechischen Religion: Eine Studie über Pallas Athene.* (Albae Vigiliae, N.S., XII.) Zurich, 1952.

——. "Licht, Wein, Honig: Die Frage nach dem minoischen Festkalender." *Kretika Chronika,* XV–XVI (1961–62), Part 1.

——. "Möglicher Sinn von *di-wo-nu-so-jo* und *da-da-re-jo-de.*" In: *Atti e memorie del 1. Congresso Internazionale di Micenologia,* II. Rome, 1967.

——. *Niobe: Neue Studien über antike Religion und Humanität.* Zurich, 1949.

——. *Prometheus: Archetypal Image of Human Existence.* Translated by Ralph Manheim. New York (Bollingen Series LXV.1) and London, 1963. (Originally published in German as *Prometheus: Die menschliche Existenz in griechischer Deutung,* 1959.)

——. *The Religion of the Greeks and Romans.* London, 1962. (A translation by Christopher Holme of *Die Religion der Griechen und Römer,* Munich, 1963. Both versions are based on *Die antike Religion,* originally published in 1940.)

——. "Die Sprache der Theologie und die Theologie der Sprache." *Areopag,* IV (1969).

——. *Töchter der Sonne.* Zurich, 1944.

——. *Umgang mit Göttlichem.* 2d edn. Göttingen, 1961.

——. "Varro über Samothrake und Ambrakia." In: *Studi in onore di Gino Funaioli.* Rome, 1955.

——. "A világfogat (Das Weltgespann)." *Egyetemes Philologiai Közlöny,* XLV (1921).

——. *Werke in Einzelausgaben.* Darmstadt and Munich, 1966 ff. 4 vols. to date. (I, *Humanistische Seelenforschung*; II, *Auf Spuren des Mythos*; III, *Tage- und Wanderbücher, 1953–1960*; VII, *Die antike Religion.*)

——. "Zeus und Hera: Der Kern der olympischen Götterfamilie." *Saeculum,* I (1950).

——, and C. G. JUNG. See under JUNG.

——, and HELLMUT SICHTERMANN. "Zeitlose Schieferbauten der Insel Andros." *Paideuma,* VIII (1962). (Text by Carl Kerényi, photographs by H. Sichtermann, drawings by Cornelia Kerényi.)

KERN, OTTO (ed.). *Orphicorum fragmenta*. Berlin, 1922.

KORNEMANN, ERNST. *Die Stellung der Frau in der vorgriechischen Mittelmeer-Kultur.* (Orient und Antike, 4.) Heidelberg, 1927.

KOUROUNIOTES, KONSTANTINOS. 'Ανασκαφαί Λυκαίου. In: 'Εφημερὶς 'Αρχαιολογική. 3d Ser. Athens, 1904.

KRAUSS, FRIEDRICH. "Paestum, Basilika. Der Entwurf des Grundrisses." In: *Festschrift Carl Weickert.* Berlin, 1955.

——, and REINHARD HERBIG. *Der korinthisch-dorische Tempel am Forum von Paestum.* (Denkmäler antiker Architektur, 7.) Berlin, 1939.

KRETSCHMER, PAUL. "Dyaus, Ζεύς, Diespiter und die Abstrakta im Indogermanischen." *Glotta*, XIII (1924).

——. "Zur Geschichte der griechischen Dialekte." *Glotta*, I (1909).

KUNZE, EMIL. *Berichte über die Ausgrabungen in Olympia*, VII. Berlin, 1961.

——. "Zeusbilder in Olympia." In: *Antike und Abendland*, II. Hamburg, 1946.

LACTANTIUS, L. CAELIUS FIRMIANUS. [Works.] Edited by S. Brandt and G. von Laubmann. (CSEL, XXIX.) Vienna, 1890. (Including *Divinae institutiones*.)

LASSERRE, FRANÇOIS. "Aux origines de l'Anthologie: I." *Rheinisches Museum*, CII (1959).

LATTERMANN, HEINRICH, and F. HILLER VON GAERTRINGEN. "Stymphalos." *AM*, XL (1915).

LIDDELL, H. G., R. SCOTT, and H. S. JONES. *A Greek-English Lexicon*. 9th edn. Oxford, 1940.

LIVY. *The War with Hannibal: Books XXI–XXX of "The History of Rome from its Foundation."* Translated by Aubrey de Sélincourt. (Penguin Classics.) Harmondsworth, 1965.

LUCIAN. *Scholia*. Edited by Hugo Rabe. Leipzig, 1906.

MAGNIEN, V. "Le mariage chez les Grecs anciens: L'Initiation nuptiale." *L'Antiquité Classique*, V (1936).

MALINOWSKI, BRONISLAW. *Myth in Primitive Psychology*. New York, 1926.

——. *The Sexual Life of Savages in North-Western Melanesia*. 2d edn. London, 1932.

MARINATOS, SPYRIDON. "Die Wanderung des Zeus." *AA*, LXXVII (1962).

MATT, LEONARD VON, and U. ZANOTTI-BIANCO. *Grossgriechenland*. Würzburg, 1961.

MENANDER. [Fragments.] In: EDMONDS, J. M. (ed.), q.v.

METTE, HANS J. (ed.). *Supplementum Aeschyleum*. Berlin, 1939.

MICHEL, CHARLES. *Recueil d'Inscriptions grecques.* Paris, 1900.

Milet. See WIEGAND, THEODOR (ed.).

MONTUORO. See ZANCANI MONTUORO, PAOLA.

MOSCATI, SABATINO. "Il sacrificio dei fanciulli." *Rendiconti della Pontificia Accademia Romana di Archeologia,* XXXVIII (1967).

MÜHLESTEIN, HUGO. *Die oka-Tafeln von Pylos.* Basel, 1956.

———. "Panzeus in Pylos." *Minos,* IV (1956).

———. Review of *Inscriptiones Pyliae,* by C. Gallavotti and A. Sacconi. *Gnomon,* XXXV (1963).

MÜLLER, KARL OTFRIED. *Geschichten Hellenischer Stämme und Städte.* 2d edn. Breslau, 1844. 3 vols.

———. *Prolegomena zu einer wissenschaftlichen Mythologie,* Göttingen, 1825. New edn. edited by C. Kerényi. Darmstadt, 1970.

NAPOLI, MARIO. *Il Museo di Paestum.* Cava de' Tirreni, 1970.

———. *Paestum.* Novara, 1970.

NAUCK, *TGF.* See the abbreviations preceding this List of Works Cited.

NILSSON, MARTIN PERSSON. *Die Entstehung und religiöse Bedeutung des griechischen Kalenders.* 2d edn. Lund, 1962.

———. *Geschichte der griechischen Religion.* (*Handbuch der Altertumswissenschaft,* V:2:i, ii.) Munich, 1941–50. 2d edn., 1955–61. 2 vols. (Unless otherwise indicated, the second edition is referred to.)

———. *Griechische Feste.* Leipzig, 1906.

———. *The Mycenaean Origin of Greek Mythology.* Berkeley, 1932.

———. "Vater Zeus." In: *Opuscula selecta,* II. Lund, 1952.

———. "Wedding Rites in Ancient Greece." In: *Opuscula selecta,* III. Lund, 1960.

NORDEN, EDUARD. *P. Vergilius Maro: Aeneis Buch VI.* 3d edn. Leipzig and Berlin, 1926.

OHLEMUTZ, ERWIN. *Die Kulte und Heiligtümer der Götter in Pergamon.* Würzburg and Giessen, 1940.

OHLY, DIETER. "Die Göttin und ihre Basis." *AM,* LXVIII (1953).

———. "Holz." *AM,* LXVIII (1953).

OPPERMANN, HANS (ed.). *Humanismus.* (Wege der Forschung, XVII.) Darmstadt, 1970.

ORTH, E. "Stier." *RE* (2d Ser.), III:2.

OTTO, WALTER FRIEDRICH. *Das Wort der Antike*. Stuttgart, 1962.

OVERBECK, JOHANNES ADOLF. *Beiträge zur Erkenntnis und Kritik der Zeusreligion*. Leipzig, 1861.

PALMER, LEONARD R. *The Interpretation of Mycenaean Greek Texts*. Oxford, 1963.

———. *Mycenaeans and Minoans*. London, 1961.

PAUSANIAS. *Pausanias's Description of Greece*. Translated with a commentary by James George Frazer. London, 1898. 6 vols.

———. See also under HITZIG, H., and H. BLUEMNER (eds.).

PAYNE, HUMPHREY, et al. *Perachora: the Sanctuaries of Hera Akraia and Limenia*. Oxford, 1940.

PHILIPPSON, PAULA. *Thessalische Mythologie*. Zurich, 1944.

PICCALUGA, GIULIA. *Lykaon. Un tema mitico*. Rome, 1968.

PINDAR. *Pindari Carmina cum fragmentis*. Edited by Cecil Maurice Bowra. (OCT.) 2d edn. Oxford, 1947.

———. *Scholia Vetera in Pindari Carmina*. Edited by A. B. Drachmann. Leipzig, 1903–1927. 3 vols.

PLUTARCH. *Moralia*. Edited, with an English translation, by F. C. Babbitt and H. N. Fowler. (LCL.) 1927 ff. 14 vols. (Including *Coniugalia praecepta*, *De facie quae in orbe lunae apparet*, and *Quaestiones graecae*.)

———. *Parallel Lives*. With an English translation by B. Perrin. (LCL.) 1914–26. 11 vols. (Including *Pyrrhus* and *Theseus*.)

PÖTSCHER, WALTER. "Hera und Heros." *Rheinisches Museum*, CIV (1961).

———. "Der Name der Göttin Hera." *Rheinisches Museum*, CVIII (1965).

POWELL, JOHANNES U. *Collectanea Alexandrina*. Oxford, 1925.

PROKLOS. *Procli Diadochi in Platonis Timaeum commentaria*. Edited by Ernst Diehl. Leipzig, 1903–1906. 3 vols.

———. *Proclus Diadochus: Commentarium in Platonis Parmenidem*. Edited by G. Stallbaum. Hildesheim, 1961.

———. *Scholium in Hesiodi Opera et dies*. In: Thomas Gaisford (ed.). *Poetae minores graeci*, III. Leipzig, 1823.

PROTT, JOHANNES DE, and LUDWIG ZIEHEN (eds.). *Leges graecorum sacrae e titulis collectae*. Leipzig, 1896–1902. 2 vols.

PUGLIESE CARRATELLI, GIOVANNI. "Riflessi di culti micenei nelle tabelle di Cnosso e Pilo." In: *Studi in onore di Ugo Enrico Paoli*. Florence, 1955.

PUHVEL, JAAN. "Eleuther and Oinoatis: Dionysiac Data from Mycenaean Greece." In: *Mycenaean Studies, Wingspread, 1961: Proceedings of the Third International Colloquium for Mycenaean Studies*. Edited by E. L. Bennett, Jr. Madison, 1964.

REITZENSTEIN, RICHARD. *Hellenistische Wundererzählungen*. 2d edn. Darmstadt, 1963.

ROBERT, CARL. *Die griechische Heldensage*, I. Berlin, 1920.

ROSCHER, WILHELM H. *Juno und Hera*. (Studien zur vergleichenden Mythologie der Griechen und Römer, II.) Leipzig, 1875.

———, *Lexikon*. See the abbreviations preceding this List of Works Cited.

RUIJGH, C. J. "Sur le nom de Poseidon." *Revue des Études Grecques*, LXXX (1967).

SÄFLUND, GÖSTA. *Excavations at Berbati, 1936–37*. Stockholm, 1965.

SÄFLUND, MARIE-LOUISE. *The East Pediment of the Temple of Zeus at Olympia*. (Studies in Mediterranean Archaeology, 27.) Göteborg, 1970.

SCHACHERMEYR, FRITZ. *Poseidon und die Entstehung des griechischen Götterglaubens*. Bern, 1950.

———. "Zum Problem der griechischen Einwanderung." In: *Atti e Memorie del 1. Congresso Internazionale di Micenologia*, III. Rome, 1967.

SCHEFFEL, HELMUT. "Eine antike Opferstätte auf dem Olymp." *AM*, XLVII (1922).

SCHLIEMANN, HEINRICH. *Mykenae*. Leipzig, 1878.

SCHOELL, R., and G. STUDEMUND (eds.). *Anecdota varia Graeca et Latina*. Leipzig, 1886. 2 vols.

SCHRÖDER, F. R. "Hera." *Gymnasium*, LXIII (1956).

SCHWENN, FRIEDRICH. *Die Menschenopfer bei den Griechen und Römern*. Giessen, 1915.

SERVIUS. *Servii Grammatici qui feruntur in Vergilii Bucolica et Georgica commentarii*. Edited by Georg Thilo. Leipzig, 1887.

SESTIERI, PELLEGRINO C. "Iconographie et culte d'Héra à Paestum." *La Revue des Arts*, V (1955).

———. "Ricerche Posidoniati." *Mélanges d'archéologie et d'histoire* (Écoles françaises d'Athènes et de Rome), LXVII (1955).

SESTIERI, PELLEGRINO C. "Il sacello-heroon Posidoniate." *Bollettino d'Arte*, XL (1955).

———. "Il sacello ipogeico di Paestum." *La Parola del Passato*, XI (1956).

———. "Statua fittile di Posidonia." *Bollettino d'Arte*, XL (1955).

SIEBS, THEODOR. "Die sogenannten subjektlosen Sätze." *Zeitschrift für vergleichende Sprachforschung*, XLIII (1910).

SIMON, ERIKA. *Die Götter der Griechen.* Munich, 1969.

SONTHEIMER, WALTHER. "Monat." *RE*, XVI:1.

SOPHOKLES. *The Fragments of Sophocles.* Edited by A. C. Pearson. Cambridge, 1917.

SORANUS. *Gynaecia.* Edited by Valentino Rose. Leipzig, 1882.

STEFFEN, V. *Karten von Mykenai.* Berlin, 1884.

STELLA, LUIGIA ACHILLEA. *La civiltà micenea nei documenti contemporanei.* Rome, 1965.

———. "La religione greca nei testi micenei." *Numen*, V (1958).

STEPHEN OF BYZANTIUM. *Ethnicorum quae supersunt.* Edited by August Meineke. Berlin, 1849.

STOOP, J. M. W. *Floral Figurines from South Italy.* Leiden diss., 1960.

STRABO. *The Geography.* With an English translation by H. L. Jones. (LCL.) 1917–32. 8 vols.

Suidae Lexicon. Edited by Ada Adler. Leipzig, 1928–35. 5 vols.

SZONDI, LIPOT. *Schicksalsanalyse.* 2d edn. Basel, 1948.

TACITUS. *The Germania of Tacitus.* Edited by Rodney P. Robinson. (American Philological Association Monographs, 5.) Middletown, Conn., 1935.

THEOKRITOS. *Scholia in Theocritum vetera.* Edited by C. Wendel. Leipzig, 1914.

USENER, HERMANN. *Kleine Schriften*, IV. Leipzig and Berlin, 1913.

VAN WINDEKENS, A. J. " ῾Ηρα '(die) junge Kuh, (die) Färse.' " *Glotta*, XXXVI (1958).

VATIN, CLAUDE. *Recherches sur le mariage et la condition de la femme à l'époque hellenistique.* (Bibliothèque des écoles françaises d'Athènes et de Rome.) Paris, 1970.

VENTRIS, MICHAEL, and JOHN CHADWICK. *Documents in Mycenaean Greek.* Cambridge, 1959.

VIRGIL. *The Works of Virgil.* With a Commentary by John Conington and Henry Nettleship. 3d edn. Hildesheim, 1963. 3 vols. (Including *Georgics* and *Aeneid*.)

List of Works Cited

———. Scholia. See under SERVIUS.

VITRUVIUS. *On Architecture.* Translated by Frank Granger. (LCL.) 1931–34. 2 vols.

WACKERNAGEL, JACOB. *Vorlesungen über Syntax*, I. 2d edn. Basel, 1926.

WALDSTEIN, CHARLES. *The Argive Heraeum*, I. Boston and New York, 1902.

WALTER, HANS. *Das griechische Heiligtum.* Munich, 1965.

WELCKER, FRIEDRICH GOTTLIEB. *Griechische Götterlehre*, I. Göttingen, 1857.

WENIGER, LUDWIG. "Das Hochfest des Zeus in Olympia." *Klio*, V (1905).

WIEGAND, THEODOR. "Die angebliche Urtempel auf der Ocha." *AM*, XXI (1896).

——— (ed.). *Königliche Museen zu Berlin. Milet.* Part I:3, *Das Delphinion in Milet.* Edited by Georg Kawerau et al. Berlin, 1914. Part I:4, *Der Poseidonaltar bei Kap Monodendri.* Edited by Armin von Gerkan. Berlin, 1915.

WILAMOWITZ-MOELLENDORFF, ULRICH VON. *Der Glaube der Hellenen.* Berlin, 1931–32. 2 vols.

———. *Griechische Tragödien.* Berlin, 1899, 1900. 2 vols.

———. "Hephaistos." In: *Kleine Schriften*, V:2. Berlin, 1962.

———. "Zeus." In: *Vorträge 1923–1924 der Bibliothek Warburg*, III. Leipzig, 1926.

ZANCANI MONTUORO, PAOLA. "Heraion alla foce di Sele." *Atti e memorie della Società Magna Grecia*, N.S., V (1964).

———. "Paestum." In: *Enciclopedia dell'Arte Antica Classica e Orientale*, V. Rome, 1963.

———. "Il Poseidonion di Poseidonia." *Archivio storico per la Calabria e la Lucania*, XXIII (1954).

———. In: *Santuari di Magna Grecia.* (Atti del quarto Convegno di studi sulla Magna Grecia.) Naples, 1965.

———, and U. ZANOTTI-BIANCO. "Capaccio. Heraion alla foce del Sele." *Notizie degli Scavi di Antichità*, 6th Ser., XIII (1937).

———. *Heraion alla foce del Sele*, I. Rome, 1951.

ZIEHEN, LUDWIG. "Olympia." *RE*, XVII:2–XVIII:1.

ZIMMERMANN, HERBERT. "Das ursprüngliche Geschlecht von *dies*." *Glotta*, XIII (1924).

INDEX

INDEX

A superior figure (e.g., 194[4]) indicates a note on the page cited. When a reference appears in both text and note on the same page, only the page is cited.

A

Achaians, 169
Acheloos, 89[113]
Adler, A., 157[37]
Admete, 153
Aegean islands, 58
Aelian, 157[38]
Aeneas, 125
Agamemnon, 41, 56
Agathokles, 23[9]
Agropoli, 168[68], 175
Ahura Mazda, 111
Aigina, 6, 154[21]
Aigisthos, 94[8]
Aigosthena, 25[20]
Aiolians, 22, 76[62]
Aischylos, 24[17]
Akrisios, 115[8]
Akropolis (Athens), 108, 109
Akusilaos, 96[13]
Alalkomenai, 115[7], 143, 144
Alkaios, 114[2]
Alkmene, 55, 137
Alpheios River, 87, 132
altar, 29, 136 (Herakles), 150; cult, 151; see also under deities' names
Altheim, F., 26[28], 175[92]
Amazon, 153
Amphitrite, 86, 89
Amphitryon, 55
Anakreon, 156[31], 157
Anaxandrides, 107
ancestor (forefather), 75, 76, 80, 89
Andros, 141
animal: frieze, 151; husband, 66, 71, 72, 81, 85, 89; sacred, 127, 170, 173[86]; sacrificial, 33, 70–76, 79, 127, 133, 135, 139, 140, 142, 158; sea, 86; symbolic, 69, 85
Anthos, 35[65]
anthropology, 52, 81, 88

anthropomorphism, 39, 59, 66, 103, 130
Antoninus Liberalis, 32[50]
Aphrodite, 59, 97, 99, 103, 112, 173
Apollo, xv, xvii[9], 24[17], 34[56], 51–56, 62, 74, 76, 95, 145, 173[86]
Apollonios (month), 139
Apollonius Rhodius, 23[8], 140[106], 156[28], 159[42], 173[86]
aporrheton, 118–19; see also secret, s.v. tale
Arcadia, 24, 27–28, 33, 35, 37, 78, 79, 82, 83, 87–89, 128, 143
archaeology/excavation, xi, 29, 42, 74, 119–120[20 24 25], 128, 132, 134, 140–141, 150, 153–154, 162[52], 163, 166, 168, 170–171, 174, 177–178; see also Mycenaea(n), s.v. Greek texts/tablets
archetypal images/archetypes, xii–xiii, xvi–xvii, 24, 26, 46, 49–50, 51, 53, 56, 66, 67, 69, 89–90, 92, 98, 114, 130, 159
Areios Didymos, 104[36]
Ares, 56, 96[14]
aretalogies, 152
Argolis, 55, 122, 137
Argonauts, 152, 168
Argos, 27, 55, 57, 58, 98, 102, 108, 109, 110, 114–128, 131, 134, 135, 137, 152, 153, 167, 168, 173, 178
Arion, 88
Aristokles, 110[62]
Aristophanes, 140[109], 157[37]
Aristotle, 31, 66[21], 131, 156[29 30]
Arnim, H. von, 129[71]
Artemidoros, 91[3]
Artemis, 51, 53, 78–79, 95, 159; statue of, 163-164
Asia, 40, 127
Asia Minor, 29, 58, 76[62], 87[108], 163
Asopos River, 145
Assyrians, 93

199

Index

Asterion, 119, 120–121, 143, 156
Åström, P., 174[66]
Athena, xv, 46, 49, 53, 59, 63, 108, 115[7], 126, 143, 144, 145, 174; Hippia, 85
Athenaios, 109[58], 152[10, 14], 157[32]
Athens/Athenian, xvii, 18, 20, 25, 72, 73–74, 104, 105–108, 109, 122[30], 126, 129[71], 131
Atreus, house of, 41–42, 94
Attica, 68, 81, 82, 97, 107[51], 108, 140, 145, 178
Augustine, 130[72]
Avellino, F. M., 175[93]
Avestan, 18

B

Babylonia, 40
bath, 98, 119, 126, 131, 143, 146, 153, 164–165, 167, 175, 178
bed of Hera, 100–102, 127, 166, 177–179
bees, 33
Bel, 111
Bérard, V., 37[73]
Berbati, 120[24], 121
Bible, 37[73]
Bieber, M., 107[51]
binding of goddess, 163–164
birth myths, 88; of Aphrodite, 59; of Hera, 153–154, 155, 159; of Zeus, 23, 27, 28, 32–33, 36
Bischoff, E., 22[2]
bisexuality, 112–113
Blegen, C. W., 120[25], 132[79]
Blomé, B., 174[88]
Bluemner, H., 119[19]
Boeotia, 25[19], 68, 79, 87, 132, 139, 140, 141–147, 155
Bolkestein, H., 104[38]
Bosshardt, E., 44[13]
Bouphonia, 72
Bowra, C. M., 41[6]
bride, 101, 126, 143, 164, 165; Hera as, 98, 145–146, 179; human, 109; becomes wife, 165; of Zeus, 109, 157, 176, 177
bridegroom (Zeus), 146, 179
bronze(s), 7, 55, 135, 138, 178
brother, 45, 61, 139; archetypal, 67; hate, 60; mother's, 47, 52

brother-husband, 51, 91–113, 129; *see also under* Zeus
brother-sister: couple, 53, 92, 95, 96, 162; love-making, 112, 123; marriage, 93–94, 96, 101, 109–113
Bruchmann, K. F. H., xv
Brugmann, K., 10
Buber, M., 37[73]
Buerchner, L., 140[107]
bull, 27[30], 69–74, 80, 81, 85, 86, 142; game, 70, 87
Buschor, E., 149, 150[2, 5], 152[12], 154, 160[46], 162[52], 164[56]

C

calendar, 22–23, 32, 33, 73, 77, 82–83, 105, 121, 131, 139, 142, 151[7], 161[47]; *see also names of Greek months*: Apollonios; Gamelion; Hekatombaion; Kronion; Parthenios
Calhoun, G. M., 46[20], 52[32]
Cape Colonne, 169
Cappadocia, 110
Carthaginians, 35
cattle, 27[30], 73, 74, 80, 127, 133, 135, 140, 142, 146, 169
cave, 23, 27[30], 28–29, 31, 32–33
Ceram, *see* Wemale
Ceres, 175
Chadwick, J., 24[16], 44[13], 64[15], 77[37], 81[58]
chain, world, 49
Chaironeia, 108[54]
Chaos, 95, 99
chapel, 27[30], 120, 141
charioteer myth, 103
child: divine, 28, 102; mysterious, 88; sacrifice, 35–37
childbirth, 28, 52, 59, 89, 173
Christians/Christian, xvi, 11, 27[30], 104, 165
Chrysippos, 129[71]
Clement of Alexandria, 125[60]
clouds, 15, 102, 103, 141
coadjutors of Great Mother, 173[86]
Collitz, H., 176[94]
colonization, 36, 169
Cook, A.B., xv, 27[30], 34[55], 35[62], 106[47], 137[97]
Corinth, 84, 86, 109, 119

cosmic/cosmogonic theme, xi, 96, 102, 112, 114, 179
cosmology, 40
couple: archetypal, xii, xvi, 51, 53, 57, 92, 104, 130; divine, 110, 133, 162, 166 (statue); d. child, 102; human, xii, xvi, 98, 101, 104–107; supreme divine, 93, 99, 130
cow, see cattle
Crete, 21–33, 70–72, 87, 123, 173[66], 176
Creuzer, F., 7, 8
cuckoo, 123–124, 166[65]
cult: and altar, 116, 151; image, 156, 158, 161–162, 171, 174, 176; see also statues, cult; objects, 150, 153, 154; and religion, xvi, 11; and temple, 117, 148, 150; see also under names of deities

D

Da, 64, 66
D'Agostino, B., 170[72]
Daidala (festival), 142–146; *daidala* (wooden statues), 162
daimon, 9–10, 16–18, 93, 173[56]
Daktyls, Idaean, 28, 136–138, 139, 173[66]
Danaë, 55
dance, 130, 141
dark god, 24[17], 88, 89
darkness, 28, 34, 36, 91, 103, 108, 126, 131, 143, 144
daughter, 53, 111, 119, 120, 156; see also under names of deities
Delos, 145
Delphi, xvii[9], 19
Demeter, 27[30], 78, 83, 85, 87–88, 93, 107, 108[54], 126, 133, 157, 159; daughter of, 79, 88
Demosthenes, 106[48]
Despoina, 78–79, 82, 84, 85, 87–89
Deubner, L., 73[61], 105[44], 108[56]
Dia, 26, 57, 58
Diana, 26[28]
Diehl, E., 114[2], 156[81], 157[83]
Diels, H., 3–9, 13[25], 16[32], 131[76]
Dikte, Mount, 23, 28
Diodorus Siculus, 27, 87[106], 139[104]
Diokles, 131
Dion Chrysostomos, 102–103, 126
Dione, 26, 58

Dionysos, xv, 24[17], 27, 28, 58, 66, 72, 82, 100, 125, 178; religion of, xi, 25, 26, 30, 145
Dioskorides, 157
Dirphys, Mount, 140
Dittenberger, L., 104[40]
Divia, 26, 27
Dodona, 5, 6, 26, 58
Dombart, B., 130[72]
Dorian(s), 38, 73, 116
doubles of Hera, 96[14]
dove, 173
dream, 12–13, 91–92
Drees, L., 132[79]
dynasty, 50, 94, 110; divine, 44, 51, 54

E

eagle, 166
earthquake, 65, 67, 72
Edmonds, J. M., 107[50]
Egypt(ian), 40, 42, 101, 110
Eileithyia, 96[14], 173
Eilmann, R., 154, 161[47], 166[64]
Eissfeldt, O., 35[67], 37[72]
Eitrem, S., 129[71], 140[108]
El (god), 36–37, 73, 132
Eleusis, 58, 78, 79, 82–84, 87, 88, 104, 108, 118
Eleuther, 25–26
Eleutherai, 25
Elias, St., 141
Elias Berbatiotikos, 120, 122
Elis, 134[85]
Elliger, W., 103[37]
Empedokles, 131
Enipeus, 75
Ennius, 45[17]
enthroned: Hera, 118, 123, 124–125, 135, 138, 172; Zeus, 176
Ephoros, 87[106]
epic, 43, 45, 48, 74, 100
Epimenides, 32
Epiphany, 30, 71, 81, 120, 138, 152, 153, 172
Epiros, 47
Eratosthenes, 97[15]
Erinyes, 45
Eros, 95
Ethiopia, 34

Index 202

Etruscan picture, 178
Etymologicum Magnum, 73[49], 74[52], 87[107]
etymology, 4, 34, 64[14], 115
Euboea, 109, 116, 122, 129[68], 140–141, 144, 145
Euphorion, 129[71]
Euripides, 11, 14[28], 71, 76[62], 91[1], 97[15], 119[19], 126[54]
Europa, 30, 71
Eurymedon, 129[71]
Eurystheus, 153
Eusebios, 142[115]

F

family: archetypal, 26, 59; matriarchal, *see* matriarchal order; Olympian divine, xii, 15, 24–27, 37, 38–59, 61, 90, 91, 95; patriarchal, *see* patriarchal order
Farnell, L. R., xiv–xv, 61, 68[24], 87[108], 146
fate, 17–18
father, 52, 95, 120, 121; archetypal, xiii, xvii, 46, 59, 60, 67, 89–90, 91–92; procreative, 45, 54, 98; *see also under* Poseidon; Zeus
fatherless birth, 46, 54, 56, 96[14]
Faure, P., 23[7], 27[30]
Fauth, W., 36[68, 69], 73[50], 85[101]
Fehrle, E., 16[32], 60[1], 157[34]
fertility, 96–97, 132[78], 159
festival, 22, 27, 73, 74[51], 82, 83, 84[95], 89, 99, 126, 139, 141; *see also under* Hera
Festus Paulus, 130[73]
figurines, 132, 136–137, 138, 170
fire god, 46
Frazer, J. G., 33[58]
freeing water, 118, 119
Freud, S., xiii
Frickenhaus, A., 121[28], 137[97, 98]
Friedrich, J., 12[23]
Frisk, H., 4, 18[39]
Frobenius, L., 98
Funaioli, G., 165[60]

G

Gaia/Ge, 59, 64, 95, 107, 117
Gaisford, T., 105[16]
Gallavotti, C., 25[17, 18]
Gamelia (festival), 105, 109
Gamelion (month), 105, 131

games, 117, 129[71]; *see also* Olympic games
Gamos, *see* wedding ceremony (Gamos)
genealogy, xvii, 76, 95–96, 155
Georgiev, V., 26[27], 64[14]
Georgius Syncellus, 153[16]
Gérard-Rousseau, M., 24[15]
Gerkan, A. von, 117[13]
Gestalt, Hera's, 56, 93
goddess: pairs, 78, 83; supreme, 108, 147; threefold, 119, 121, 145, 156; *see also* trinities
god(s): assembly of, 40–42, 44, 46, 48; family of, *see* family *s.v.* Olympian divine; grouping of, 22, 39, 40; Homeric, 17, 25, 29, 39, 42, 58; state of, *see* state, Olympian divine; supreme, 15, 30, 35, 36; *see also under* Zeus
Goethe, 7
Great Goddess, 78, 82, 84, 85, 89, 93, 112, 157; Aphrodite, 59; Hera, 27, 54, 119, 148, 156; Rhea, 29; Themis, 41
Great Mother, 29, 59, 172–173
Greek language, xi–xv, 4–6, 9–12, 16–17, 21, 22, 34, 44, 64–65, 83–84, 131
Greek light, 14
Greek philosophy, xii, xvii[9], 5
Greek religion: as correlation, xi, xiii, xvi, 6, 11, 13, 21, 37, 38–39, 47, 50, 92, 114, 148; growth of, 21–27, 30, 58–59, 92–93, 123, 132–135; history of, xi–xvii, 3, 7–9, 11–12, 16–17, 19, 33, 38–40, 42–44, 50–51, 60–62, 65–66, 69–70, 96–97, 114, 127, 128[65], 133, 179
Greeks, earliest existence of, 5, 6, 13, 18, 21, 27, 38, 47
Gruben, G., 118[14], 151[6]
Guarducci, M., 176[96]
Guthrie, W. K. C., 82[88]
gynecologists, 131

H

Hades, 61, 125, 174
Hadrian, 108
hair, 80, 135
Hamp, E. P., 64[14]
Havers, W., 10[14]
Hebe, 96[14]
hecatomb, 62, 70–76, 127, 139, 140, 161
Heden, E., 17[37]

Index

Heisenberg, W., xvii
Hekate, 79
Hekatombaia (festival), 73
Hekatombaion (month), 73
Helikon, Mount, 69[34]
Helios, 15
Helladic periods, 38, 132
Hellenes, 5, 6, 7, 139
Hellespont, 19
Hephaistos, 41, 46, 51, 56, 96[11], 129[71]
Hera: archetypal woman and wife, 51, 56, 59, 67, 98, 114, 128–132, 136;
   altars: 116–117, 120[20], 133, 134, 145, 146, 150–151, 154, 161, 166, 169, 170–171, 175;
   association with moon: 117–118, 121–122, 124–128, 130–132, 134, 138–139, 148, 159, 162; birth: 153–154, 155, 159; character (Gestalt): 56, 93;
   cults: xii, 56, 57, 97, 109; Argos, 98, 102, 108, 110, 114–128, 135; Boeotia, 141–146; Euboea, 140–141; Karia, 159; Mount Kithairon, 162; Olympia, 132–139, 169; Paestum, 171–179; Samos, 110, 148–167, 169; Stymphalos, 128–132; Tiryns, 137[97];
   daughters: of H., 94, 96[11]; H. as eldest daughter, 56;
   epithets: Akraia, 119–120, 122, 124, 167; Antheia, 155–156, 177; Bunaia, 119[10]; Chera, 129, 131, 167; "cow-eyed," 128; Dirphya, 140; Euboia, 119, 120, 127, 140, 167; Hippia, 133; Imbrasia, 159; Leukolenos, 120[20], 131[78]; Limenia, 119[10], 131; Pais, 129, 167, 175, 176; Parthenia, 156, 159–160, 165; Parthenos, 122, 129; Prosymna, 119, 120, 124–126, 164, 167; Teleia, 98, 104, 108, 109, 122, 129, 145, 167; Toneia, 164;
   festivals: 99, 102, 104–105, 116, 119, 122, 131, 152, 157, 159[11], 179[100]; see also Daidala; Gamelia; Heraia; wedding ceremony (Gamos); H. as mother: 46, 51, 114, 172–173;
   myths: xii, 56, 63–64, 97, 99, 110, 118–119, 122–124, 129, 135, 140, 145, 149, 155–156, 159–160; name: 24, 114–115, 119, 137, 140, 155; H. as playmate of Zeus: 129[71], 160; see also lovemaking s.v. of Zeus and H.; H. as queen of heaven: 109, 110, 121, 125, 127, 135, 160[15], 168, 178;
   religion: 100; Argos, 110, 114–128, 168; Boeotia, 142–147; Euboea, 140–141; Olympia, 132–139; Poestum, 148, 168–179; Samos, 110, 148–167; Stymphalos, 128–132; relationship to r. of Zeus, 26–27, 51, 57, 133–137, 138, 166, 176, 179; spread of, 115, 123, 139–140, 144, 148, 152, 155, 159, 167–171, 175;
   sanctuaries: 115; Argos, 27, 55, 58, 152, 178; Kroton, 169; Samos, 149, 152–154, 166–167; Paestum, 167–168, 177; Perachora, 109;
   separation (withdrawal) from Zeus: 114, 124–125, 129, 143–144, 160, 162, 178; sons of H.: 24–25, 46, 56, 129[71]; statues: 118–119, 123, 124, 125, 126, 135, 138, 141, 142, 143–144, 146, 147, 152, 153, 165, 166, 172; see also cult s.v. image; H. the supreme goddess: 147;
   temples: 127; Argive Heraion, 115–128, 134, 137, 140, 150, 155–156, 160, 165–166, 167, 168, 170, 179; in Athens, 108–109; Basilica (Paestum), 171, 174, 176; Classical (Paestum), 171, 175, 176; Doric (Paestum), 134, 171, 174; in Hermione, 122–124; Italic (Paestum), 174; in Kroton, 169; Ionic (Paestum), 161, 171; on Mount Kithairon, 145; on Mount Oche, 140; in Olympia, 134, 135, 138; in Paestum, 122, 148, 171, 174–176, 178–179; in Perachora, 131; in Samos, 122, 148, 154, 157, 161–162, 168; by the Sele estuary, 170–171, 174; in Sparta, 115[8]; in Stymphalos, 128–132; in Tiryns, 137;
   underworld aspect of H.: 125–126, 129[71], 171–172, 174, 175, 178; H. as wife of Zeus: 26, 92–110, 113, 123, 129, 130; see also union, s.v. of Zeus and H.; wedding ceremony (Gamos)
Heraia (festival), 27, 134, 140, 152, 164, 165
Herakles, 19, 55, 96[11], 136–139, 153, 178
Heraklion, 72, 173[86]

Index

Herbig, R., 174[88]
Hermes, 41, 81, 155
Hermione, 110[62], 122–124, 129[68], 166[65]
Herodotos, 19, 75[81]
heroes, 31–32, 42–43, 54–55, 75, 89, 100, 137, 138, 174, 177
heroines, 89
Herrmann, H.-V., 133[82], 135[90], 138[101]
Hesiod, xvii, 5, 17[36], 25[19], 41[6], 46, 51[30], 56[42], 59, 69[34], 70, 79, 95, 96, 105[46]
Hesychios, 47[25], 105[44], 127[59], 129[71]
Heubeck, A., 44[13]
hieros gamos, see under marriage
hieros logos, see sacred story
Hiller von Gaertringen, F., 128[68]
Hippokrene spring, 69[34]
hippomorphism, 69, 86, 87
Hittites, 12
Hitzig, H., 119[19]
Höfer, O., 98[20], 126[52]
Hofmannsthal, H. von, 14
Hölderlin, F., 18
Holdt, H., 14
Homann-Wedeking, E., 154[19]
Homer, 5[6], 6, 12, 15, 17, 18, 25, 29, 30–31, 34[55], 38–59, 60–64, 70, 73, 74–77, 81, 86, 92–93, 95, 96–97, 99–102, 104, 108, 109, 112, 114, 115, 124, 127[64], 129, 133, 135, 137, 138, 160[45]; and creation of Olympian divine family, 43, 50, 56, 58–59
homogastrioi, 94, 109, 110
honey, 33, 178
horns, 72[41], 127–128
horse, 61, 67–69, 81, 86, 88; breeding, 68, 86, 87
Humboldt, W. von, 7
husband, 50, 64–68, 85, 92, 98, 160; archetypal, 51, 66–67, 88, 90, 92; as father, 52; not father, 67; *see also* brother-husband; *and under names of deities*
Hypereides, 145[121]
Hypnos, 100

I

Ida, Mount, 28, 100
Idaean Cave, 28
Ilievski, P. H., 22[4]

Illyrians, 47
Imbrasos, 154, 155, 156, 158, 160, 161, 166, 167
Immerwahr, W., 35[52]
immortality, 32–34
incest, 53, 94, 109, 110, 111–113
indecent behavior, 99
Indians, 10, 47
Indo-European: language, 3–4, 8, 11, 34; religion, 8, 10, 47
Indonesia, 158
initiation, 104, 118, 160[45]
intoxication, 178
Ionia(n), 73, 152
Iphigeneia, 26[27]
Iris, 45, 101
Isler, H. P., 89[113], 162[52]
Israel: language, 11; religion of, xvi, 13, 37, 115
Italy/Italic, 168, 172, 174, 176
Ithaka, 44

J

Jacoby, F., 23[9], 32[49], 96[13], 151[8], 152[10]
Jaeger, W., 131[76]
Jason, 168
Jensen, A. E., 158[39]
Jerusalem, temple in, 115
Jews, *see* Israel
Johnson, F. P., 141[112]
Jörgensen, O., 17[35]
journey: to Olympos, 178; through underworld, 125–126
Jung, C. G., xii, 113[71]
Juno, 96[11], 125, 130, 142, 168[70], 169, 173; *Iuno inferna*, 164, 172; Iuno Lucina, 173
Juppiter, 45, 47, 130

K

Kabeiroi, 173[80]
Kähler, H., 116[9], 134[84], 161[48], 171[75], 175[91]
Kallimachos, 27, 28, 33, 104[40], 129[70], 156[28, 29], 160[45], 161[49]
Kanathos spring, 98, 119, 126
Karia(ns), 87[106], 153[14], 157, 159
Karo, G., 137[97]
Kazantzakis, N., 72
Keller, O., 123[30]

Index

Kern, O., 176[95]
king, 30, 31, 35, 41–46, 48, 61, 115[8], 160[45]; of gods, *see under* Zeus
kingdom, Mycenaean, as model for Olympian divine, 42–46, 50, 57, 58, 93–94, 137
Kithairon, Mount, 142–146, 162, 179
Knossos, 27, 30–31, 44, 72, 81[84], 85; palace of, 22; tablets, 21–25, 28; *see also* Mycenaea(n), *s.v.* Greek texts/tablets
Kore, 85, 107, 126
Kornemann, E., 94[7 10], 110[64]
Korybantes, 173[86]
Kos, 69[38], 104[40]
Kouretes, 136, 138
Kourouniotes, K., 33[58]
Krauss, F., 174[88], 175[90]
Kretheis, 75[61]
Kretheus, 75[58 61]
Kretschmer, P., 4, 9–10, 64[14]
Kronia (festival), 73
Kronion (ancient name), 9, 18; (month), 73
Kronos, 18, 35, 36, 45, 46, 56, 59, 61, 73, 95, 99, 107, 132, 133, 135[90]
Kroton, 169
Kunze, E., 135[92], 136[94], 138[101]
Kybele, 172

L

Lactantius, 165[61]
Lady (title), 77, 78, 83, 84, 85
Lakedaimon, 115[8]
Lakinion, 169
Lakonia, 85
landscape, xii, 115, 168
Laomedon, 62
Lasserre, F., 101[31]
Latin language, xiii, 16, 64
Lattermann, H., 128[66]
Lattimore, R., 49[26], 62[8], 63[9 10], 102[34], 124[43]
law, 31, 41, 44, 93, 108
legend, 42–43, 76[62], 89, 94[8], 116, 149, 168, 178; distinguished from myth, 43; sacred, *see* sacred story (*hieros logos*)
Lehmann, K., 128[65]
Leleges, 152, 153[14]
Lemnos, 153[14]
Lenaia (festival), 84[95]

Leonidas, 19
Lerna, 125
Lesbos, 22
Leto, 51–58, 145
life: broader origin of, 52–55, 89; cult, 30; and death, beyond, 31–34
light, 5, 14–15, 23, 31, 33, 71, 91–92, 103, 172; myths, 34–36; *see also* moonlight
lighting up, 4–6, 9–10, 13, 15, 18, 20, 23, 27–29, 31, 32, 46, 54, 59, 64, 86, 103, 108, 117, 146–147
lightning, 7, 15, 91, 103
Lindsay, W. M., 130[73]
linguistics, xii–xiv, 4, 9–12, 14, 16, 22, 26[27 28], 44, 64–66, 92, 155, 175[92]
lion, 173[86]
Livy, 169
love-making, 52, 75, 98, 112; of Zeus and Hera, 43, 53, 96–97, 99–102, 112, 129, 160
Lucian, 93, 99[24]
lunar year, 142
lute playing of Apollo, 51
lygos, 126, 152, 153–159, 163–164, 178
Lykaion, Mount, 24, 28, 33–37, 38[1], 87, 88, 132
Lykaon, 35
Lykosoura, 37, 78–80, 83, 87, 88

M

Macedonia, 6, 22, 37
Macrobius, 34[55], 74[51]
Madonna cult, 179[106]
maenad, 178
magic, 111–112, 151
Magnien, V., 101[29]
Makris, 140, 145
Malinowski, B., 52[35], 94, 111
Marinatos, S., 24[12]
marriage, 92–110; archetypal, 51; myth, 97; sacred (*hieros gamos*), 97, 101–107, 177[101]; of Zeus, 23, 41; of Zeus to Hera, 26–28, 93, 94, 129; *see also* wedding ceremony (Gamos)
masculinity, 16, 26, 43, 47, 138
matriarchal order, 45–58, 67, 88, 89, 94–95, 108–112, 123
Matt, L. von, 172[82], 173[85]
Maximus Confessor, 104[38]

Index

meal, common, *see* sacrifice/sacrificial, s.v. meal
medical literature, 130, 157
Megalopolis, 89
Mekone, 70
Melanippe, 76⁶²
Meles, 75⁶¹
men: correlated to Zeus as archetype, 51, 136, 139, 179; and temple building, 133
Menander, 11, 105¹² ⁴⁰, 108⁵⁴
Menodotos, 151–154
menstruation (*katamenia*), 130, 131, 157–159, 163
Mesopotamia, 40, 42, 110
Metonic cycle, 32
metope relief (Paestum temple), 170, 171⁷⁷, 174
Mette, H. J., 64¹³
Michel, C., 161⁵⁰, 165⁵⁹
Midea, 117
Milesia, 117
Minoan culture, xi, 21, 25, 27³⁰, 30–31, 34, 70, 71, 96¹⁴, 108, 128, 138, 151⁷
Minos, King, 30–31
miracle/miraculous image, 150–152, 153, 161, 170
missionary activity, 152
Mistress (title), 78, 79, 115, 117, 128, 139, 157
Mnemosyne, 18³⁸, 25¹⁹, 79
Moloch, 35
monogamy, 109, 129⁷¹
monotheism, xv–xvi, 8
Monti Alburni, 168, 179¹⁰⁶
moon, 105¹⁶, 117–118, 121–122, 124, 126–128, 130–132, 134, 142, 144, 151⁷, 158, 159, 162, 164; goddess, 26, 53, 72, 158; *see also* Hera, s.v. association with moon; myths, 118, 121
moonlight, 118, 122, 128, 143, 148, 163, 176
Moscati, S., 37⁷⁰
mother, 45, 55, 67, 75, 78, 82–83, 98, 111, 123, 172; archetypal, xiii, 47, 51; common, 94, 95, 109; goddess, 89, 117, 137–138; of gods, 133, 137; Hera as, 46, 51, 172; of Homer, 75⁶¹; of Zeus, 28, 36
motherless birth, 53

mountain, 6, 23, 27, 28, 29, 31, 33, 34, 37, 47, 87, 100, 102, 117, 119–120, 122–123, 129, 141, 145, 146, 167
Mühlestein, H., 22¹, 25⁷¹, 132⁸¹
Müller, K. O., 8–9, 142¹¹⁴
music, 18, 146; *see also* songs
Mycenae(an), 42, 56, 94, 115, 117, 118, 173⁹⁶; culture, 43, 45, 55, 58, 61, 69–70, 74, 79, 92, 132, 171⁷⁶; M. Greek texts/tablets, 21–27, 44, 57, 60, 64, 72, 74, 77–85. 86; origins, 21, 42–46, 57, 88; titles, 57
mysteries, 78–80, 83, 84, 87–89, 102, 104, 165
mystic(al), 102³⁵, 107, 108, 118–119, 126
mythologem, 23, 29, 36, 40, 46, 95, 97, 99, 102, 112
myth(ology), xvi, 3, 8, 19, 28, 31, 33, 36, 39, 40–41, 42–44, 48, 50, 52, 54–55, 58–59, 67, 69, 87–89, 93, 95–96, 99, 102, 110–113, 118, 121, 123, 137, 138, 144, 158, 166, 174; *see also under deities' names*

N

Naiads, 89
name, 17, 25, 27, 30, 34, 35, 41, 45, 58, 66, 70, 72, 77, 78, 81⁸⁴, 82, 83, 84, 85, 88, 117, 120, 125–126, 138, 145, 177; Greek, 156, 168, 175
Napoli, M., 178¹⁰³ ¹⁰⁵
nature, xv, 8, 10, 11, 13, 14, 15, 19, 47, 95, 131, 147
Nauck, A., 71⁴¹
Nauplion, 119
Naxos, 160⁴⁵
Neleus, 74
Neoplatonism, 105⁴⁶, 107
Nereids, 89
Nereus, 46
Nestor, 76; palace of, 60, 74
Nikainetos (Samian poet), 109⁵⁸, 157, 176
Nile River, 40
Nilsson, M. P., 39², 42⁸ ⁹, 47²¹, 73⁴⁵, 75⁵⁰, 79⁷⁷, 105¹⁶, 122³⁵, 144¹²², 146¹²⁶
Norden, E., 125⁴⁵
nurses/nursing, 27, 119, 145, 172
nymph, 41, 81, 99, 142–143, 146, 152, 153¹⁴, 160⁴⁶
nymphe, 109, 157, 176, 177

Index

O

oaristes, 30
obstetricians, 28, 173[66]
Oche, Mount, 122, 140–141
Odysseus, 62, 143
Ohlemutz, E., 173[66]
Ohly, D., 152[11], 153[17], 154[18], 162[51], 166[65]
Okeanos, 41, 43, 95, 99, 102, 114
Olympia, 7, 109, 132–139, 150, 169, 173[50]
Olympian divine family, *see* family, *s.v.* Olympian divine
Olympic games, 133–135, 139
Olympos, Mount, 6, 29, 37, 39–42, 48–49, 58, 101, 178
Onkios, King, 88
Oppermann, H., xii[9]
oracle, 5, 6, 12, 19, 69[32], 144
Orient(al), 7, 30, 48, 49, 94
origin: of gods, 95–96; Hera as, 114; of life, broader, 52–55, 89; non-maternal, 54–55; *see also* under Mycenae(an)
Orlandos, A. K., 128[66]
Orphics, 176
Orth, E., 127[64]
Otto, W. F., 72[45]
Ouranos, 59, 107
Overbeck, J. A., xv[7]

P

Paestum, 109[59], 122, 167–179
Palmer, L. R., 23[4], 24[16], 38[1], 72[45], 74[46], 77[67], 78[69], 80[80], 81[84], 82[87,88]
Panhellenic: Hera, 109; Zeus, 6, 109, 139
Panzeus, 22[4]
Parthenios (month), 139
parthenogenesis, 56, 96
Pasiphaë, 71–72
patria potestas, 45, 48, 49
patriarchal order, 45–58, 60, 86, 90, 91, 95, 108, 109
Pausanias, 33, 34–45, 37[71,74], 78, 79[72,74,75], 82, 87, 88, 108[55], 109[57], 115[6], 118–121, 122[38], 124[42], 125, 126[61,67], 127, 128, 133[58], 134[86], 135, 136, 138, 139[104], 142–145, 152[13], 154, 155, 163[58], 166[62]
Payne, H., 119[19], 127[61], 131[79]
Pearson, A. C., 44[14]
Peisistratids, 108

Pelasgos, 128
Pelias, 75
Peloponnese, 26, 33, 57, 86, 87, 132, 139
Perachora, 109, 119, 131, 178
perfective aspect (*actio perfectiva*), 4, 9, 14, 16, 64
Pergamon, 150
periodicity, 98, 127–128, 130, 158, 159, 163
Persephone, 27[30], 78, 82, 85, 87, 88, 125
Perseus, 55
Persia, 93, 94, 103, 109, 110
Persian, Old, 18
Persian Wars, 18, 19
Persson, A. W., 120[21]
Phaiakians, 62–63, 99
Phaleron, 108[56]
Pheidias, 133
Phigalia, 88
Philippson, P., 69[33], 87[106]
Philochoros, 74[51]
Phoenicians, 30, 35, 37
Phoinix, 30
Pindar, 68[30,31], 127[63], 129[68], 139[103], 159[43], 163[54]
Piraeus, 163
pirate stories, 152, 153
Pirate War, 165
Pithoigia (festival), 82
plant, 69, 121, 128, 130, 154, 155
plasticity, xvi, 7, 13
Plataia, 142, 143, 145
Plato, 30–31, 33[52], 35, 44[11], 85, 106, 107
playmates Zeus and Hera, 129[71], 160
Pliny, 35[66], 157[35], 168
Plutarch, 33[51], 34[59,61], 65[17], 108[54], 142–145
Polemon, 163[54]
Polybios, 34[60]
polygamy, 129
Polykleitos, 118, 124
Polykrates, 149, 157, 162
Polymnos, 126
polytheism, xv, 13, 39, 50
pomegranate, 118, 172
Poseidippos, 101[31]
Poseidon: altars, 79, 88, 117; animal form, 66–69; *see also* animal(s), *s.v.* husband; cult, 60–63, 69, 76, 87; cult association, 66, 70, 77–84, 85, 86;

Index

Poseidon (cont.):
  epithets: Earthshaker, 64–65, 69, 72, 76, 87; Hippios, 79, 88, 133;
  as father, 60, 75, 76, 79, 86, 88, 89, 93, 98; Greeks dear to, 61, 62; as husband, 64–68, 71–72, 81, 85–86, 87–89, 92, 93; myths, 60, 61, 63–64, 68, 86, 87–89; name, 64–66, 76, 77, 115;
  religion, 60-66, 71, 76–77, 86–87; sanctuaries, 68, 80, 168[98]; and the sea, 60, 61–64, 76, 86; sons of, 75, 89; temples, 79, 89, 175; wife of, 64, 65, 79
Poseidonia (Paestum), 168
Posidaeia, 83
Potnia/potnia, 77–78, 80, 82–85, 127[64], 128
Pötscher, W., 115[5]
Powell, J. U., 129[71]
procreation, 45, 54, 98, 103
Proklos, 105[10], 107, 108
Prometheus, xv, 70, 129[71]
Proserpina, 125
Prosymnos, 125
Prott, J. de, 74[58], 105[15]
Ptolemy Philadelphos, 101
puberty, 96[11]
Pugliese Carratelli, G., 22[1], 23[5]
Puhvel, J., 25[18]
Punic Wars, 169
purification, 101, 118, 126, 131, 152, 164
Pylos/Pylians, 21, 24–26, 44, 57–58, 60, 74–76, 78–86, 117, 132

Q

queen, 44, 50, 57, 111, 133, 136; see also Hera, s.v. queen of heaven

R

races, 133, 134–135
raven, 144
Reitzenstein, R., 152[9]
religio, xiii
religion, see Greek religion; see also under names of deities
repression, 52
republic, 42
Rhea, 28, 29, 33, 36, 61, 95, 99, 107, 133, 137, 138, 139
rite/ritual, 36, 70, 84, 99, 118–119, 147, 149, 152, 159–167; see also wedding ceremony (Gamos)
river god, 41, 75, 89[113], 119, 120, 156, 160
Robert, C., 71[42], 76[62], 94[8]
Robinson, R. P., 69[52]
Rome/Roman, xi, 35, 45, 47, 73, 96[11], 130, 165
Roscher, W. H., xv, 130[75]
Rose, V., 131[78], 156[29, 30]
Ruijgh, C. J., 64[41]

S

sacred story (hieros logos), 97, 98, 102, 111[67], 122, 151, 160
sacrifice/sacrificial, 23, 29, 33–34, 69[51], 79, 105, 117, 120[29], 134, 145, 146, 148, 150–151, 170[25], 171; cakes, 152, 153; gifts, 166; human, 35–37; meal, 70, 76, 127, 139; see also hecatomb
Säflund, G., 120[21]
Säflund, Marie-Louise, 136[93]
Salerno Gulf, 167
Salmoneus, 75[58]
Samos, 109, 110, 122, 126, 129, 148–167, 168, 169, 171, 178, 179
Samothrace, 84, 128[65], 165
sanctuaries, 149, 150; Eleusis, 79; Hermione, 110[62]; Lykosoura, 88, Pylos, 80; see also under names of deities
Sanskrit, 10, 16, 18, 64
Sardinia, 31, 32
Saturnalia (festival), 73
scepter, 41, 124
Schachermeyr, F., 38[1], 63[11]
Scheffel, H., 29[30]
Schleif, H., 162[52]
Schliemann, H., 121
Schoell, R., 28[26]
Schröder, F. R., 115[5]
Schwenn, F., 35[45]
science, xvi–xvii, 9, 14
sea, 19, 59, 61, 63, 64, 65, 66, 71, 76, 81[71], 86, 117, 161, 164–165, 167, 168; god, 46, 60
secret, 82, 118; love-making, 53, 99, 129; rite, 35, 37, 84, 103, 128; tale, 98, 125, 126, 156, 160
Sele (Silaros) River, 120[29], 167–171, 174, 175, 177

Index

Selene, 118
Semites/Semitic, 36–37, 132; god, 35
sensuous transmission, xii
Servius, 68[29]
Sestieri, P. C., 167[60], 173[84], 176[98], 177[100 101 102]
sexuality, 157, 163
sharing, 18; by lot, 61
siblings, 94; *see also* brother-sister
Sichtermann, H., 141[112], 174[80]
Siebs, T., 10[15]
silenus, 81[81]
silver, 175–176
Simon, E., 127[61], 173[80]
Sirius, 28, 151[7]
sisters, 121; *see also* brother-sister
Sisyphos, 174
sky, 15, 19, 28, 31, 91, 117, 121, 122, 131, 134, 151, 162; god, xv, xvi, 5–7
slate buildings, 141
slaves and masters, 73
Slavic, Old Church, 18
sleep, 12, 31–32, 100
snake, 108
sobriety, 157, 158, 178
Socrates, 106
solar year, 131
son: archetypal, 67; eldest, 45, 50, 51, 56, 61; *see also under names of deities*
songs, 102, 103, 104, 126, 157, 160
Sontheimer, W., 121[29]
Sophokles, 11, 19–20, 44[14], 140
Soranus, 131
Sounion, 145
Sparta, 57, 104, 115[8], 163, 173[86]
stadium, 117, 133
state, Olympian divine, 39–42, 44, 46, 50
statues, cult, 150, 151, 162, 166; *see also under names of deities*
Steffen, V., 120[22]
Stella, L. A., 24[18 17]
Stephen of Byzantium, 122[33], 123[40], 140[110]
Sterope, Queen, 136
Stoic view, 102, 103
Stone Age, 52
Stoop, J. M. W., 172[82]
Strabo, 120, 168
Studemund, G., 28[36]
Stymphalos, 121, 128–132, 167, 176

Suidas Lexicon, 25[22], 157[77]
sun, 4, 15, 31, 32, 33, 34, 53, 105[46]; solar year, 131
sweetness, 31, 178
symbol change, 69, 81, 86, 87
syncretism, 23

T

Tacitus, 69[32]
Tantalos, 35
tauromorphism, 69, 71, 76[62], 81, 87, 89[113]
Telesterion, 118
Temenos, 128, 143
temple, 115, 116, 117, 136, 148, 150, 177; *see also under names of deities*
Tenos, 141
terrace of Argive Heraion, 116–118, 120
Tethys, 43, 95, 99, 102
thalamos, 100–102
Thales, 13
Thebes, 55, 69, 137, 139, 173[56]
Thelpusa, 87, 88
Themis, 41, 44
Theogamia, 105
Theokritos, 99, 101, 104[40], 110[62], 123[36]
theology, xiii, 39, 40, 42
Theopompos of Chios, 32[19]
theos, xiii–xiv, 9, 11–13, 16–18
Theren River, 27
theriomorphism, 67, 69
thesauros/treasure house, 171[77], 174
Thesmophoria (festival), 157, 159[11]
Thessaly, 22, 68, 75[58], 76, 87
Thetis, 46
Thilo, 68[29]
throne, 29–30, 61, 123, 128[66], 135
Thukydides, 116[11]
Thyestes, 94
timelessness, 31–33
Timotheos of Miletos, 18
Tiryns, 55, 117, 132[79], 137
Titanomachia, 48, 49[29]
tragedy, xvii[9], 18, 19–20
trenches (*bothroi*), 171
triangle (matriarchal) of Leto-Apollo-Artemis, 50–58; *see also* matriarchal order; patriarchal order
tribes, Greek, 21, 22, 36, 38, 74, 152, 168
trident, 86

Index

trinities, 57, 78, 79, 81, 83, 95, 121
Triton River, 143
Trobriand Islands, 94, 111–112
Trojan War, 49, 57, 62, 100
twins, 76⁶², 92, 112⁷⁰
Tymphaians, 47
Typhaon, 56, 96¹⁴, 129⁷¹
Tyro, 75

U

uncle, 47
underworld, 75, 82, 108, 125–126, 129⁷¹, 171–172, 174, 175, 178
union: of god and goddess, 85; of Zeus and Hera, 24, 27, 51, 55, 57, 90, 92–94, 96–97, 126, 162
Usener, H., 91²

V

Van Windekens, A. J., 115⁵
Varro, 130⁷², 165
Vatin, C., 101³⁰
Veda, 4, 10
Ventris, M., 24¹⁶, 44¹³, 64¹⁵, 77⁶⁷, 81⁸³
Vesuvius, 170⁷⁵
Virgil, 11, 45¹⁷, 68²⁶, 99, 125, 142
virgin(ity), 51, 53, 98, 108, 119, 122, 126, 129, 131, 156, 159
Vitruvius, 116¹⁰

W

Wackernagel, J., 4, 10, 11
Waldstein, C., 118¹¹, 124⁴¹
Walter, H., 151⁷, 154¹⁸, 161⁴⁷
weather god, 6, 10, 47
wedding ceremony (Gamos), 96, 103–107, 122, 124, 126–127, 131, 140–146, 160, 164, 165, 178–179
weddings in Athens, 105–108, 131
Welcker, F. G., 7–9, 15–16, 18, 141, 175⁸³
Wemale of West Ceram, 158
Weniger, L., 134⁸⁷
werewolves, 35
widow, 129, 130
Wiegand, T., 117¹³, 141¹¹¹, 155²⁶
wife, 98, 106, 111; archetypal, 51, 59, 98, 114; first, 50, 55, 96; goddess, 96¹⁴, 128, 132, 173; *see also under deities' names*

Wilamowitz-Moellendorff, U. von, 3, 6–11, 16³², 17³⁴, 67²², 81⁸⁶, 136, 155²⁵, 164²⁷, 176⁸⁴
wine, 26, 82–83, 178
wolf, 34, 35
woman/female: correlated to Hera as archetype, xi, 26, 51, 52, 54, 59, 67, 97–98, 110, 114, 121–122, 128–132, 136, 148, 163, 173; deity, 29, 58, 59, 92, 114, 126, 133; form (gender), 16, 86, 155; isolation (withdrawal) from men, 99, 157–159; *see also* Hera, *s.v.* separation (withdrawal) from Zeus
world soul, 103
wreath, 121, 135, 156

X

Xenophon, 91
Xerxes, 19

Z

Zancani Montuoro, P., 168⁶⁷ ⁶⁸, 170⁷⁴ ⁷⁵, 171⁷⁶ ⁷⁷ ⁷⁹, 174⁹⁷, 179¹⁰⁶
Zanotti-Biano, U., 171⁷⁸ ⁷⁹, 172⁸², 179¹⁰⁶
Zeus: archetypal man and father, xvii, 46, 51, 59, 60, 89–90, 92; *see also below, s.v.* husband;
  altars: 33, 134, 139, 150; beguiling of, by Hera: 43, 100, 112; *see also* lovemaking, *s.v.* of Z. and Hera, birth: see birth myths, *s.v.* of Z.; Z. as brother-husband to Hera: 51, 91–113; childhood: 23, 30;
  cults: xii, xv, 6, 23, 24, 26, 51; daughters: 45, 49, 59;
  epithets: Diktaios, 23, 28; Dodonaean, 5; Enalios, 64; Heraios, 90, 97, 105; Kithaironios, 146¹²⁷; Lykaios, 33, 35; Naios, 5; Panhellenios, 6, 109, 139; Phanaios, 91; Teleios, 98, 104, 108, 109;
  Z. as father: xvii, 3, 18, 23, 26, 27, 37, 40, 45, 46–59, 60, 89–90, 92, 98, 108; as god of Greek men: 136, 139, 179; as husband to Hera (Z. Heraios): 57, 65, 90, 92, 97, 105, 135, 160, 176, 179; *see also* marriage, *s.v.* of Z.; of Z. to Hera; union, *s.v.* of Z. and Hera; as king of gods: 41–42, 44–46, 48, 61,

160[45]; masculine quality of: 26, 138; moral and spiritual content in Z.: xv, 6, 7, 19, 54, 89, 91, 139, 147; myths: xii, xv, 23, 29, 30–31, 33–36, 54–55, 61, 71, 97, 99, 122–123; and Poseidon: 45, 60–66, 71, 76, 87[108]; religion: xv–xvi, 9, 13, 19, 21–39, 46–47, 54, 57, 59, 60–65, 97, 108, 132–139, 179; sanctuary of Olympian Z.: 108; sons of Z.: 19, 24–26, 27, 28, 30, 45, 51–56, 82, 137, 178; statues: 7, 133, 135–138, 166, 176; Z. the supreme god: xvii, 3, 8, 22, 40, 45, 49, 50, 59, 91–92, 113, 135, 147, 177; temples: Argos, 115; Athens, 108; Olympia, 133, 134, 136, 139; wife of Z.: 26, 51, 82, 109, 123, 129, 130; word and name Z.: xiv, 3–20, 23, 26, 29, 38, 46–47, 65, 92, 115

Ziehen, L., 74[53], 105[45], 135[88], 136[95], 139[102]
Zimmermann, H., 4, 9, 16[81]
Zoega, J., 7
Zoroaster, 110

GPSR Authorized Representative: Easy Access System Europe - Mustamäe tee 50, 10621 Tallinn, Estonia, gpsr.requests@easproject.com